TRINITY S

AKINARI NAO

Translation: Christine Dashiell

Lettering: Anthony Quintessenza

TRINITY SEVEN SHICHININ NO MASHO TUKAI Volume 9
© AKINARI NAO 2014
© KENJI SAITO 2014
First published in Japan in 2014 by KADOKAWA CORPORATION, Tokyo.
English translation rights arranged with KADOKAWA CORPORATION, Tokyo, through TUTTLE-MORI AGENCY, INC., Tokyo.

English translation © 2017 by Yen Press, LLC

Yen Press
1290 Avenue of the Americas
New York, NY 10104

Visit us at yenpress.com
facebook.com/yenpress
twitter.com/yenpress
yenpress.tumblr.com
instagram.com/yenpress

First Yen Press Edition: May 2017

Yen Press is an imprint of Yen Press, LLC.
The Yen Press name and logo are trademarks of Yen Press, LLC.

Library of Congress Control Number: 2015952616

ISBNs: 978-0-316-47076-6 (paperback)
       978-0-316-47084-1 (ebook)

10 9 8 7 6 5 4 3 2 1

BVG

Printed in the United States of America

PREVIEW OF THE NEXT VOLUME

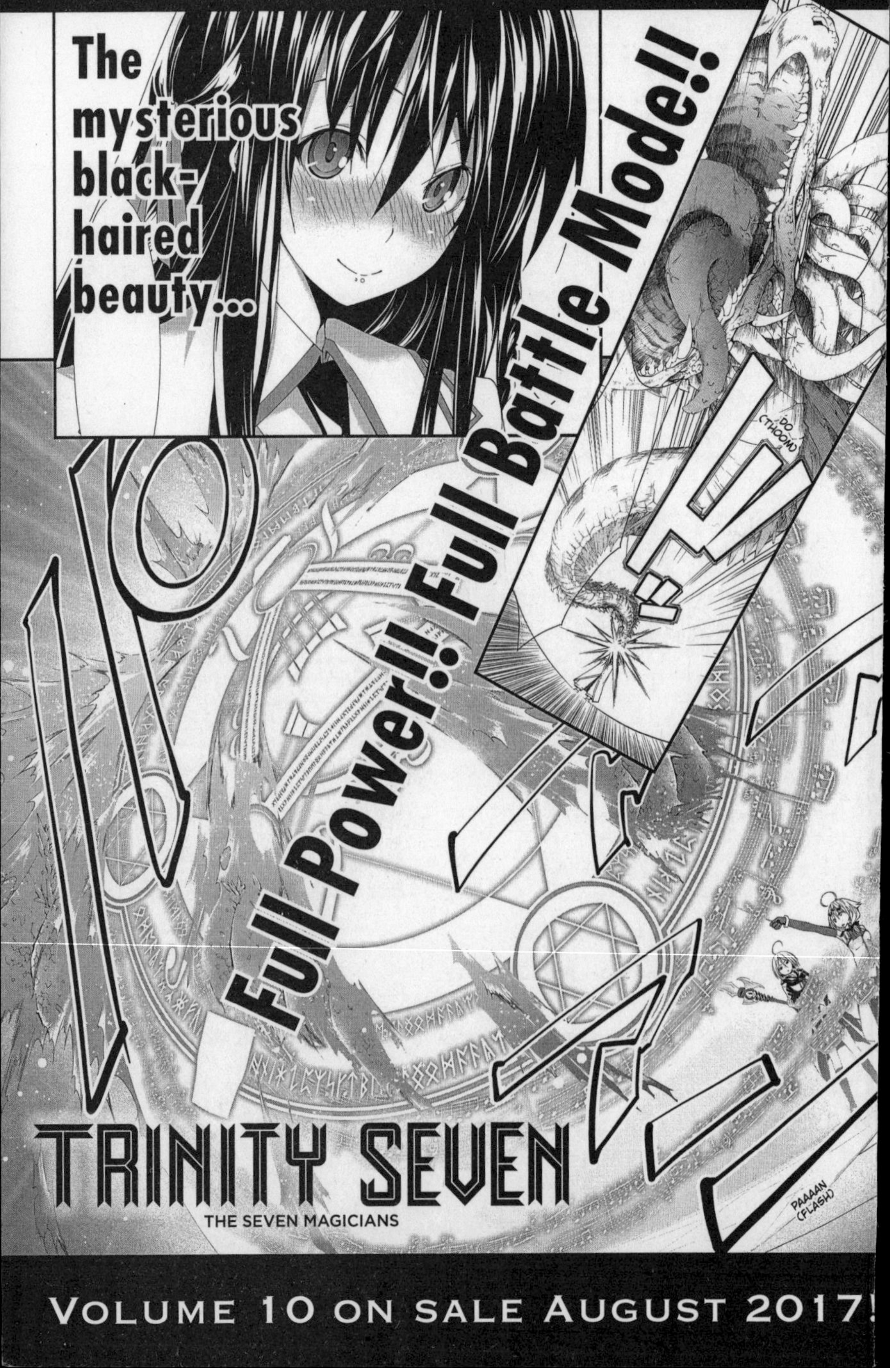
DO (THOOM)
The mysterious black-haired beauty...
Full Power!! Full Battle Mode!!
PAAAAN (FLASH)
TRINITY SEVEN
THE SEVEN MAGICIANS

VOLUME 10 ON SALE AUGUST 2017!

36. Aeshma & Malkuth

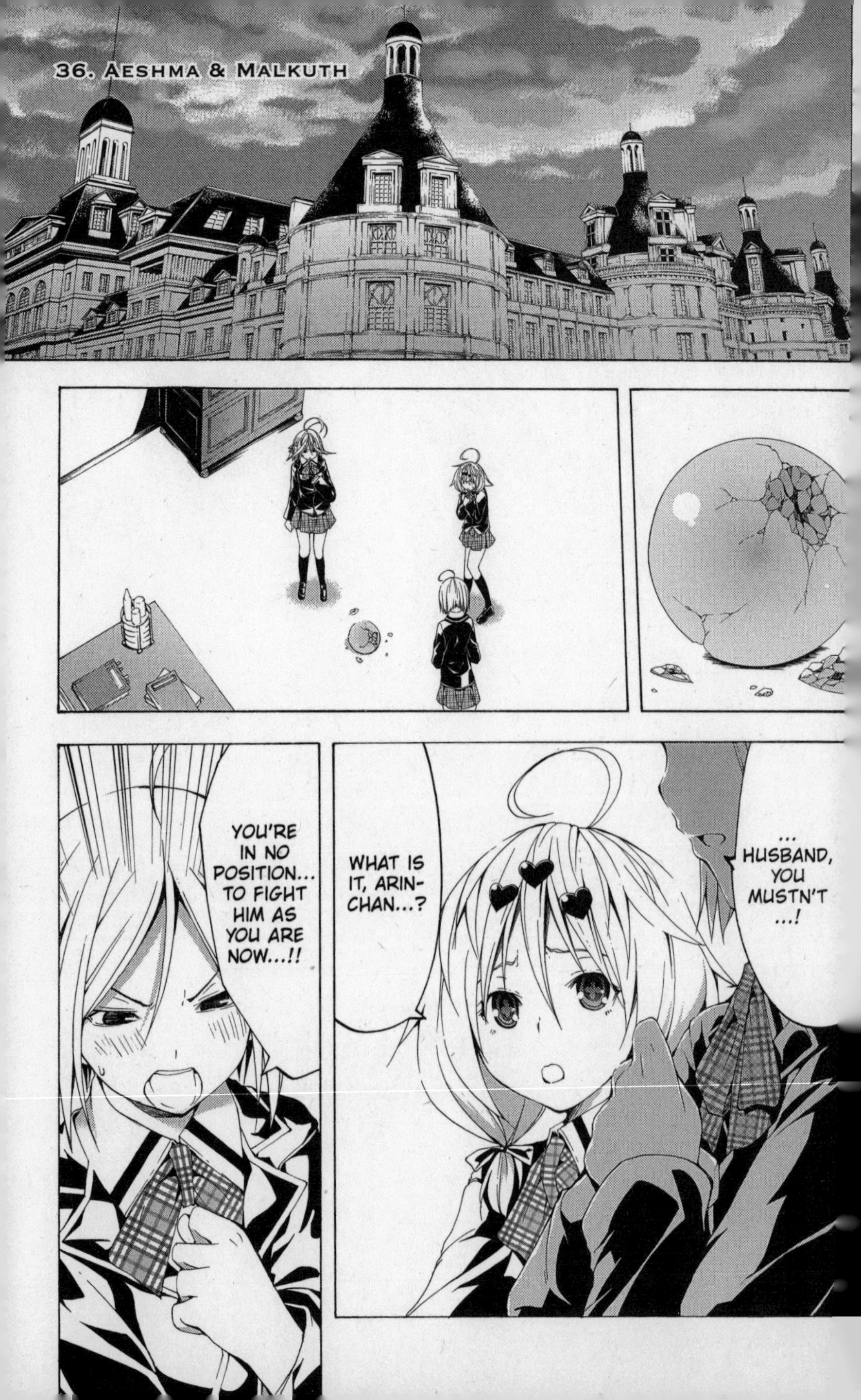
... HUSBAND, YOU MUSTN'T ...!
WHAT IS IT, ARIN-CHAN...?
YOU'RE IN NO POSITION... TO FIGHT HIM AS YOU ARE NOW...!!

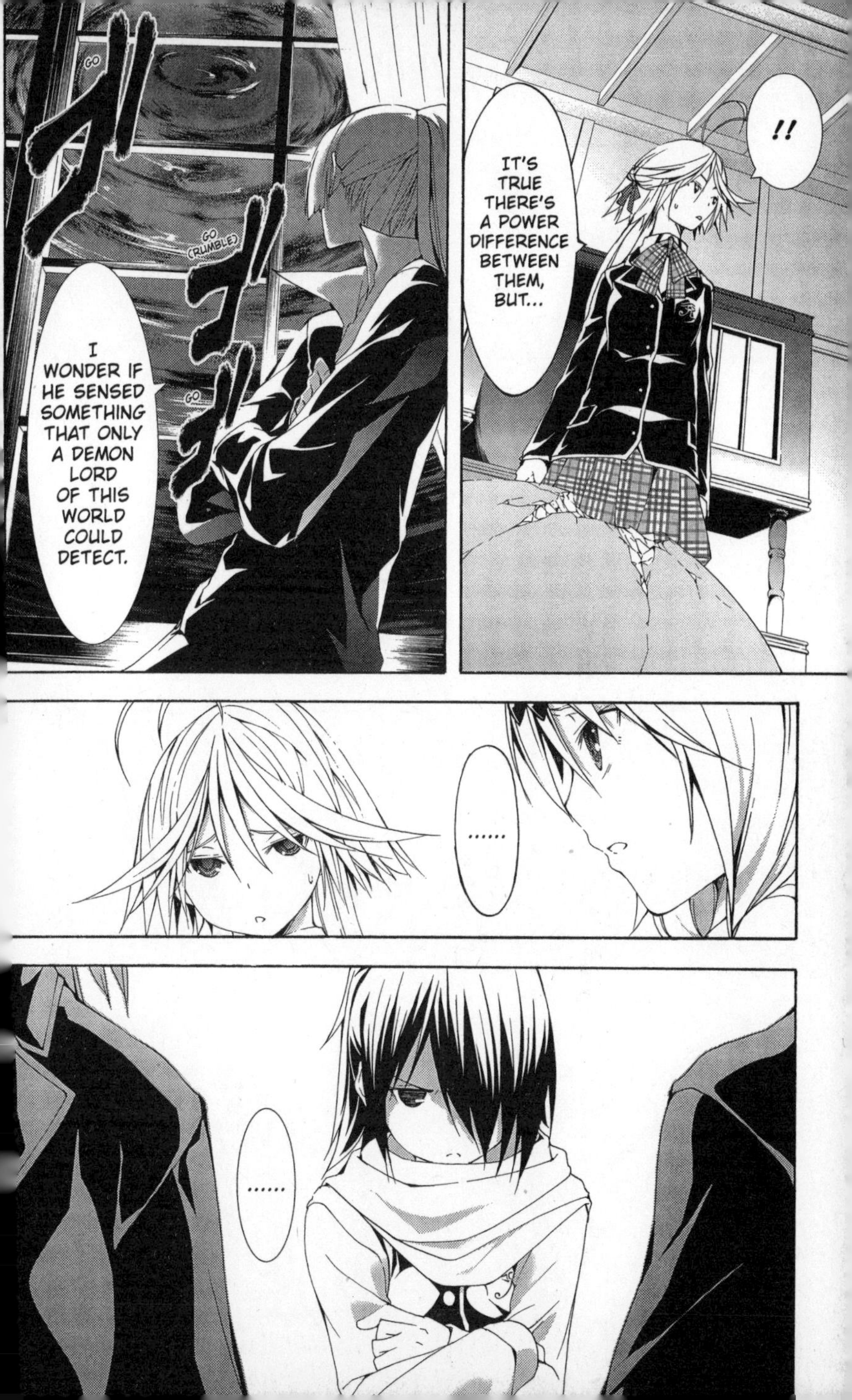
!!
IT'S TRUE THERE'S A POWER DIFFERENCE BETWEEN THEM, BUT...
GO
GO (RUMBLE)
GO
I WONDER IF HE SENSED SOMETHING THAT ONLY A DEMON LORD OF THIS WORLD COULD DETECT.
......
......

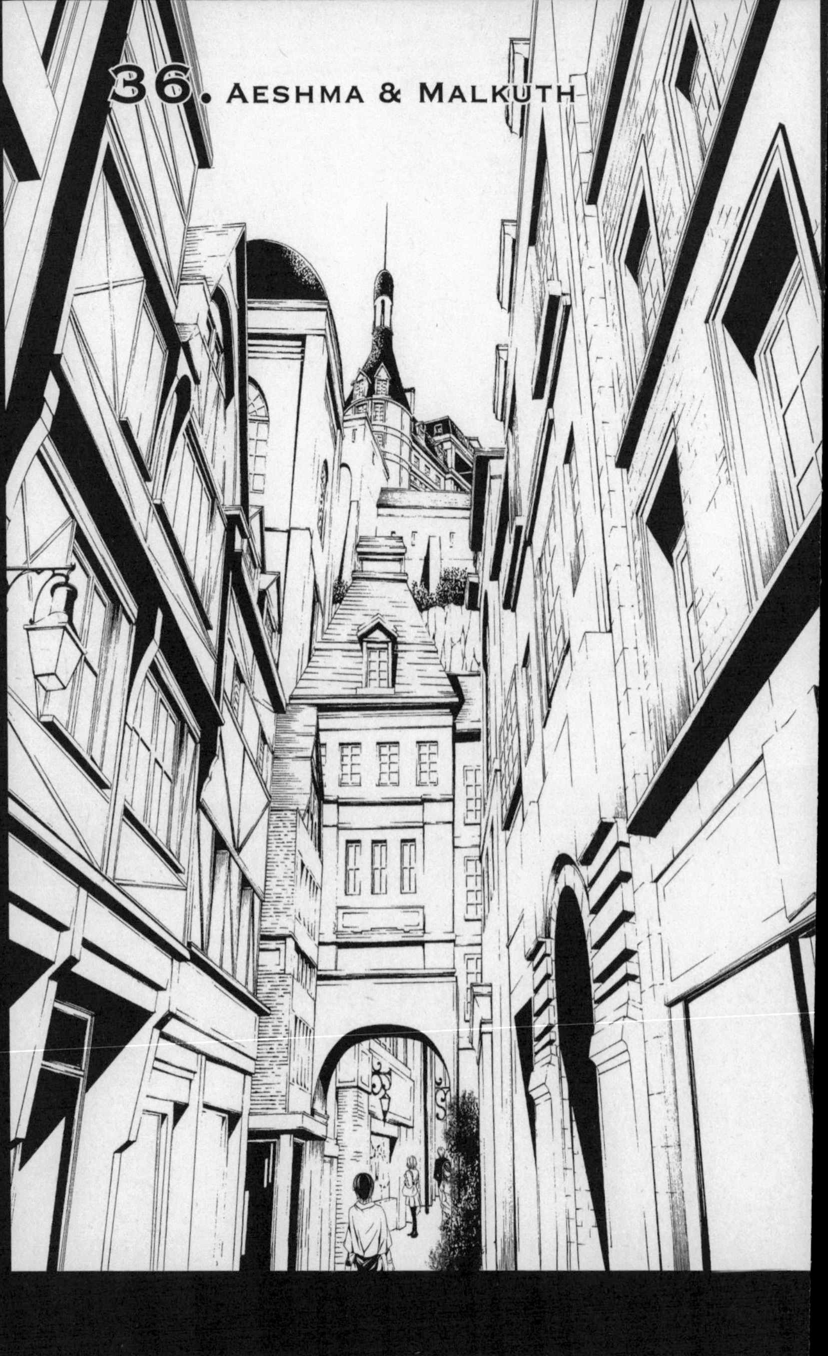
36. Aeshma & Malkuth

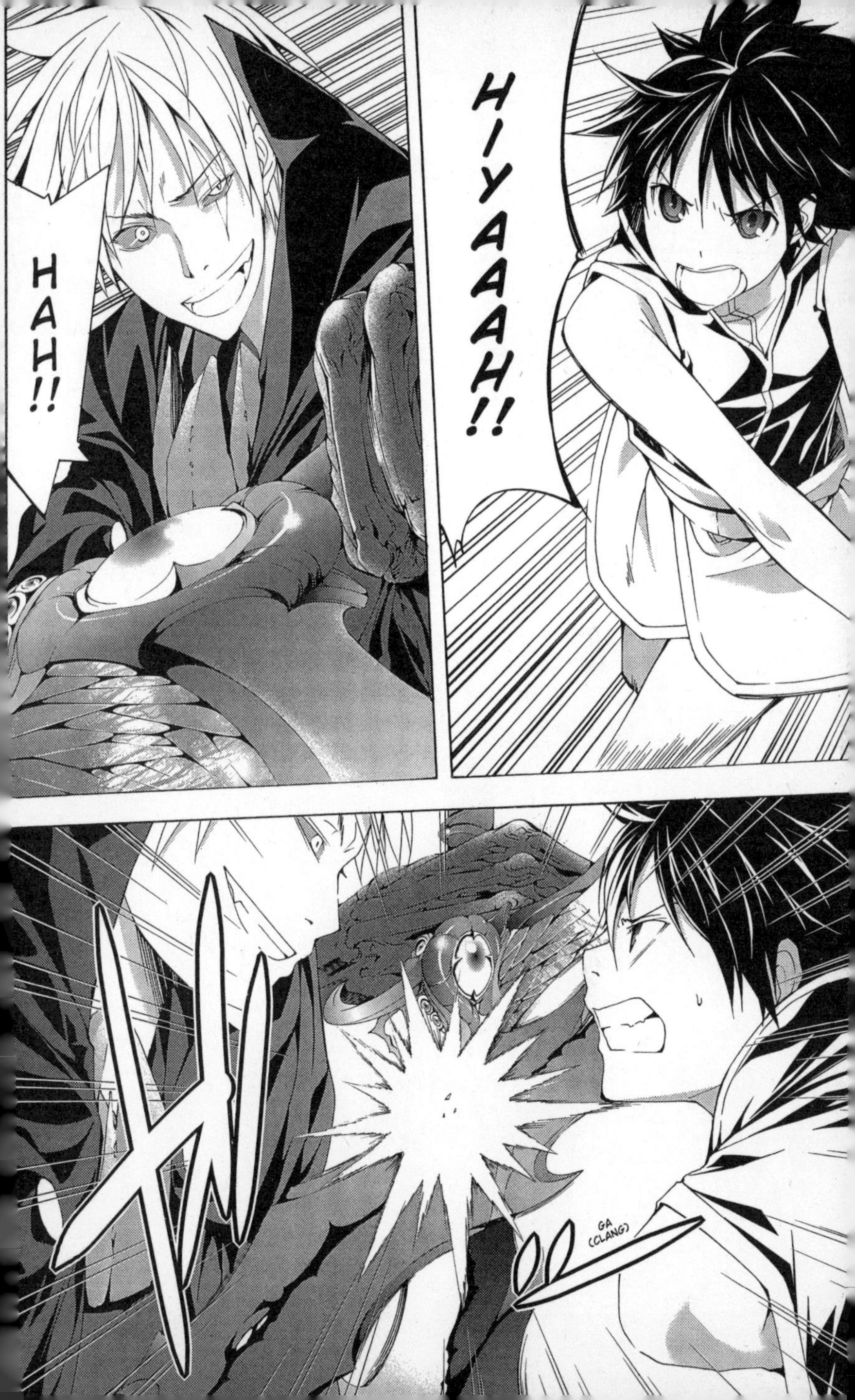
HIYAAAAH!!
HAH!!
GA (CLANG)

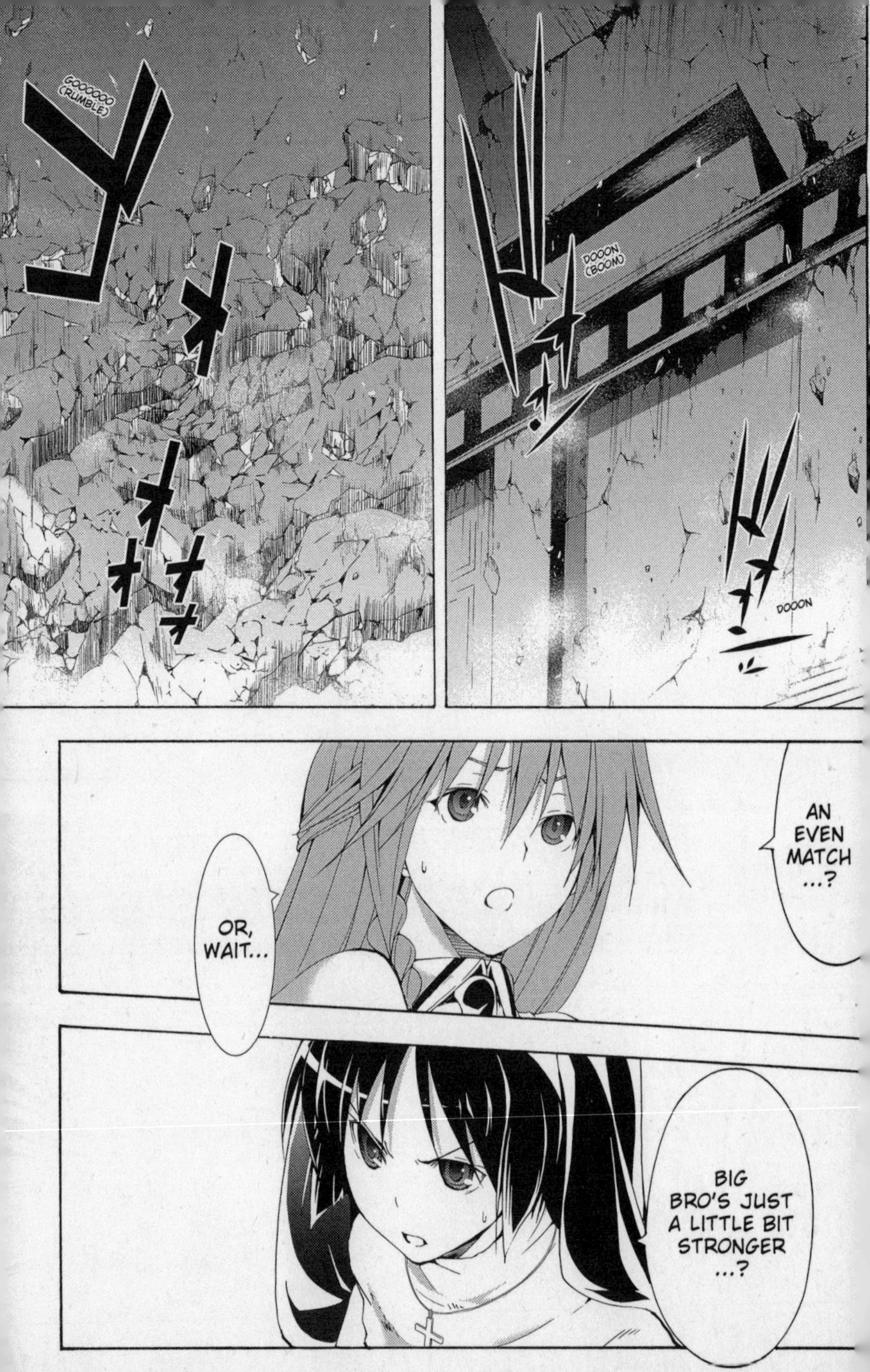
DOOON (BOOM)
DOOON
GOOOOOO (RUMBLE)
AN EVEN MATCH ...?
OR, WAIT...
BIG BRO'S JUST A LITTLE BIT STRONGER ...?

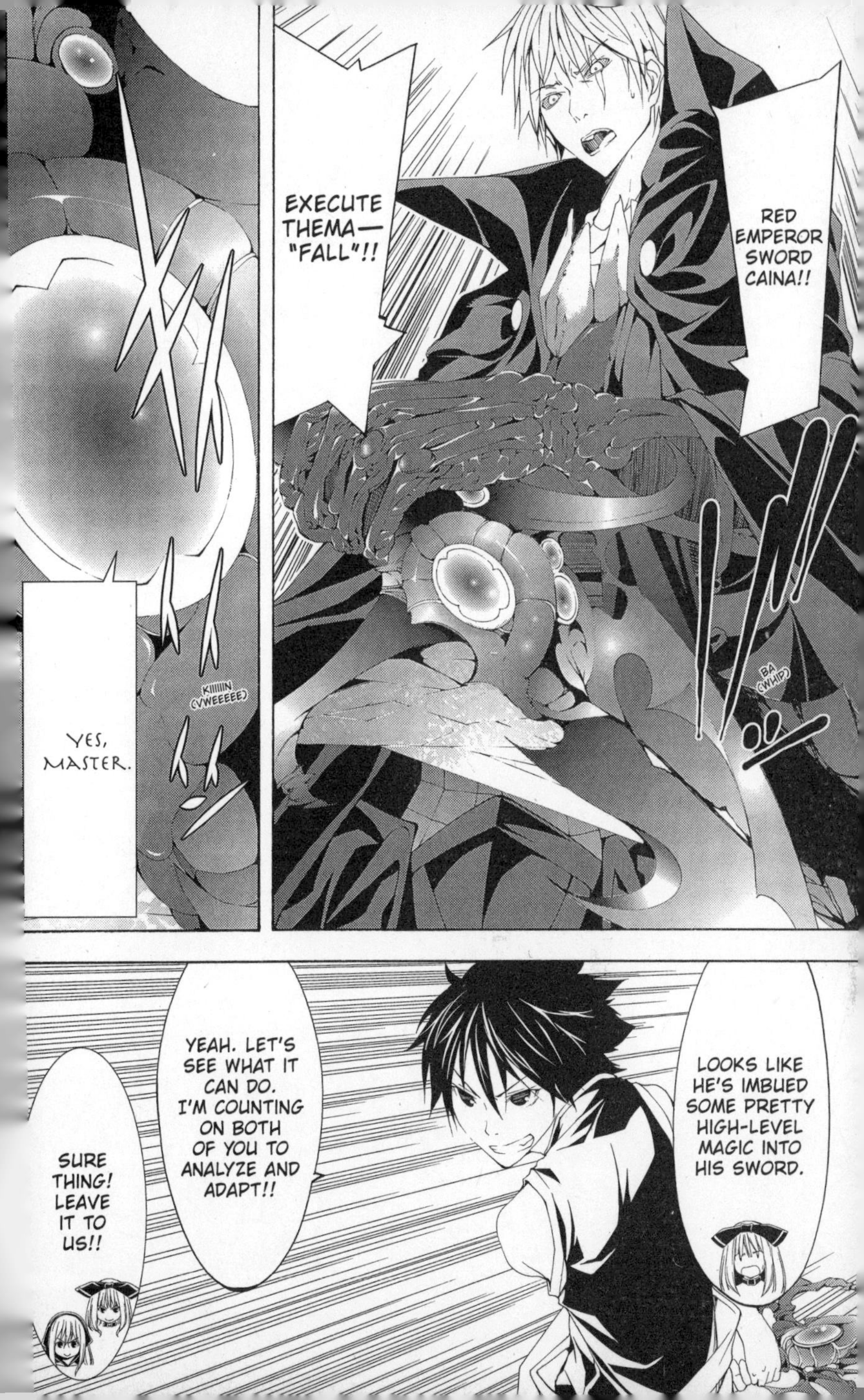
RED EMPEROR SWORD CAINA!!
EXECUTE THEMA— "FALL"!!
BA (WHIP)
KIIIIIN (VWEEEEE)
YES, MASTER.
LOOKS LIKE HE'S IMBUED SOME PRETTY HIGH-LEVEL MAGIC INTO HIS SWORD.
YEAH. LET'S SEE WHAT IT CAN DO. I'M COUNTING ON BOTH OF YOU TO ANALYZE AND ADAPT!!
SURE THING! LEAVE IT TO US!!

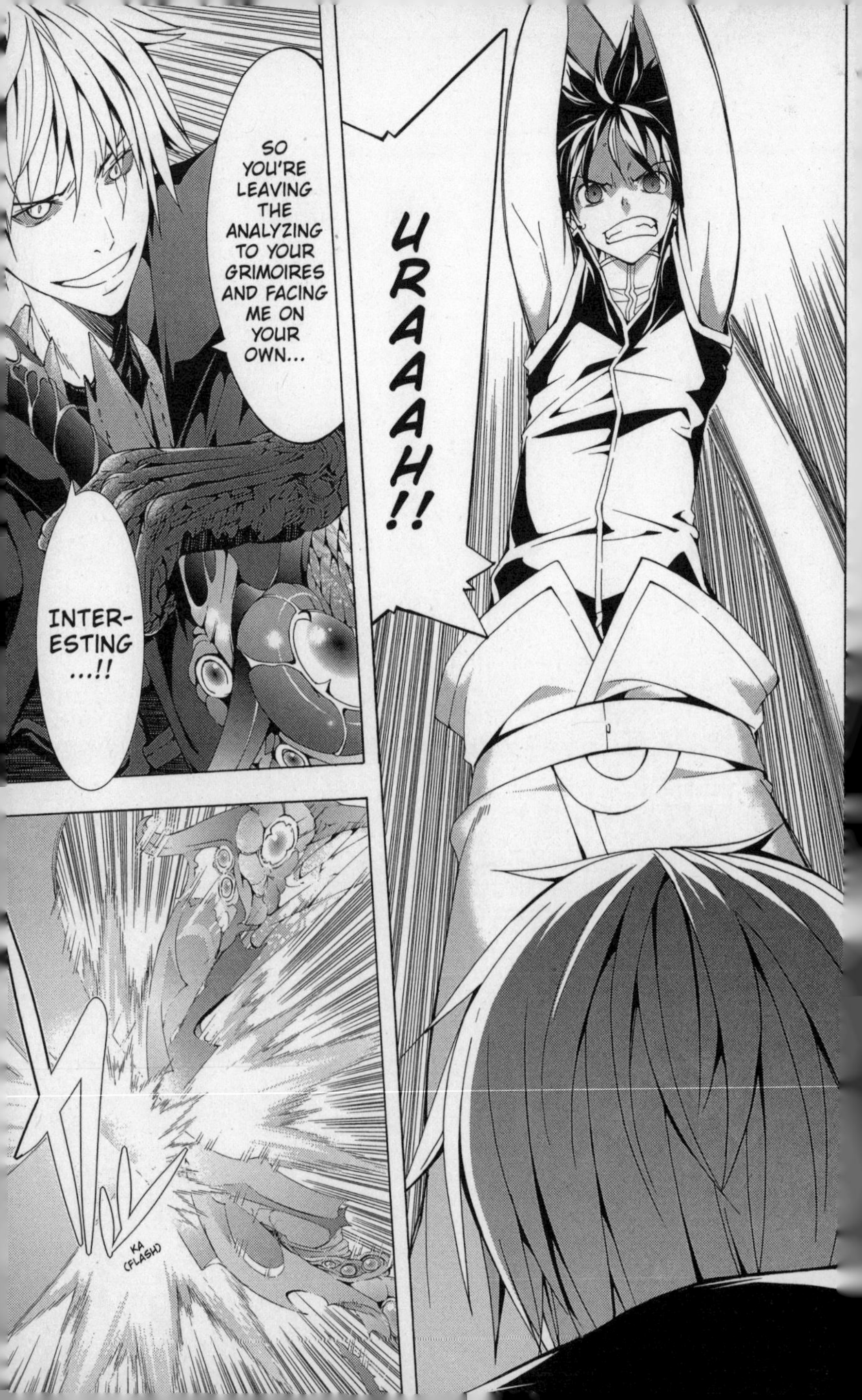
URAAAH!!
SO YOU'RE LEAVING THE ANALYZING TO YOUR GRIMOIRES AND FACING ME ON YOUR OWN...
INTER-ESTING ...!!
KA (FLASH)

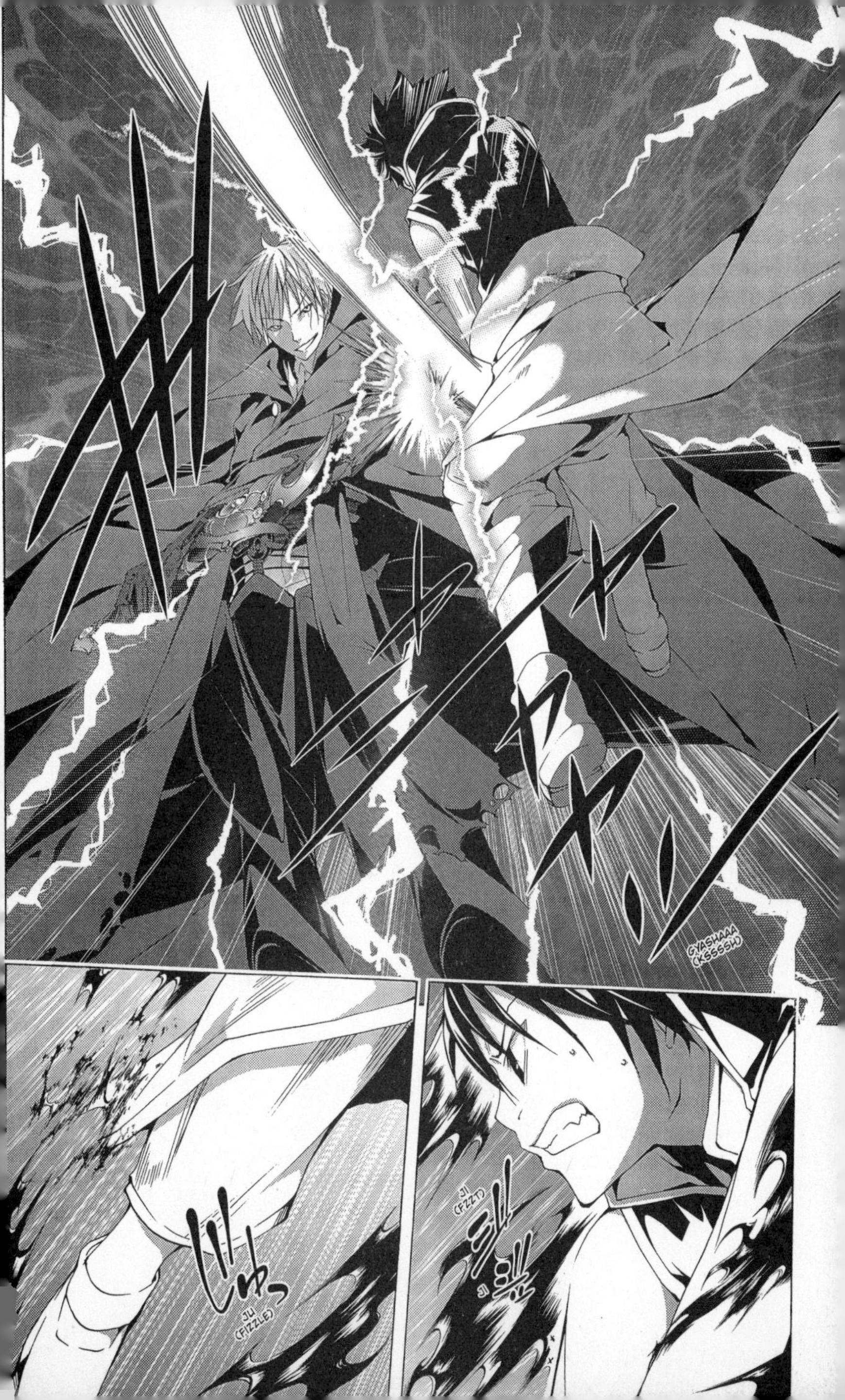
GYASHAAA
(KSSSSH)
JI
(FZZT)
JI
JU
(FIZZLE)

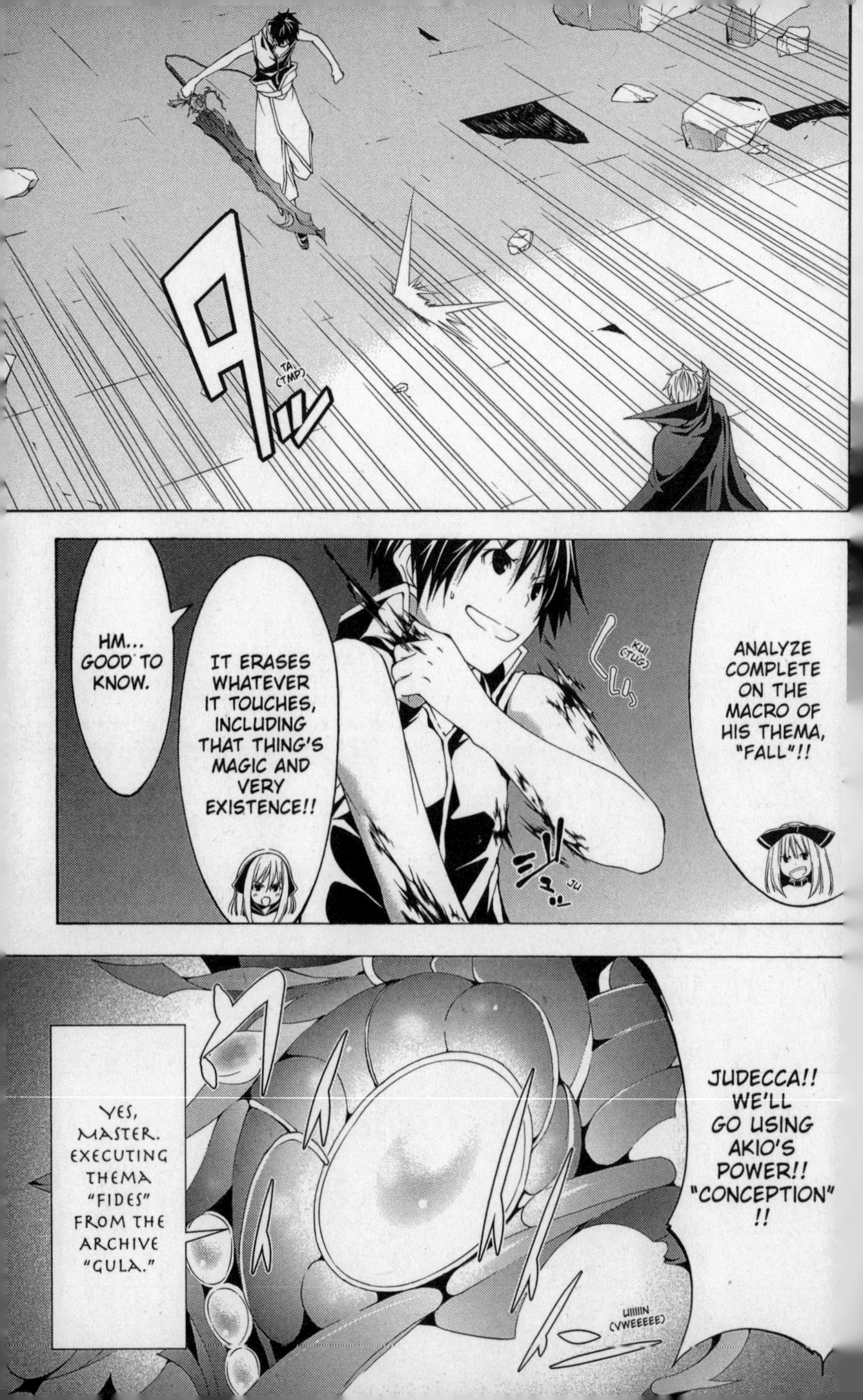
TA (TMP)
ANALYZE COMPLETE ON THE MACRO OF HIS THEMA, "FALL"!!
KUI (TUG)
IT ERASES WHATEVER IT TOUCHES, INCLUDING THAT THING'S MAGIC AND VERY EXISTENCE!!
HM... GOOD TO KNOW.
JU
JUDECCA!! WE'LL GO USING AKIO'S POWER!! "CONCEPTION"!!
YES, MASTER. EXECUTING THEMA "FIDES" FROM THE ARCHIVE "GULA."
UIIIIN (VWEEEEE)

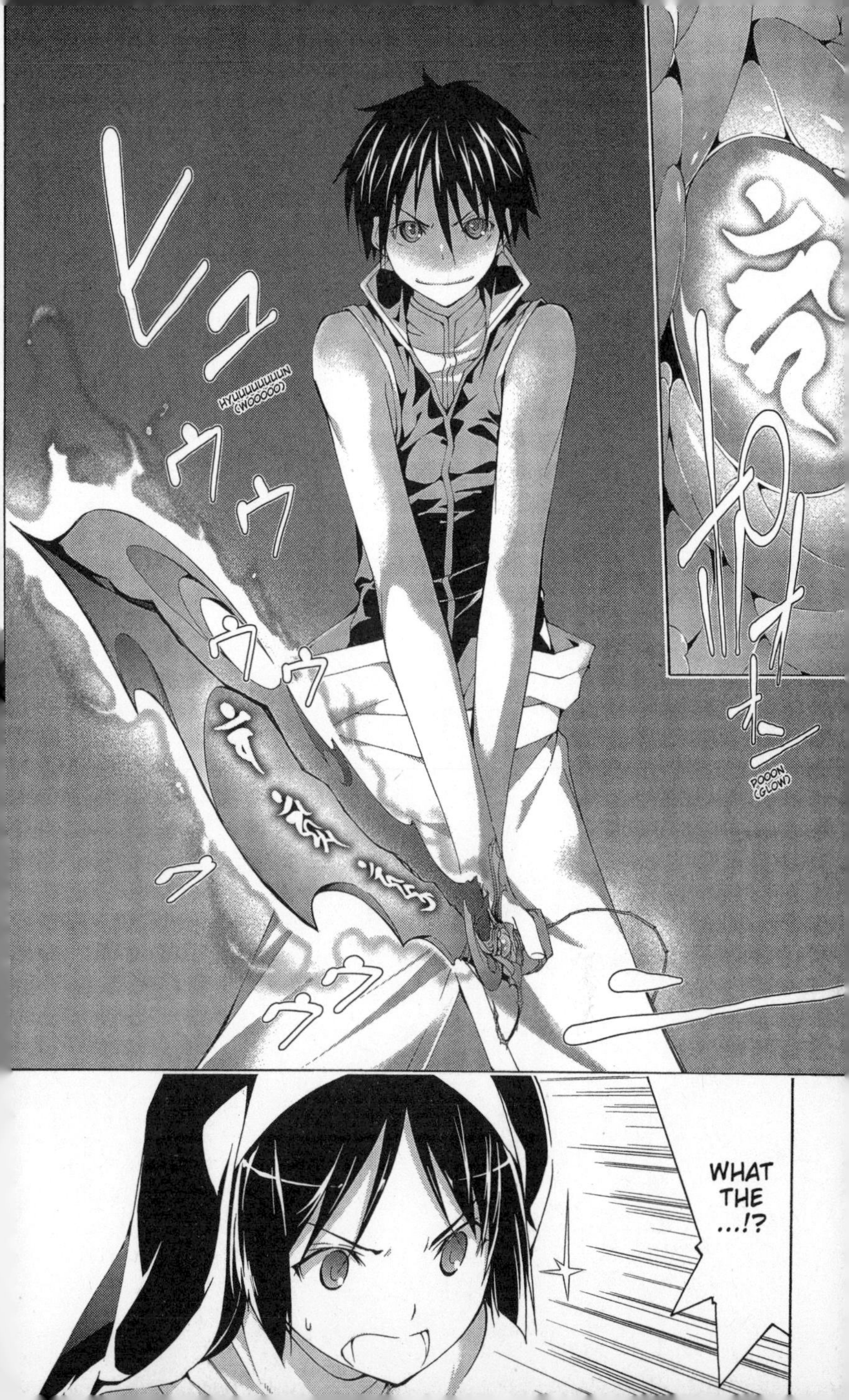
POOON (GLOW)
HYUUUUUUUUN (WOOOOO)
WHAT THE ...!?

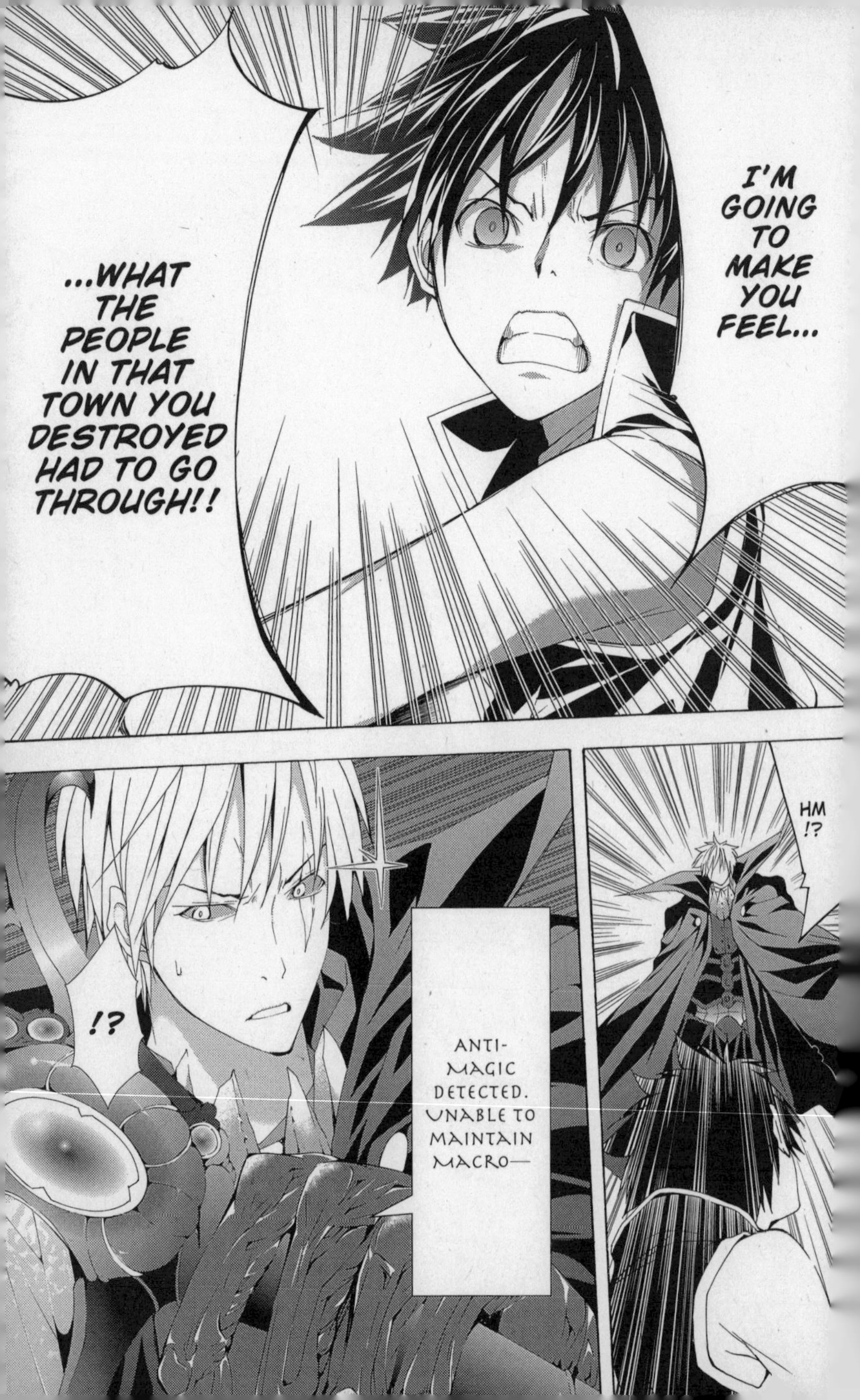
I'M GOING TO MAKE YOU FEEL...
...WHAT THE PEOPLE IN THAT TOWN YOU DESTROYED HAD TO GO THROUGH!!
HM !?
ANTI-MAGIC DETECTED. UNABLE TO MAINTAIN MACRO—
!?

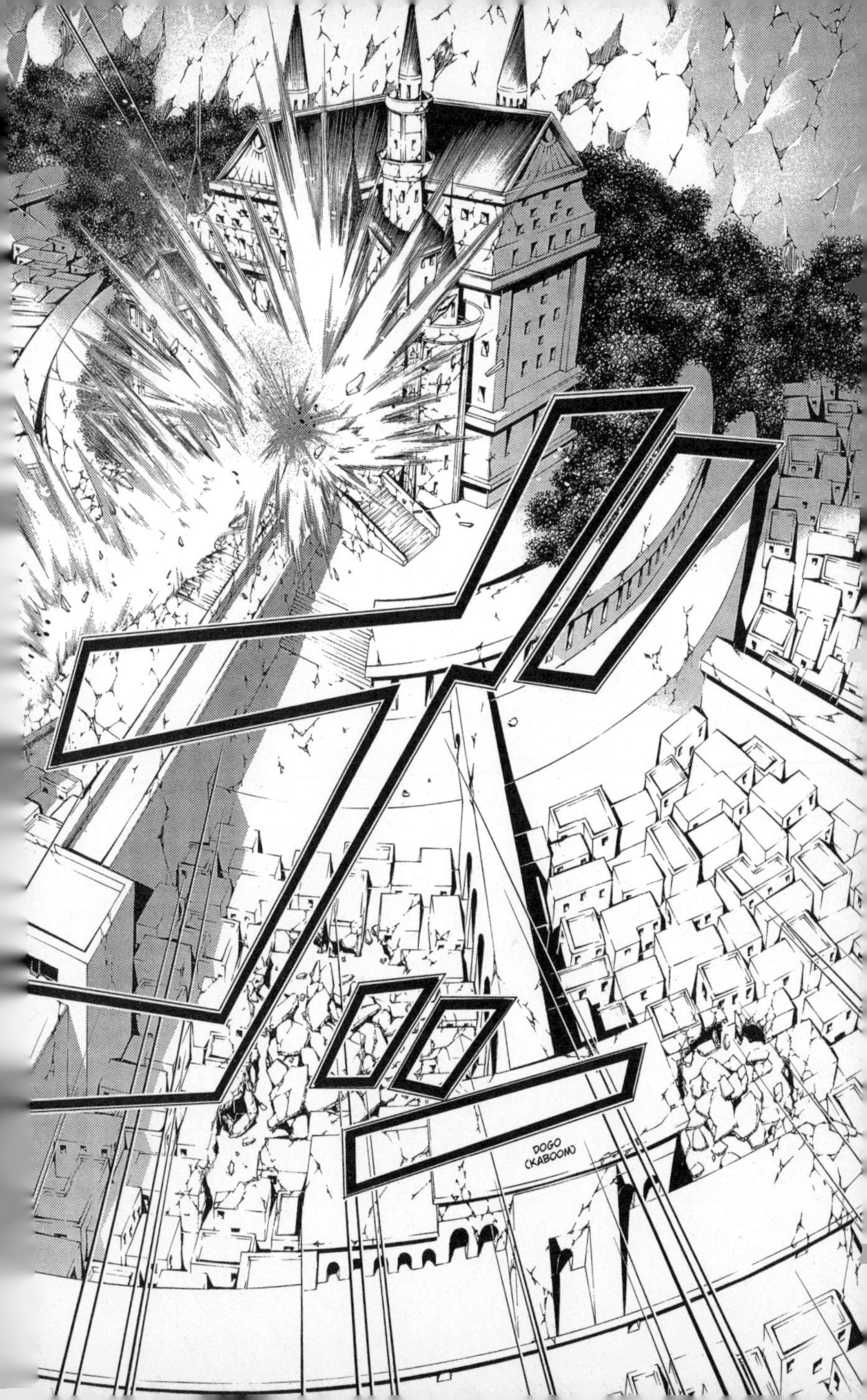
DOGO
(KABOOM)

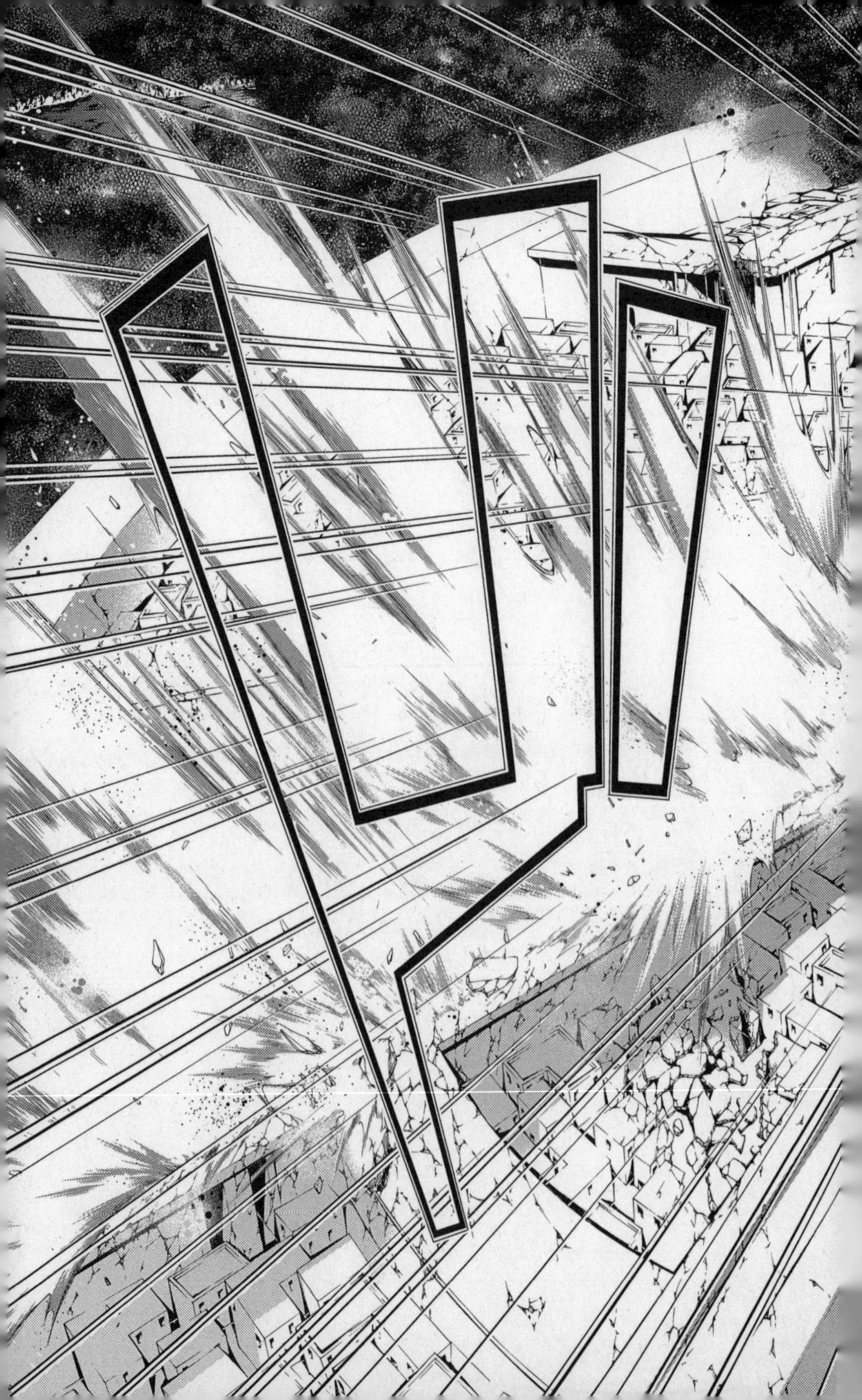

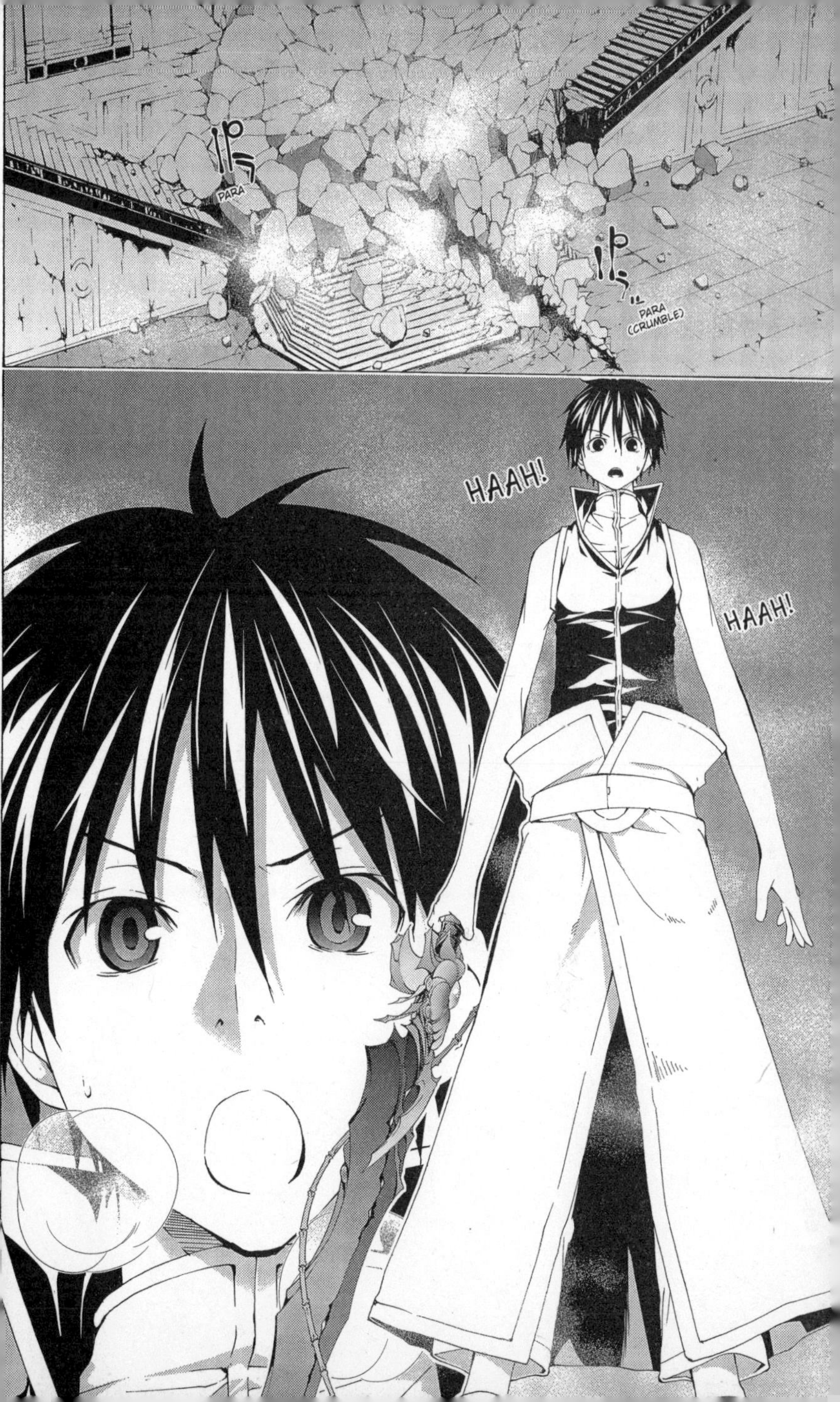
PARA (CRUMBLE)
PARA
HAAH!
HAAH!

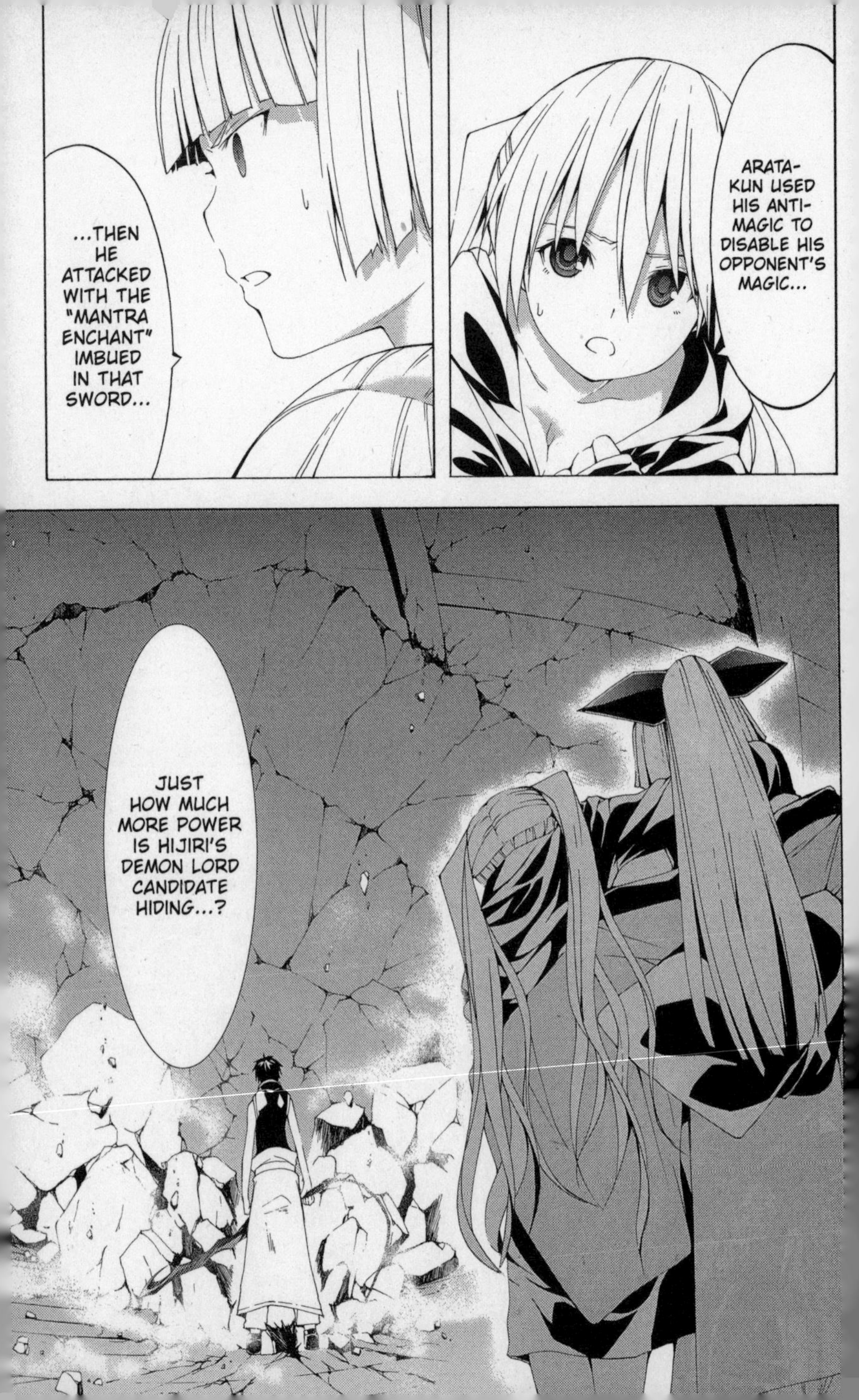
ARATA-KUN USED HIS ANTI-MAGIC TO DISABLE HIS OPPONENT'S MAGIC...
...THEN HE ATTACKED WITH THE "MANTRA ENCHANT" IMBUED IN THAT SWORD...
JUST HOW MUCH MORE POWER IS HIJIRI'S DEMON LORD CANDIDATE HIDING...?

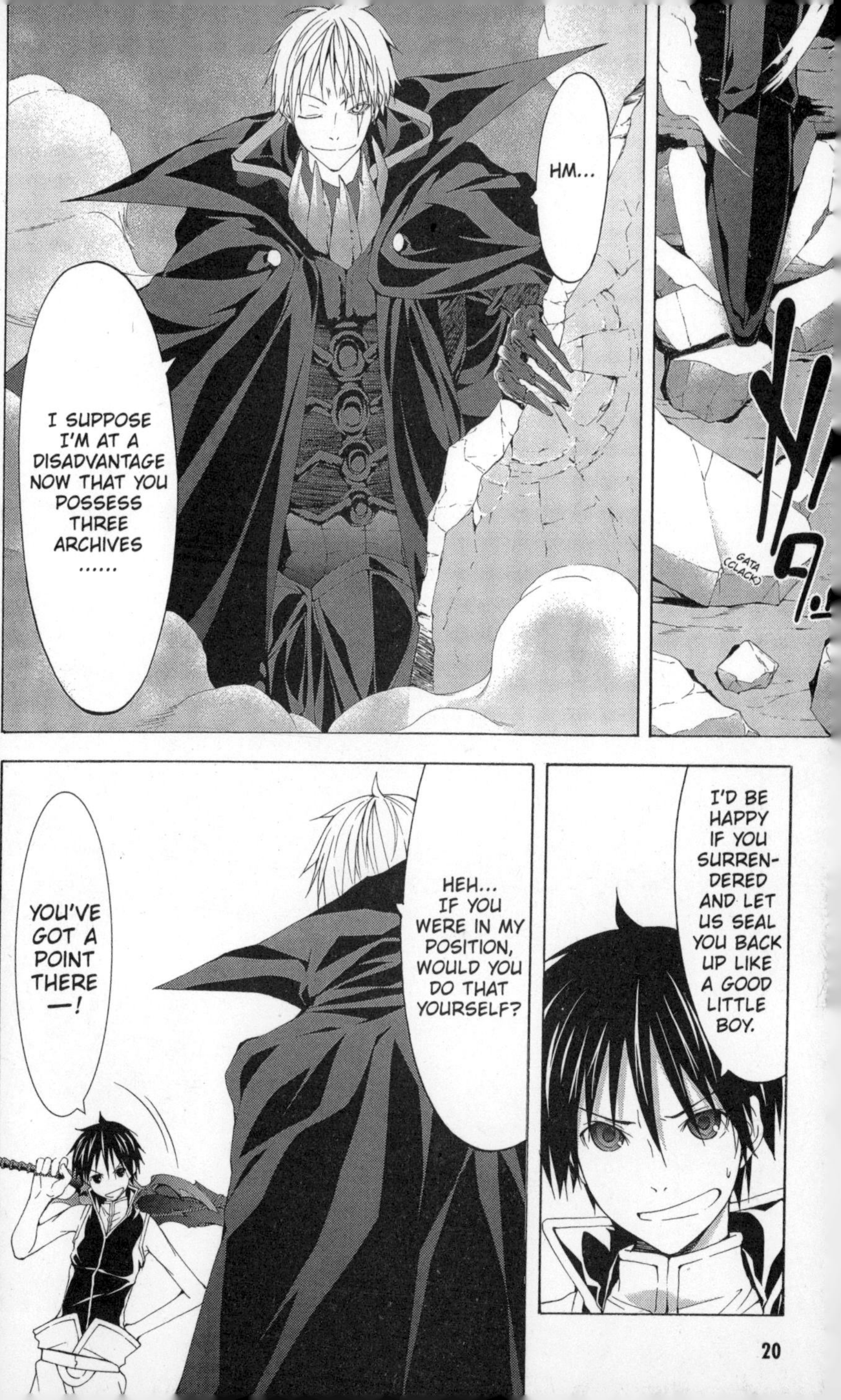
GATA (CLACK)
HM...
I SUPPOSE I'M AT A DISADVANTAGE NOW THAT YOU POSSESS THREE ARCHIVES ......
I'D BE HAPPY IF YOU SURREN-DERED AND LET US SEAL YOU BACK UP LIKE A GOOD LITTLE BOY.
HEH... IF YOU WERE IN MY POSITION, WOULD YOU DO THAT YOURSELF?
YOU'VE GOT A POINT THERE —!

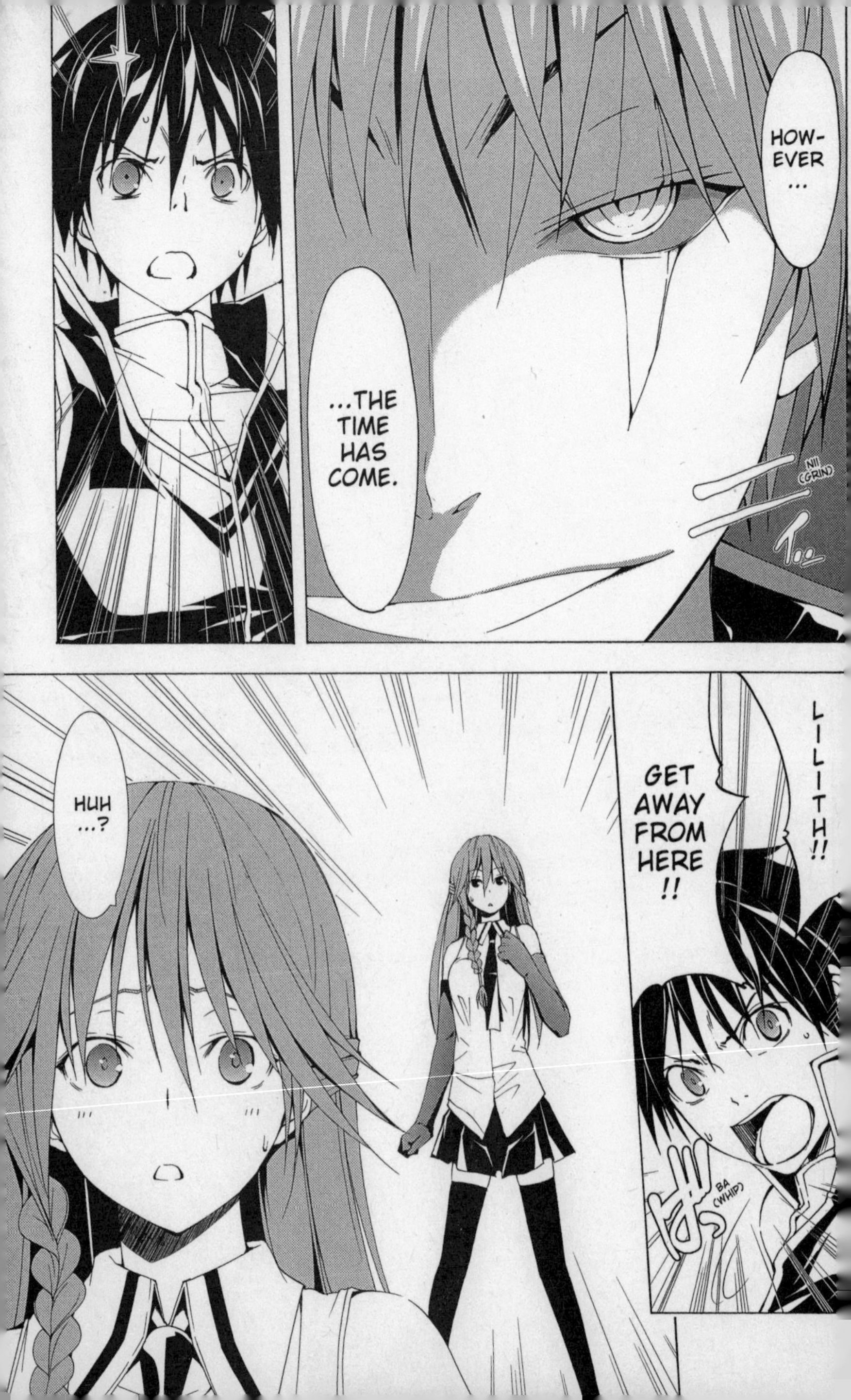
HOW-EVER...
...THE TIME HAS COME.
NII (GRIN)
LILITH!!
GET AWAY FROM HERE!!
BA (WHIP)
HUH...?

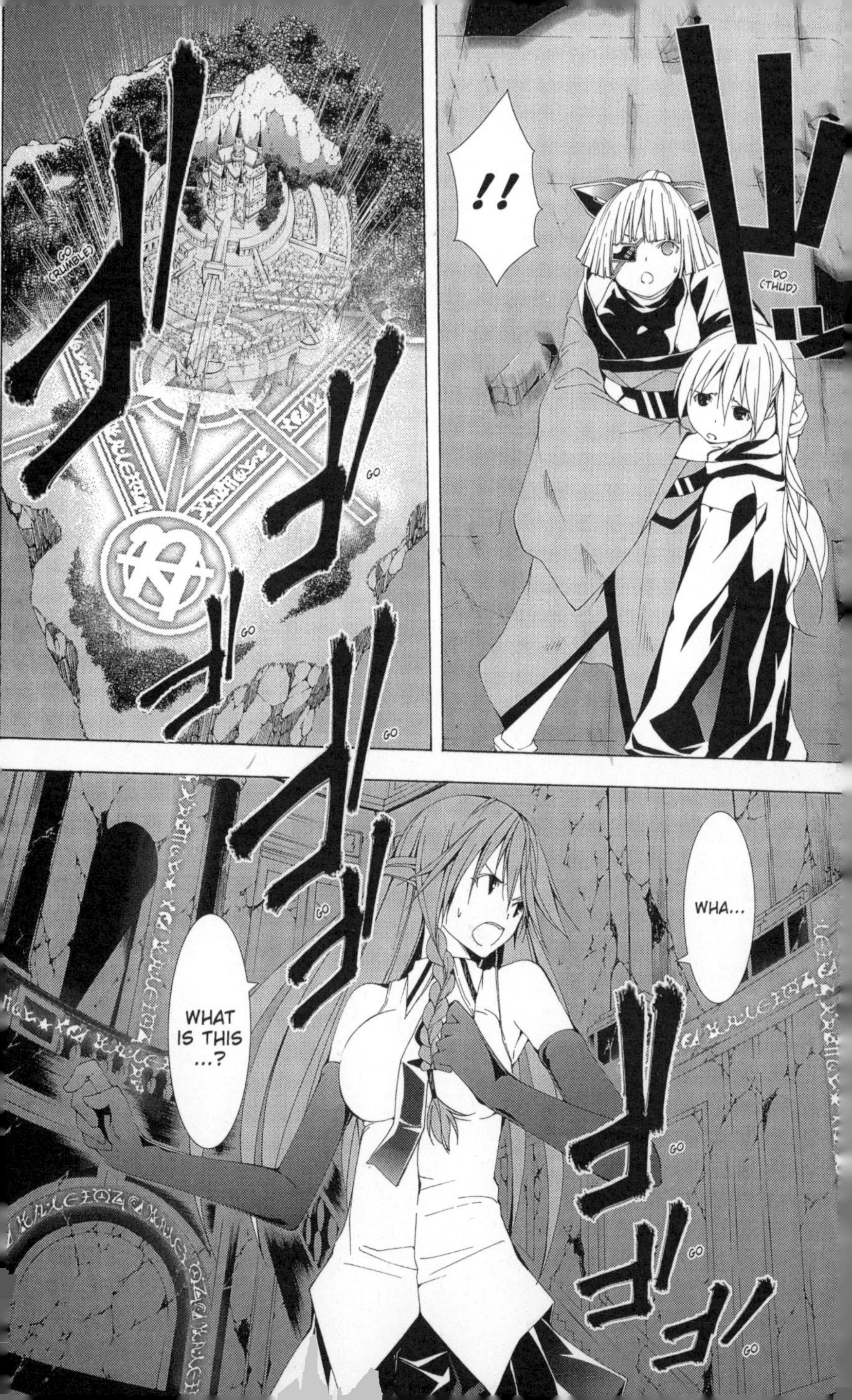
!!
DO (THUD)
GO (RUMBLE)
GO
GO
GO
WHA...
GO
WHAT IS THIS ...?
GO
GO
GO

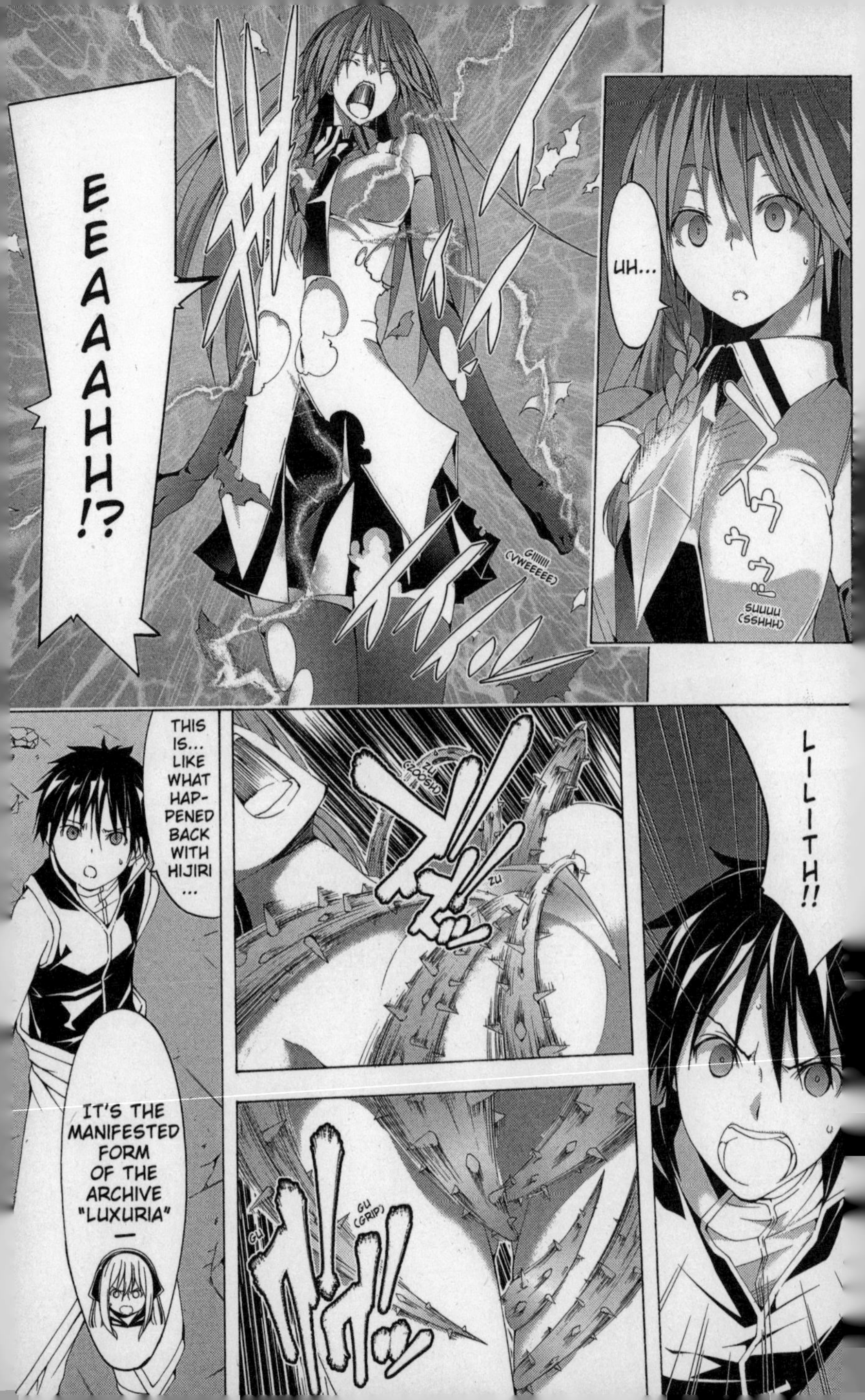
UH...
SUUUU (SSHHH)
EEAAAAHH!?
GIIIIII (VWEEEEE)
LILITH!!
ZU (ZOOSH)
ZU
GU (GRIP)
GU
THIS IS... LIKE WHAT HAP-PENED BACK WITH HIJIRI ...
IT'S THE MANIFESTED FORM OF THE ARCHIVE "LUXURIA" —

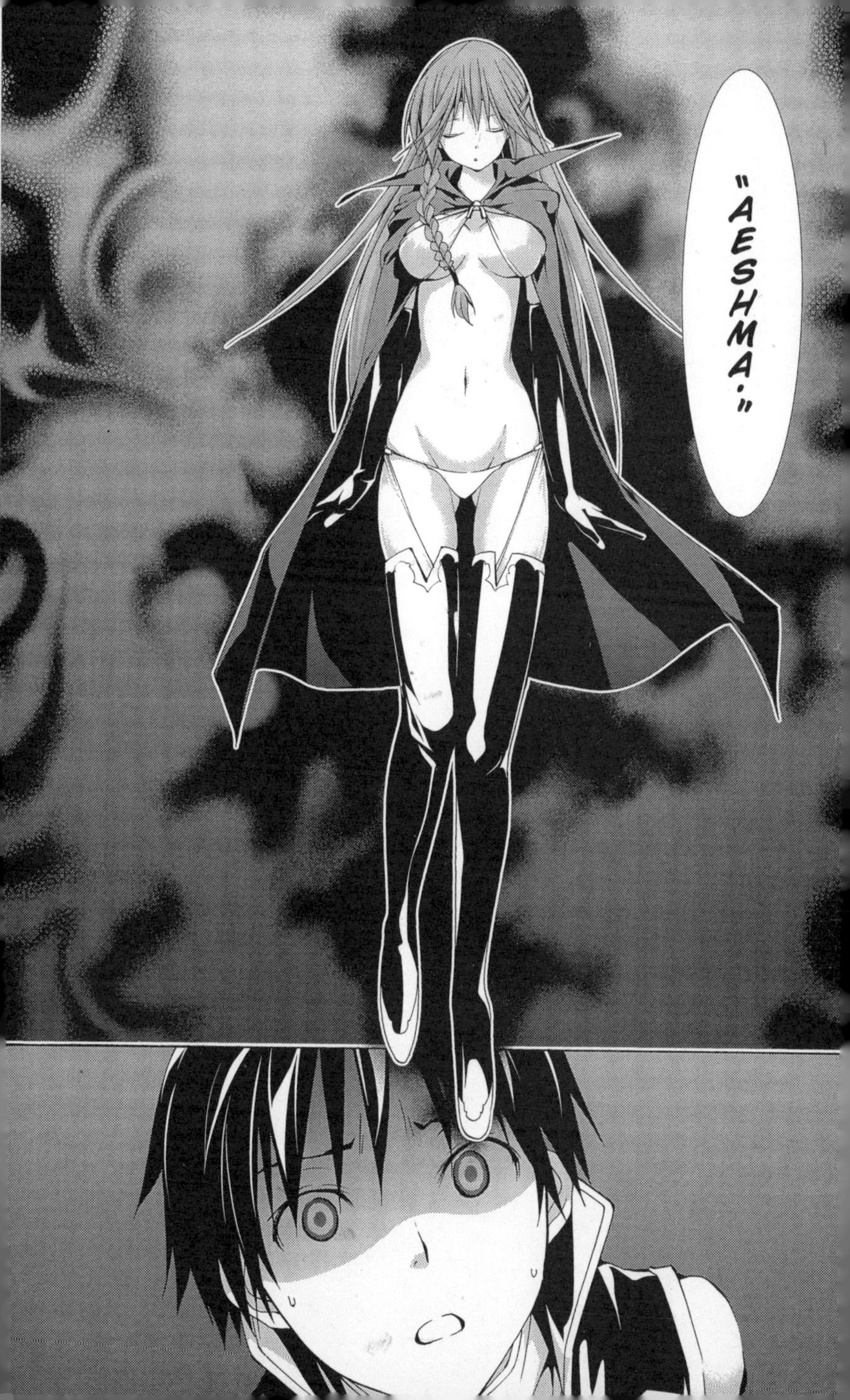
"AESHMA."

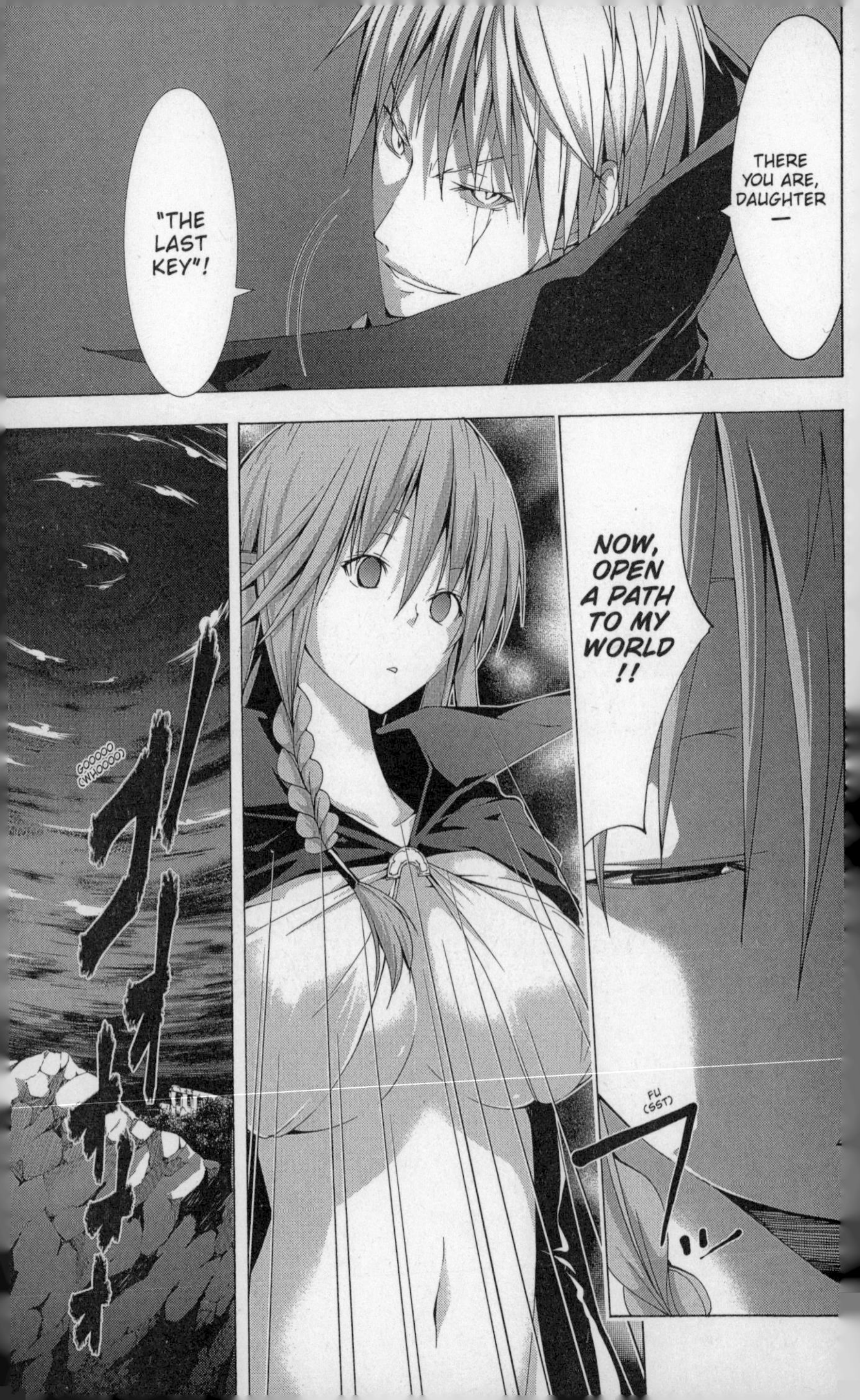
THERE YOU ARE, DAUGHTER —
"THE LAST KEY"!
NOW, OPEN A PATH TO MY WORLD!!
FU (SST)
!!
GOOOOO (WHOOOO)

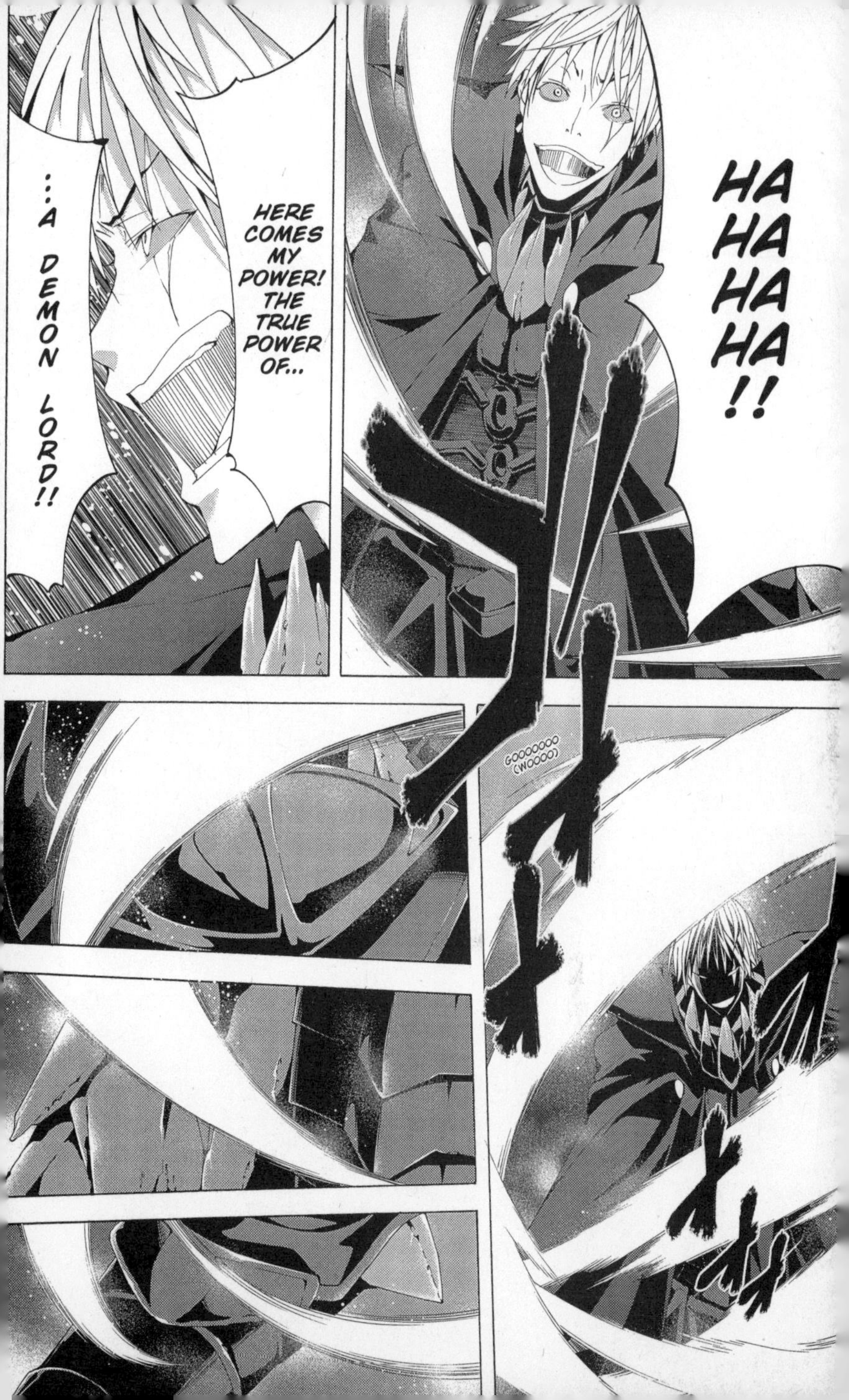
HA HA HA HA!!
HERE COMES MY POWER! THE TRUE POWER OF...
...A DEMON LORD!!
GOOOOOOO (WOOOO)

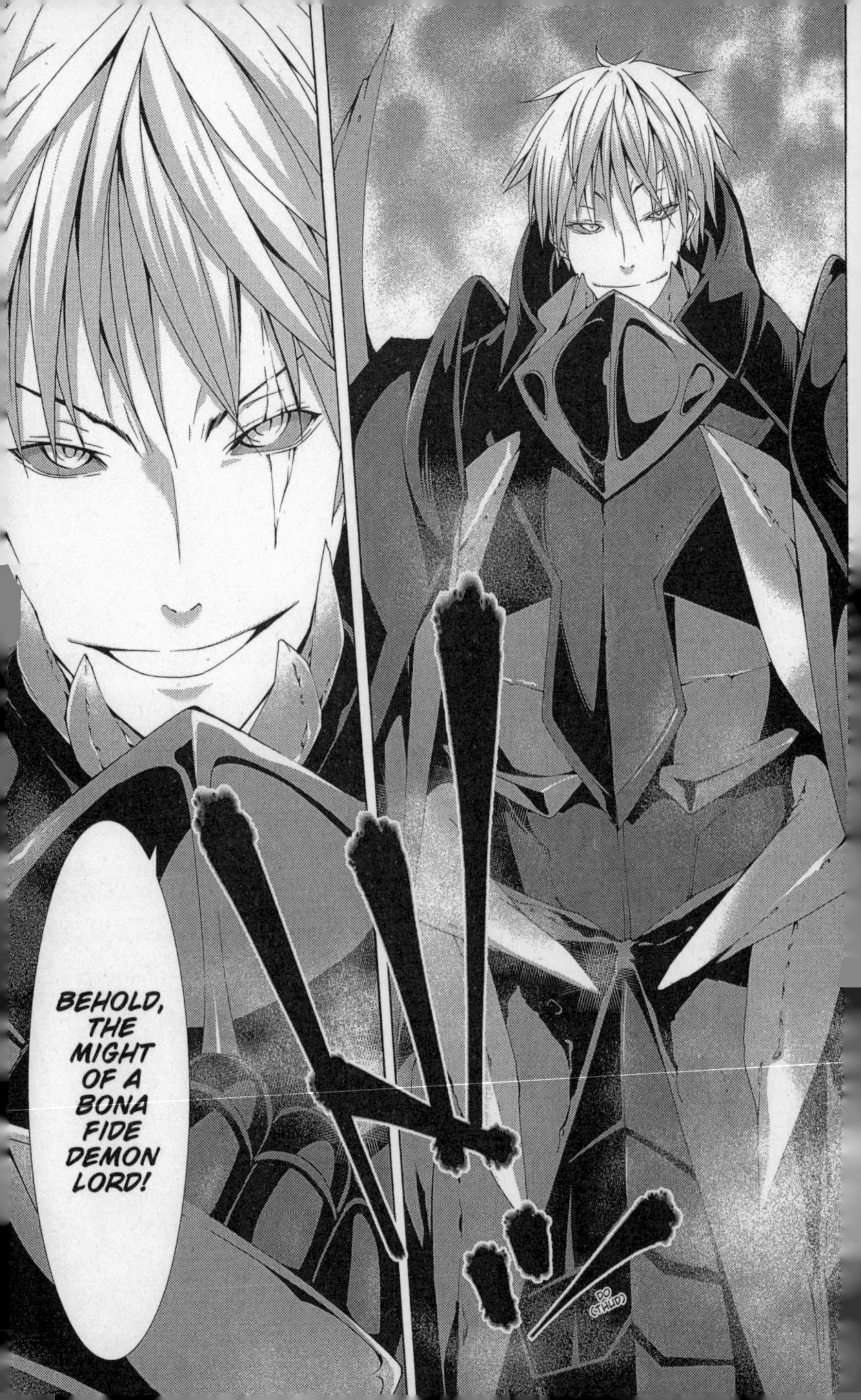
DO (THUD)
BEHOLD, THE MIGHT OF A BONA FIDE DEMON LORD!

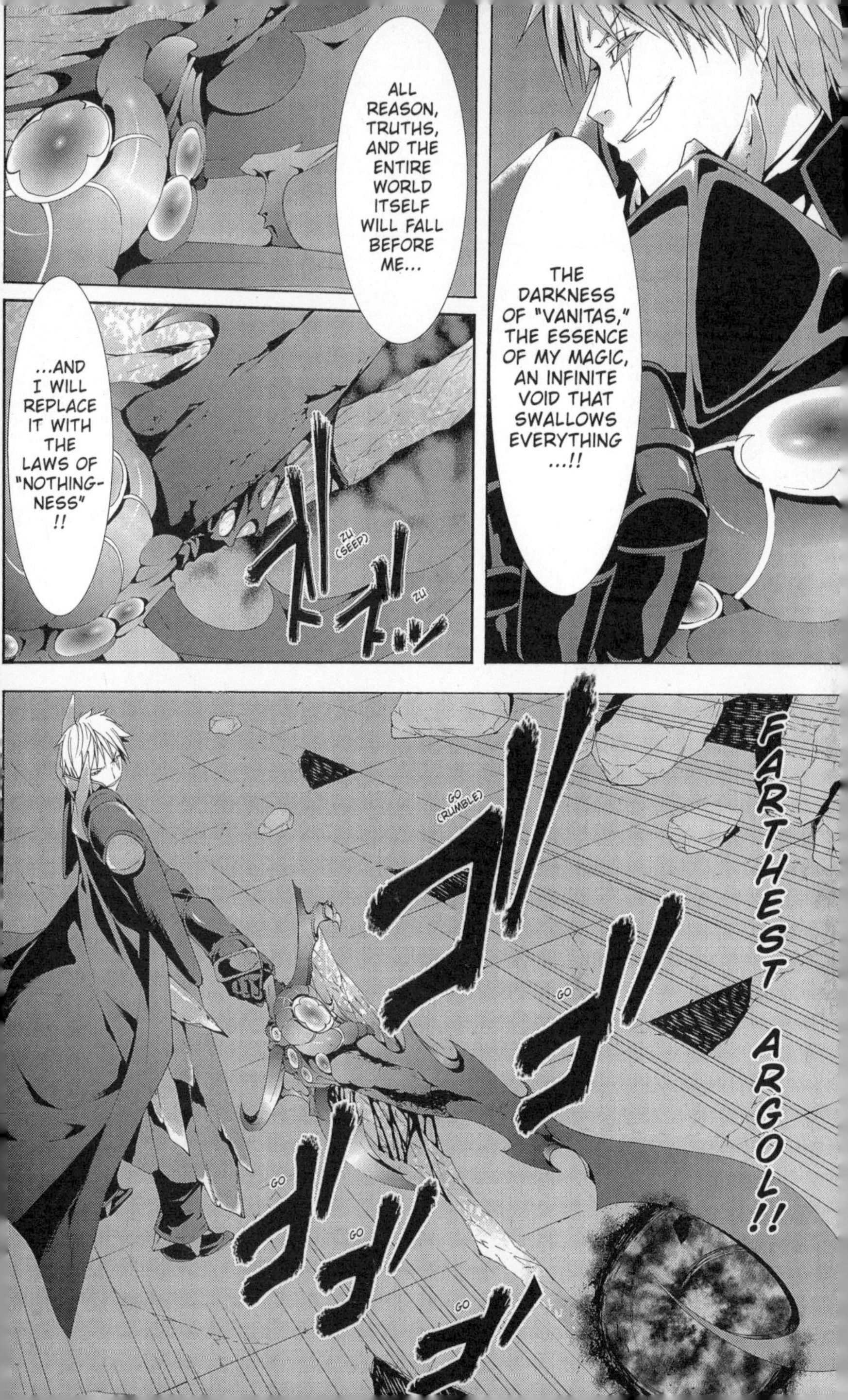
THE DARKNESS OF "VANITAS," THE ESSENCE OF MY MAGIC, AN INFINITE VOID THAT SWALLOWS EVERYTHING ...!!
ALL REASON, TRUTHS, AND THE ENTIRE WORLD ITSELF WILL FALL BEFORE ME...
...AND I WILL REPLACE IT WITH THE LAWS OF "NOTHING-NESS" !!
ZU (SEEP)
ZU
FARTHEST ARGOL!!
GO (RUMBLE)
GO
GO
GO
GO

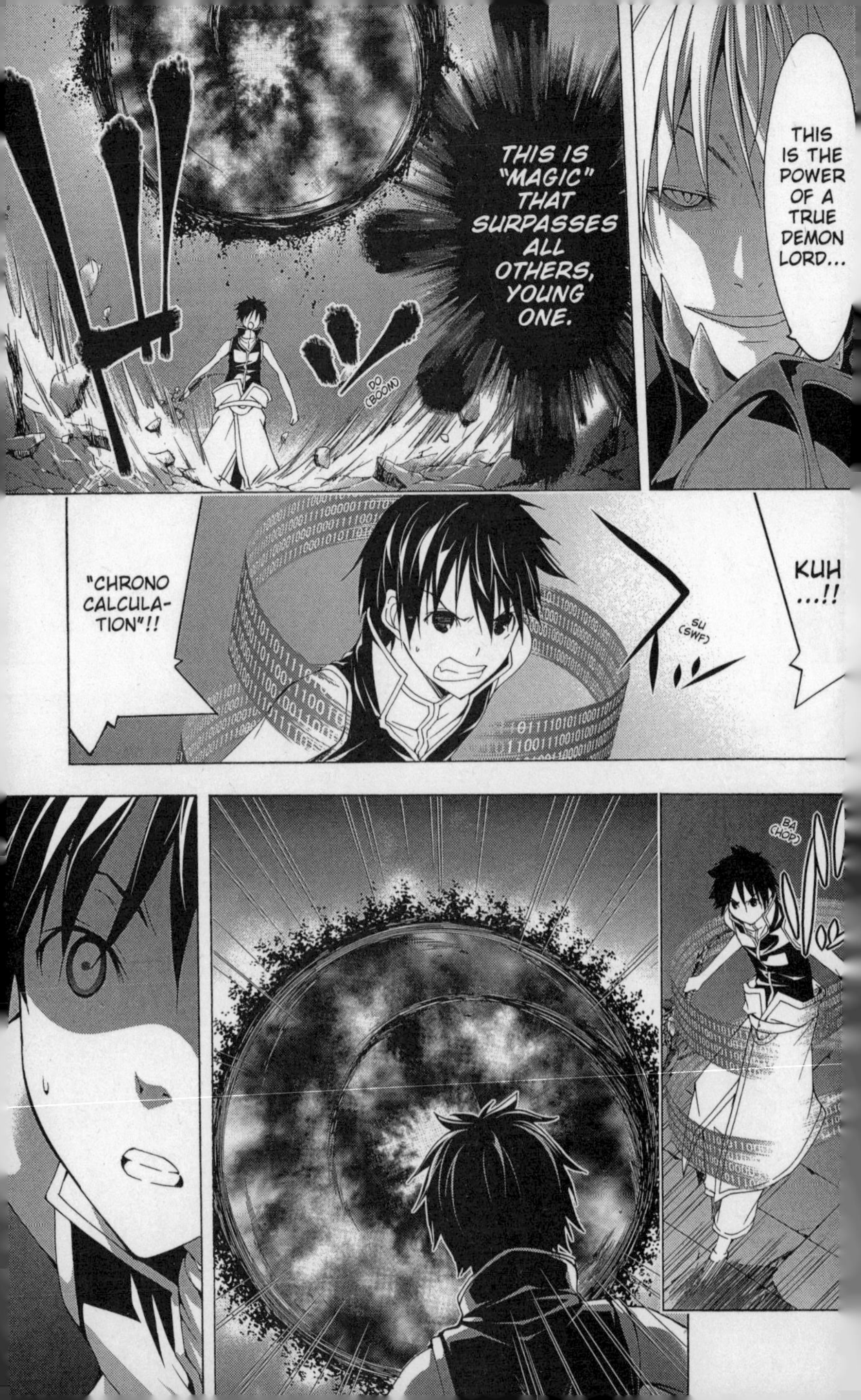
THIS IS THE POWER OF A TRUE DEMON LORD...
THIS IS "MAGIC" THAT SURPASSES ALL OTHERS, YOUNG ONE.
DO (BOOM)
KUH ...!!
SU (SWF)
"CHRONO CALCULA-TION"!!
BA (HOP)

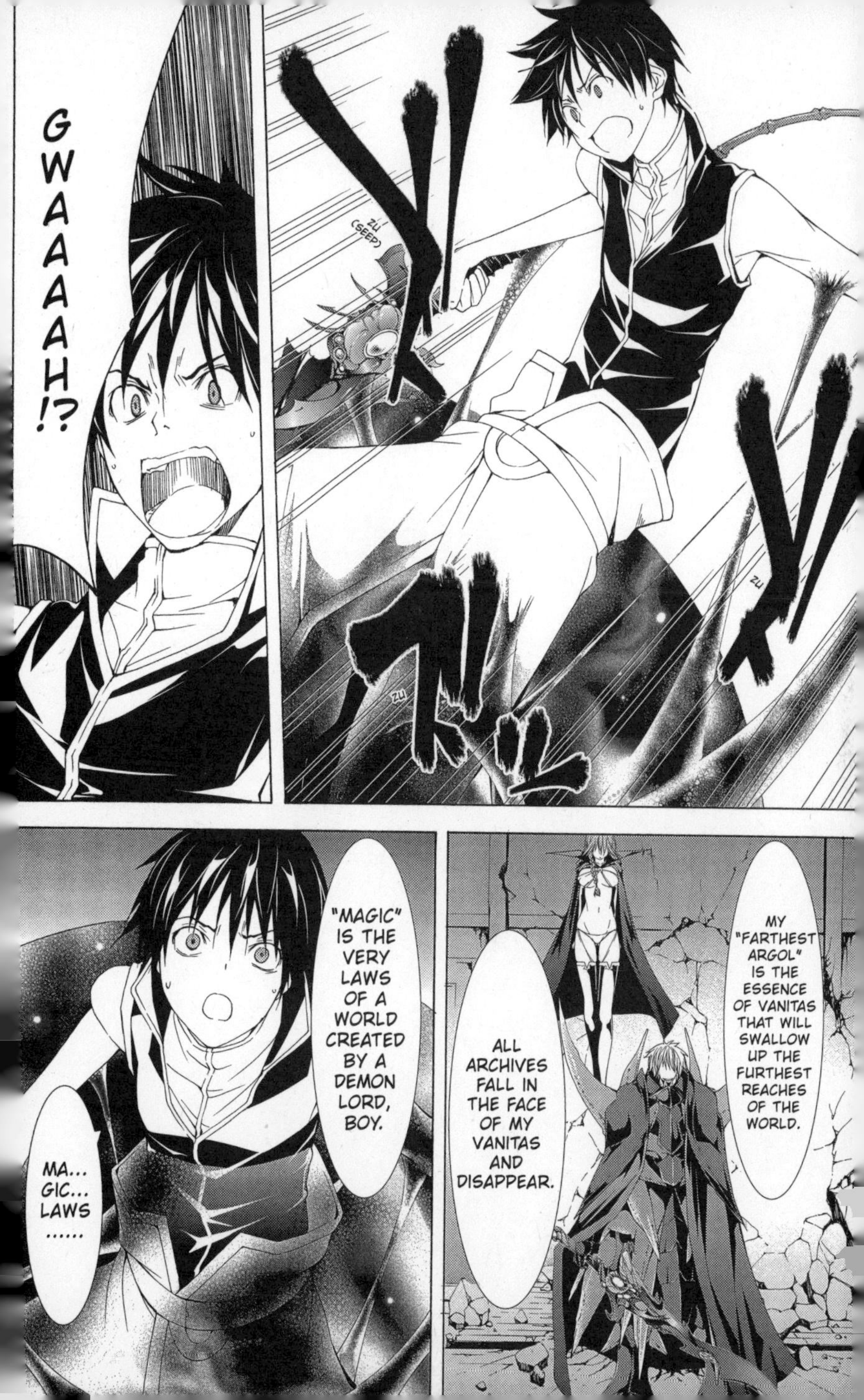
ZU (SEEP)
ZU
ZU
GWAAAAAH!?
MY "FARTHEST ARGOL" IS THE ESSENCE OF VANITAS THAT WILL SWALLOW UP THE FURTHEST REACHES OF THE WORLD.
ALL ARCHIVES FALL IN THE FACE OF MY VANITAS AND DISAPPEAR.
"MAGIC" IS THE VERY LAWS OF A WORLD CREATED BY A DEMON LORD, BOY.
MA... GIC... LAWS ......

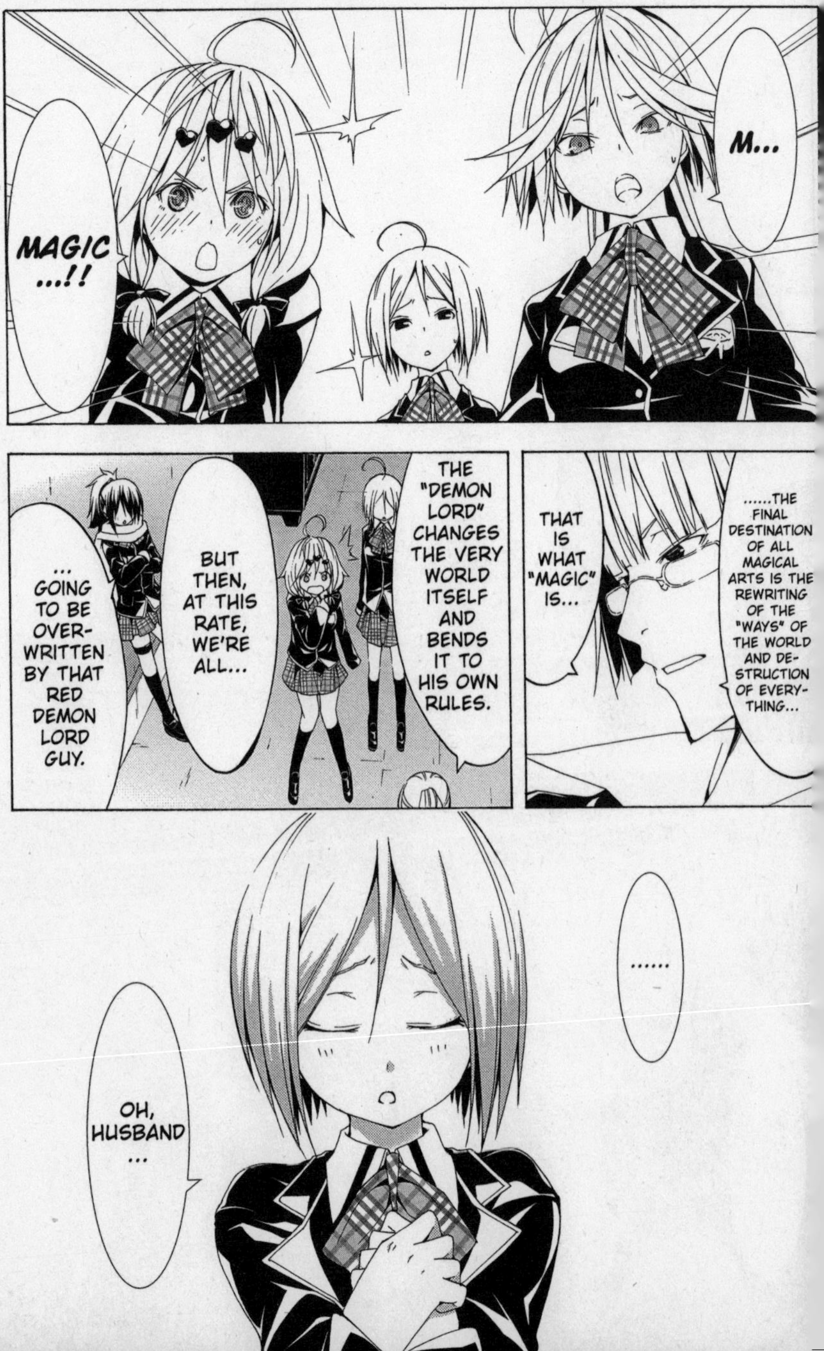
M...
MAGIC ...!!
......THE FINAL DESTINATION OF ALL MAGICAL ARTS IS THE REWRITING OF THE "WAYS" OF THE WORLD AND DE-STRUCTION OF EVERY-THING...
THAT IS WHAT "MAGIC" IS...
THE "DEMON LORD" CHANGES THE VERY WORLD ITSELF AND BENDS IT TO HIS OWN RULES.
BUT THEN, AT THIS RATE, WE'RE ALL...
... GOING TO BE OVER-WRITTEN BY THAT RED DEMON LORD GUY.
......
OH, HUSBAND ...

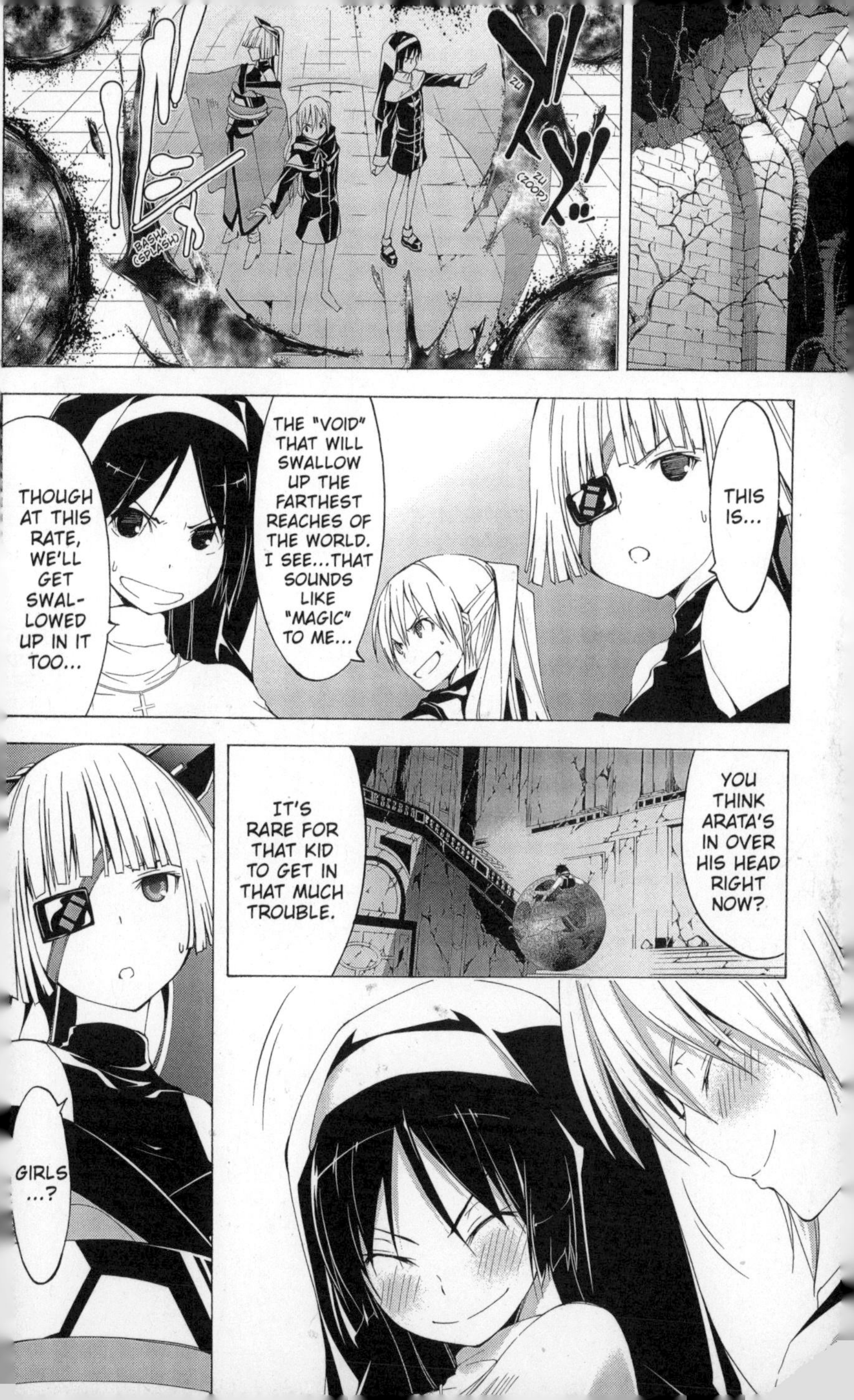
ZU
ZU (ZOOP)
BASHA (SPLASH)
THIS IS...
THE "VOID" THAT WILL SWALLOW UP THE FARTHEST REACHES OF THE WORLD. I SEE...THAT SOUNDS LIKE "MAGIC" TO ME...
THOUGH AT THIS RATE, WE'LL GET SWAL-LOWED UP IN IT TOO...
YOU THINK ARATA'S IN OVER HIS HEAD RIGHT NOW?
IT'S RARE FOR THAT KID TO GET IN THAT MUCH TROUBLE.
GIRLS ...?

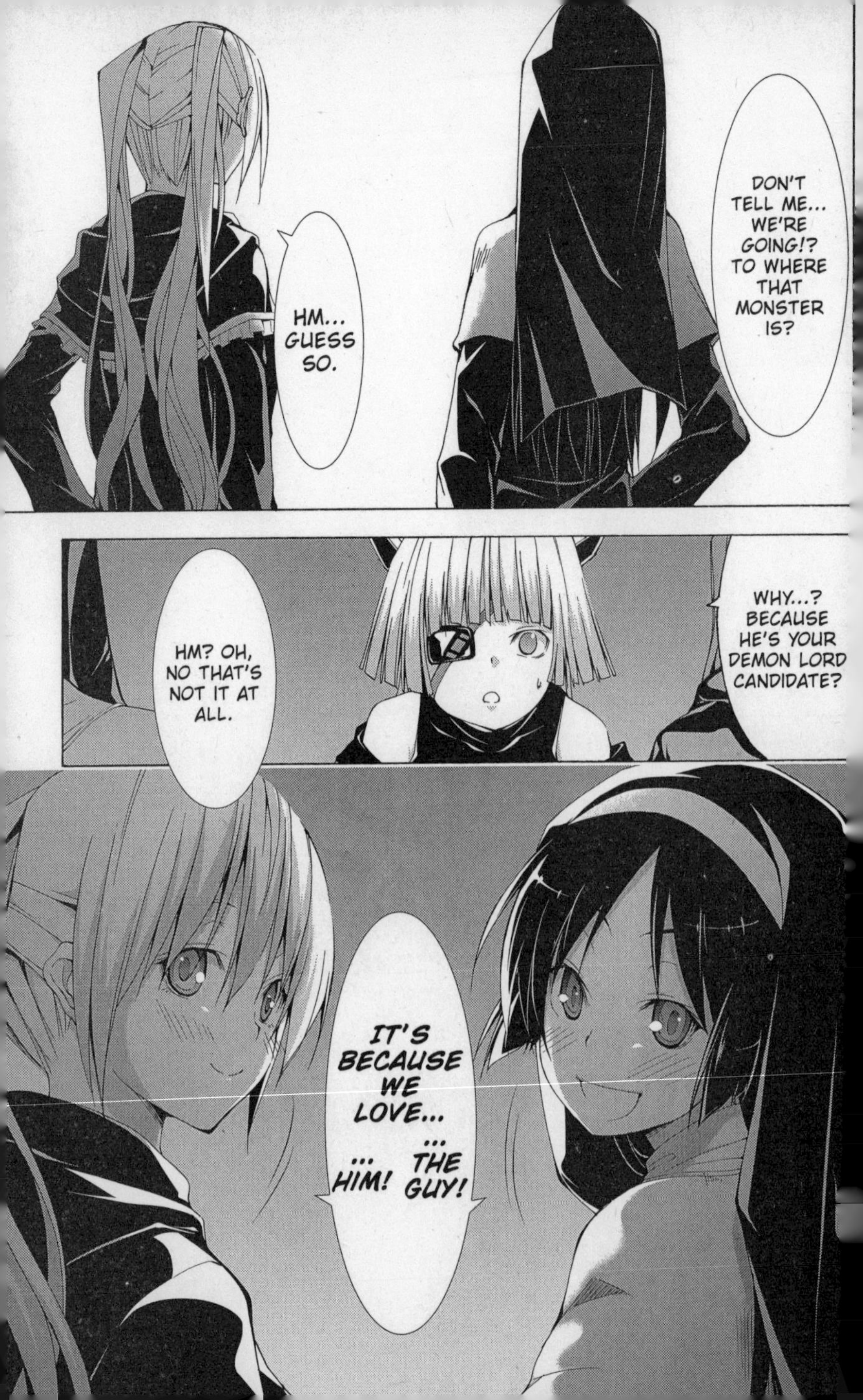
DON'T TELL ME... WE'RE GOING!? TO WHERE THAT MONSTER IS?
HM... GUESS SO.
WHY...? BECAUSE HE'S YOUR DEMON LORD CANDIDATE?
HM? OH, NO THAT'S NOT IT AT ALL.
IT'S BECAUSE WE LOVE...
... THE GUY!
... HIM!

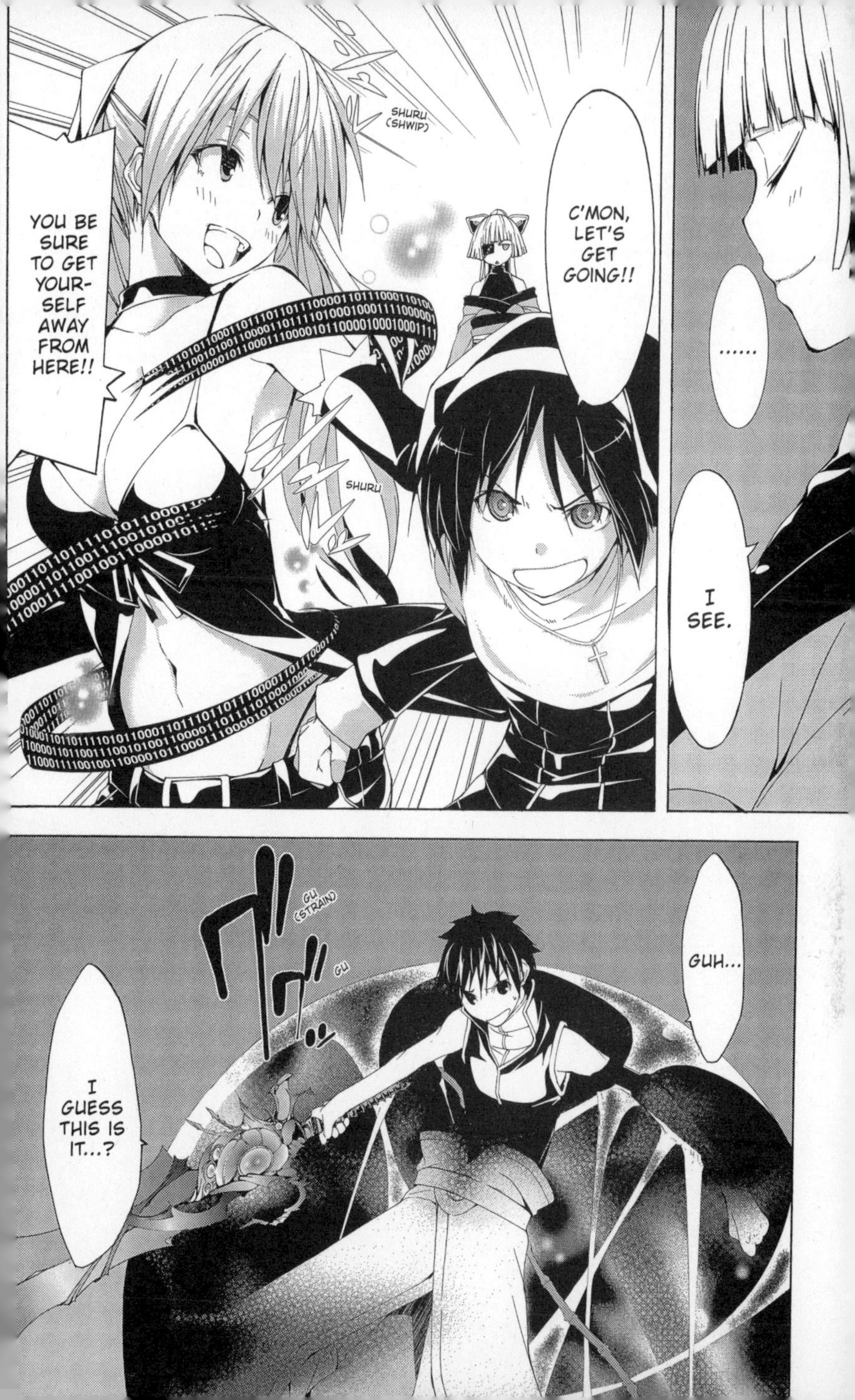
......
I SEE.
C'MON, LET'S GET GOING!!
SHURU (SHWIP)
YOU BE SURE TO GET YOURSELF AWAY FROM HERE!!
SHURU
GUH...
GU (STRAIN)
GU
I GUESS THIS IS IT...?

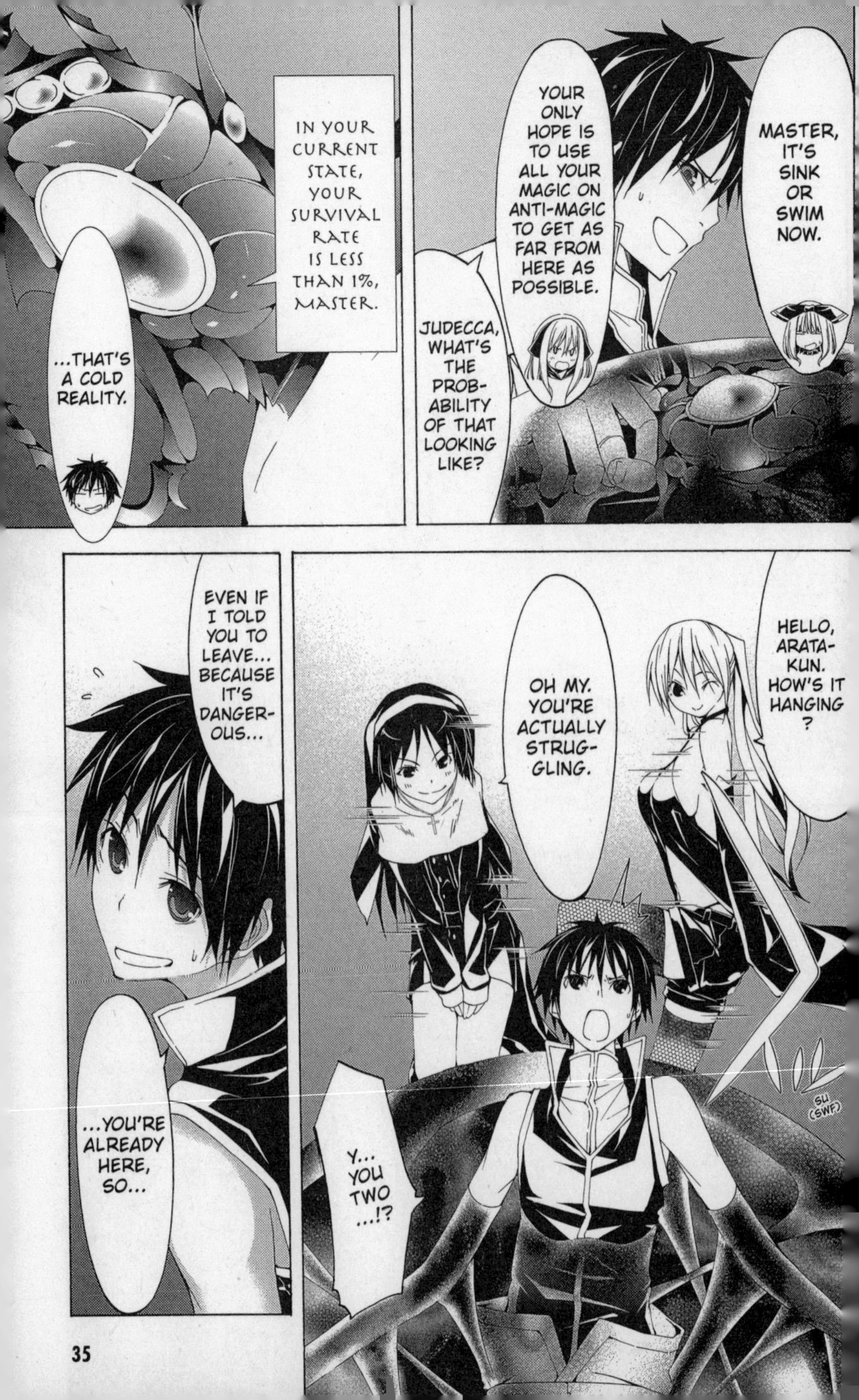
MASTER, IT'S SINK OR SWIM NOW.
YOUR ONLY HOPE IS TO USE ALL YOUR MAGIC ON ANTI-MAGIC TO GET AS FAR FROM HERE AS POSSIBLE.
JUDECCA, WHAT'S THE PROB-ABILITY OF THAT LOOKING LIKE?
IN YOUR CURRENT STATE, YOUR SURVIVAL RATE IS LESS THAN 1%, MASTER.
...THAT'S A COLD REALITY.
HELLO, ARATA-KUN. HOW'S IT HANGING?
OH MY. YOU'RE ACTUALLY STRUG-GLING.
SU (SWF)
Y... YOU TWO ...!?
EVEN IF I TOLD YOU TO LEAVE... BECAUSE IT'S DANGER-OUS...
...YOU'RE ALREADY HERE, SO...

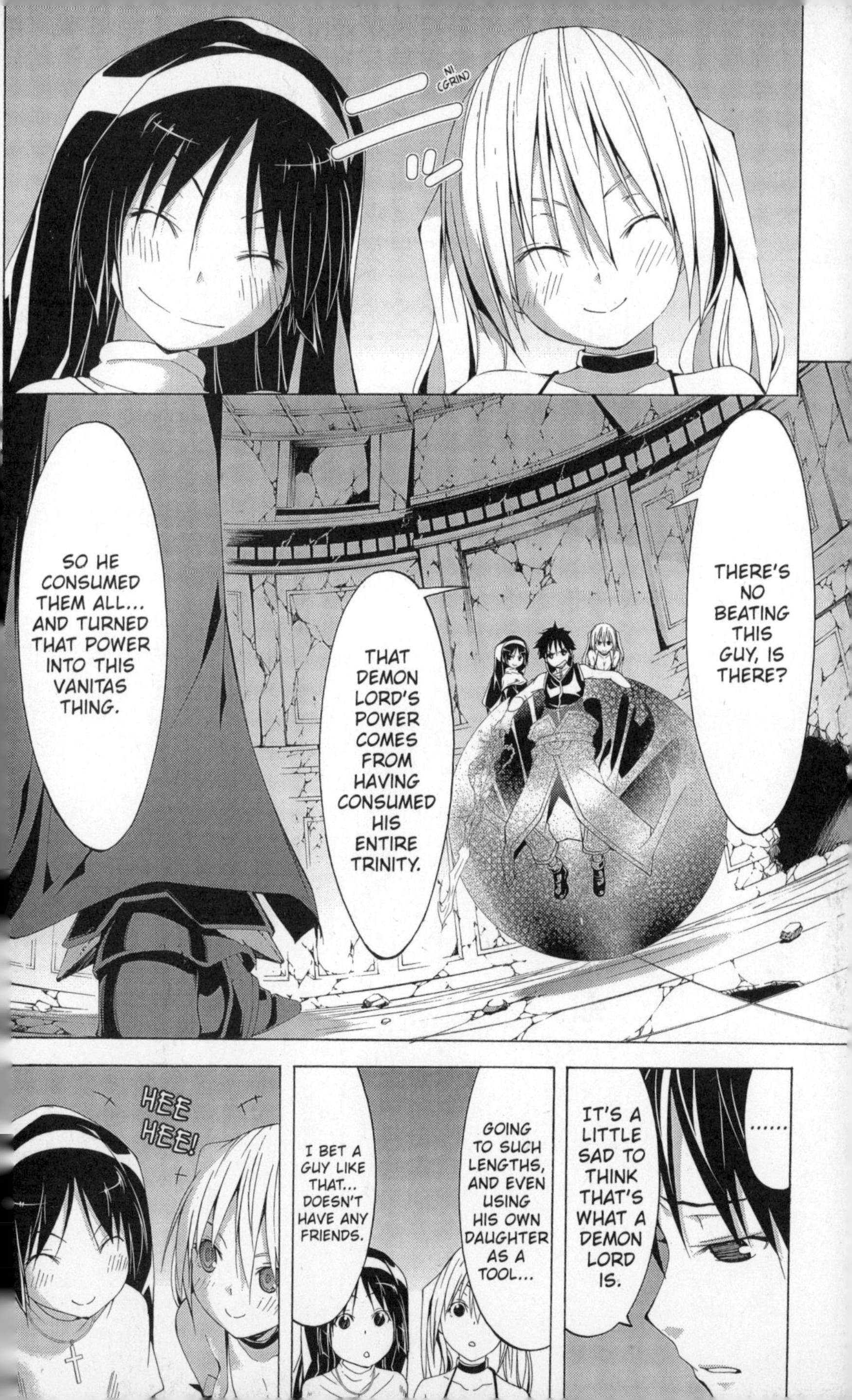
NI (GRIN)
THERE'S NO BEATING THIS GUY, IS THERE?
THAT DEMON LORD'S POWER COMES FROM HAVING CONSUMED HIS ENTIRE TRINITY.
SO HE CONSUMED THEM ALL... AND TURNED THAT POWER INTO THIS VANITAS THING.
......
IT'S A LITTLE SAD TO THINK THAT'S WHAT A DEMON LORD IS.
GOING TO SUCH LENGTHS, AND EVEN USING HIS OWN DAUGHTER AS A TOOL...
I BET A GUY LIKE THAT... DOESN'T HAVE ANY FRIENDS.
HEE HEE!

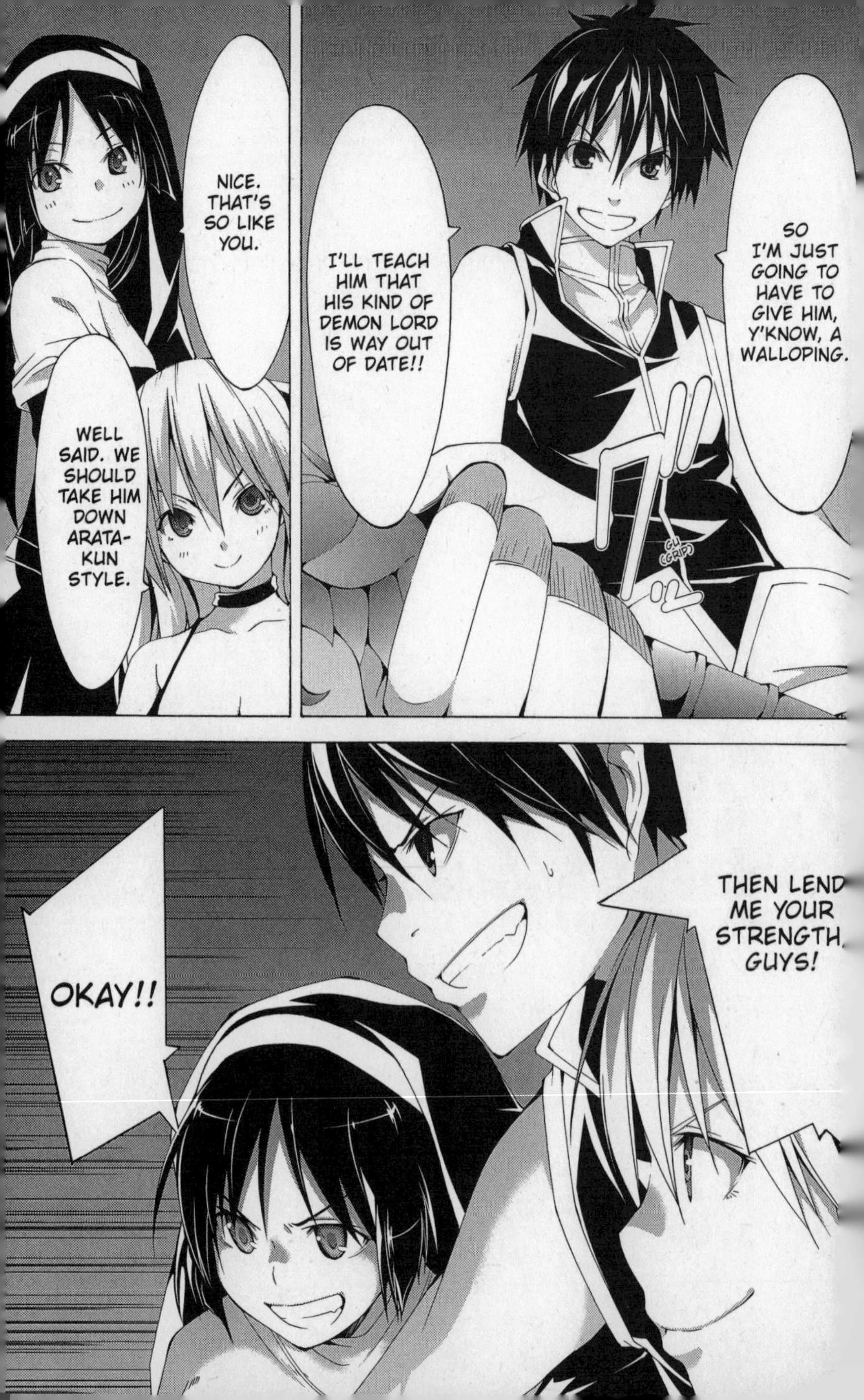
SO I'M JUST GOING TO HAVE TO GIVE HIM, Y'KNOW, A WALLOPING.
GU (GRIP)
I'LL TEACH HIM THAT HIS KIND OF DEMON LORD IS WAY OUT OF DATE!!
NICE. THAT'S SO LIKE YOU.
WELL SAID. WE SHOULD TAKE HIM DOWN ARATA-KUN STYLE.
THEN LEND ME YOUR STRENGTH, GUYS!
OKAY!!

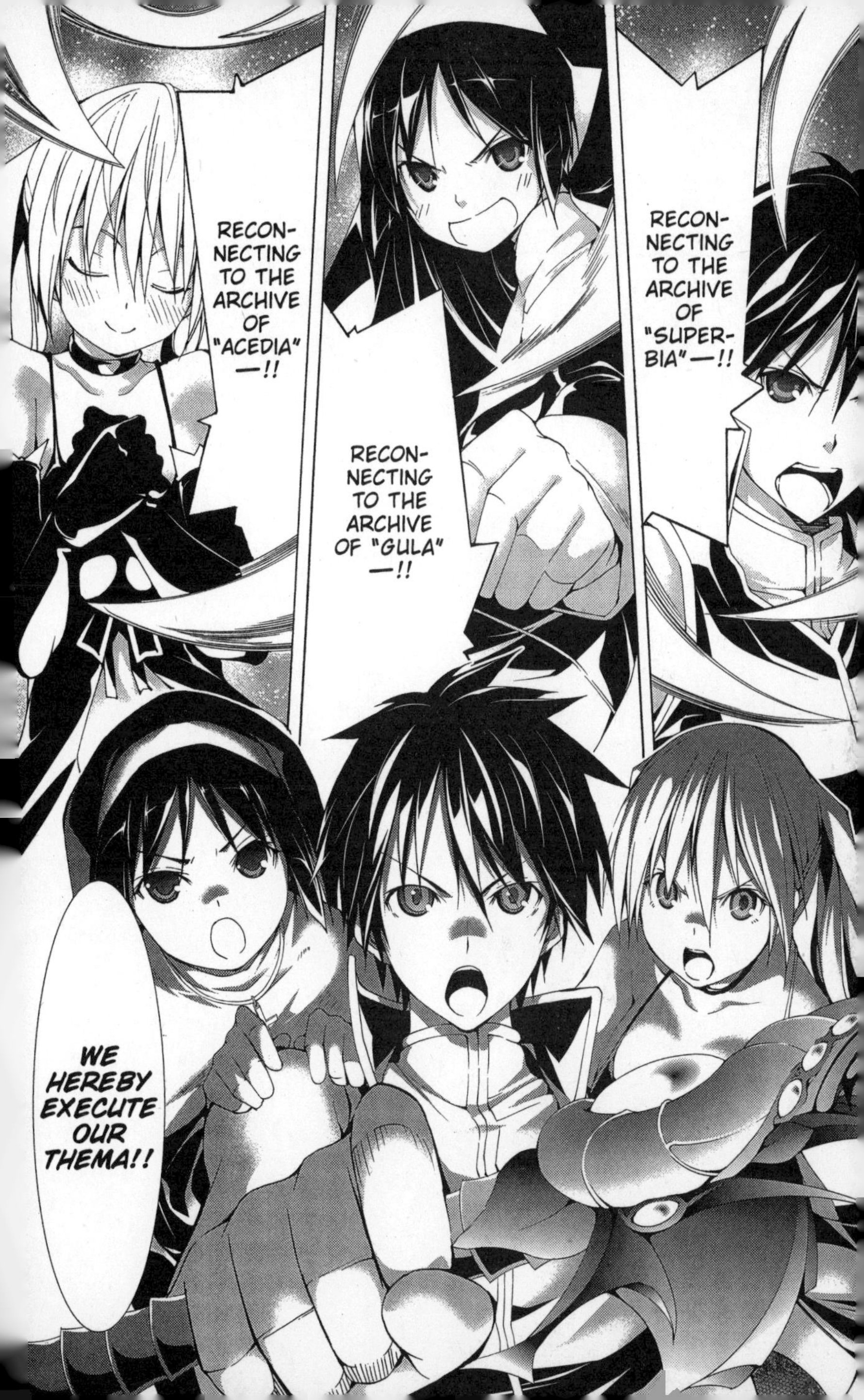
RECON-NECTING TO THE ARCHIVE OF "SUPER-BIA"—!!
RECON-NECTING TO THE ARCHIVE OF "GULA" —!!
RECON-NECTING TO THE ARCHIVE OF "ACEDIA" —!!
WE HEREBY EXECUTE OUR THEMA!!

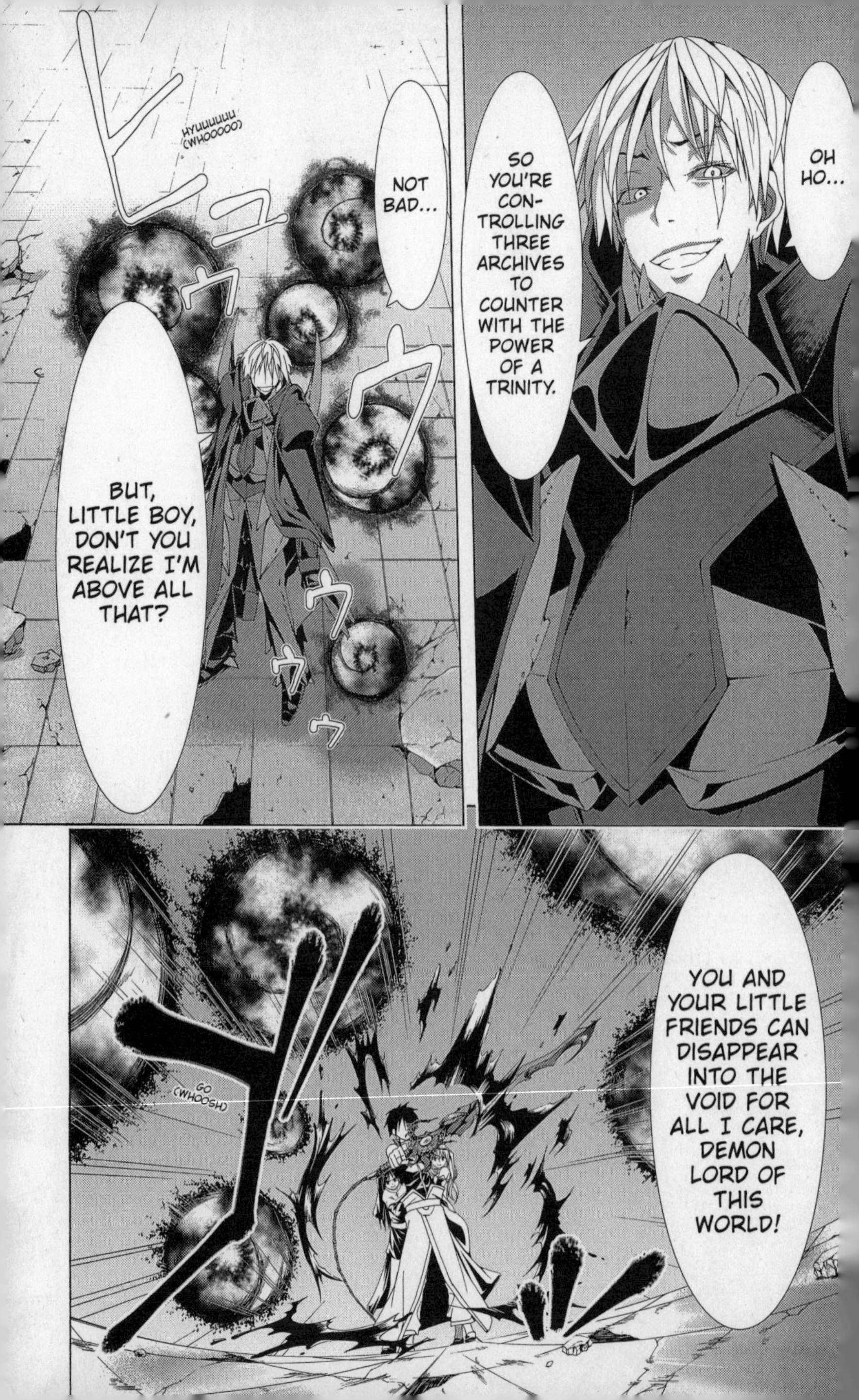
OH HO...
SO YOU'RE CON-TROLLING THREE ARCHIVES TO COUNTER WITH THE POWER OF A TRINITY.
HYUUUUUU (WHOOOOO)
NOT BAD...
BUT, LITTLE BOY, DON'T YOU REALIZE I'M ABOVE ALL THAT?
YOU AND YOUR LITTLE FRIENDS CAN DISAPPEAR INTO THE VOID FOR ALL I CARE, DEMON LORD OF THIS WORLD!
GO (WHOOSH)

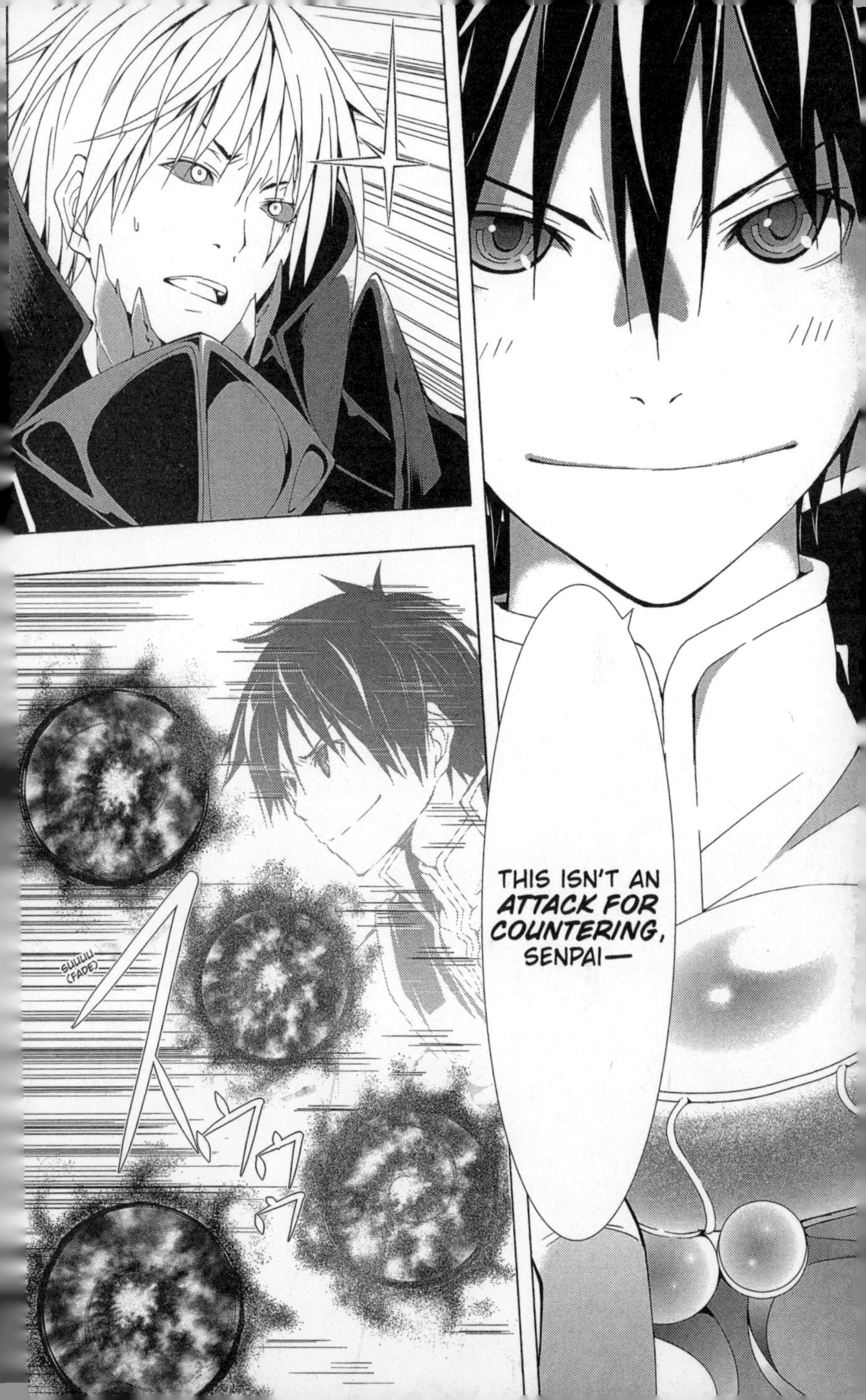
THIS ISN'T AN ATTACK FOR COUNTERING, SENPAI—
SUUUU (FADE)

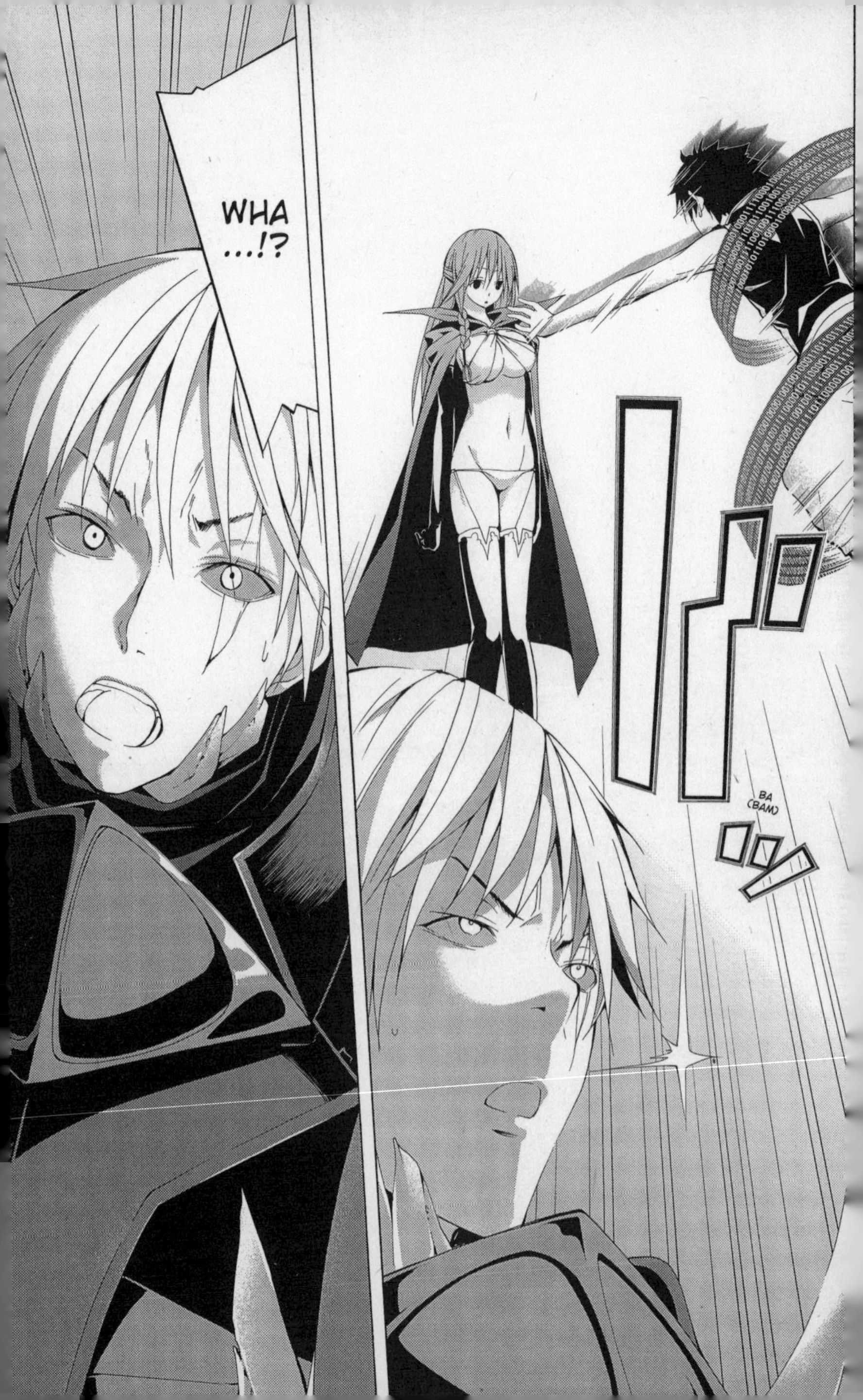
BA
(BAM)
WHA
...!?

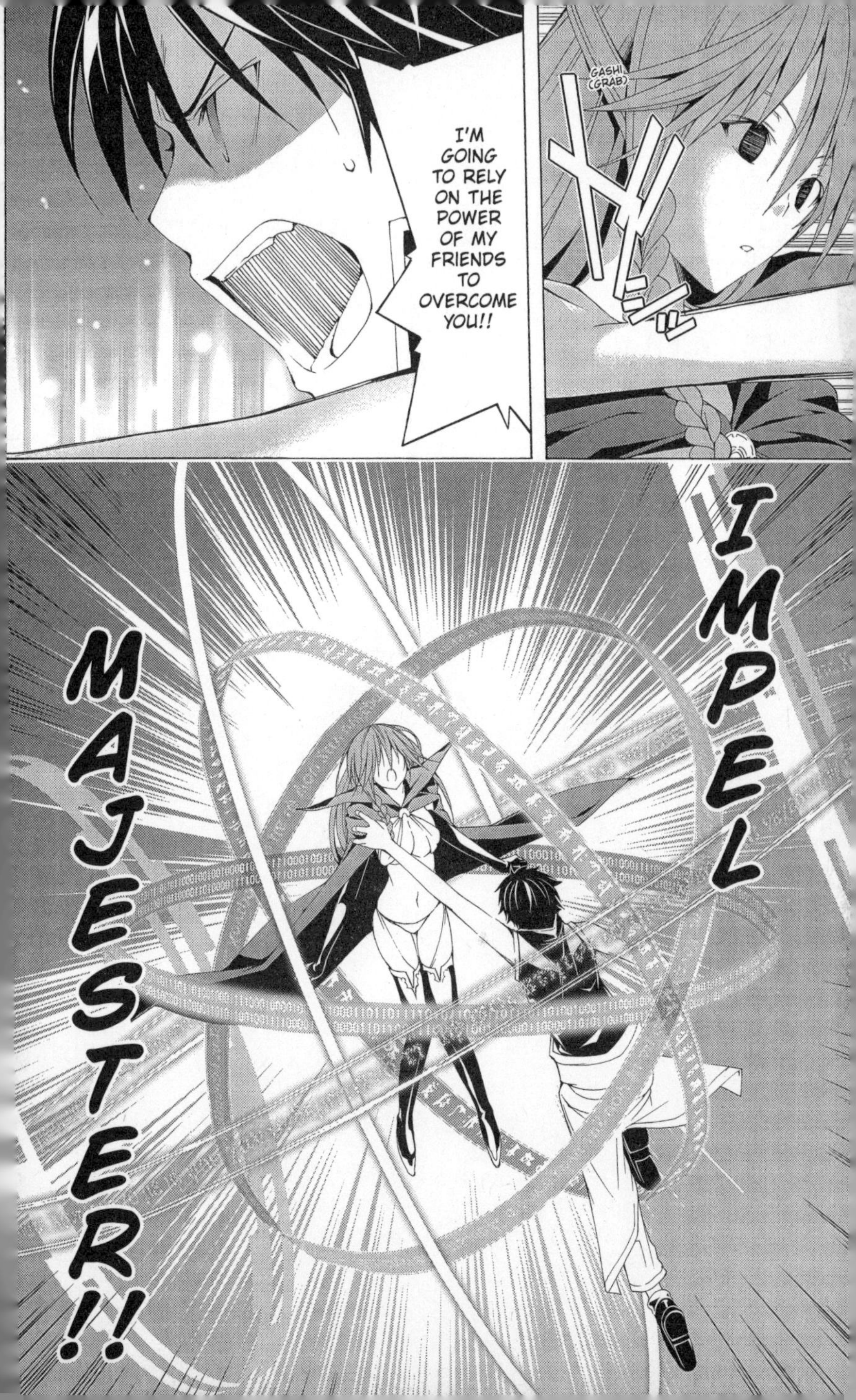
GASHI (GRAB)
I'M GOING TO RELY ON THE POWER OF MY FRIENDS TO OVERCOME YOU!!
IMPEL
MAJESTER!!

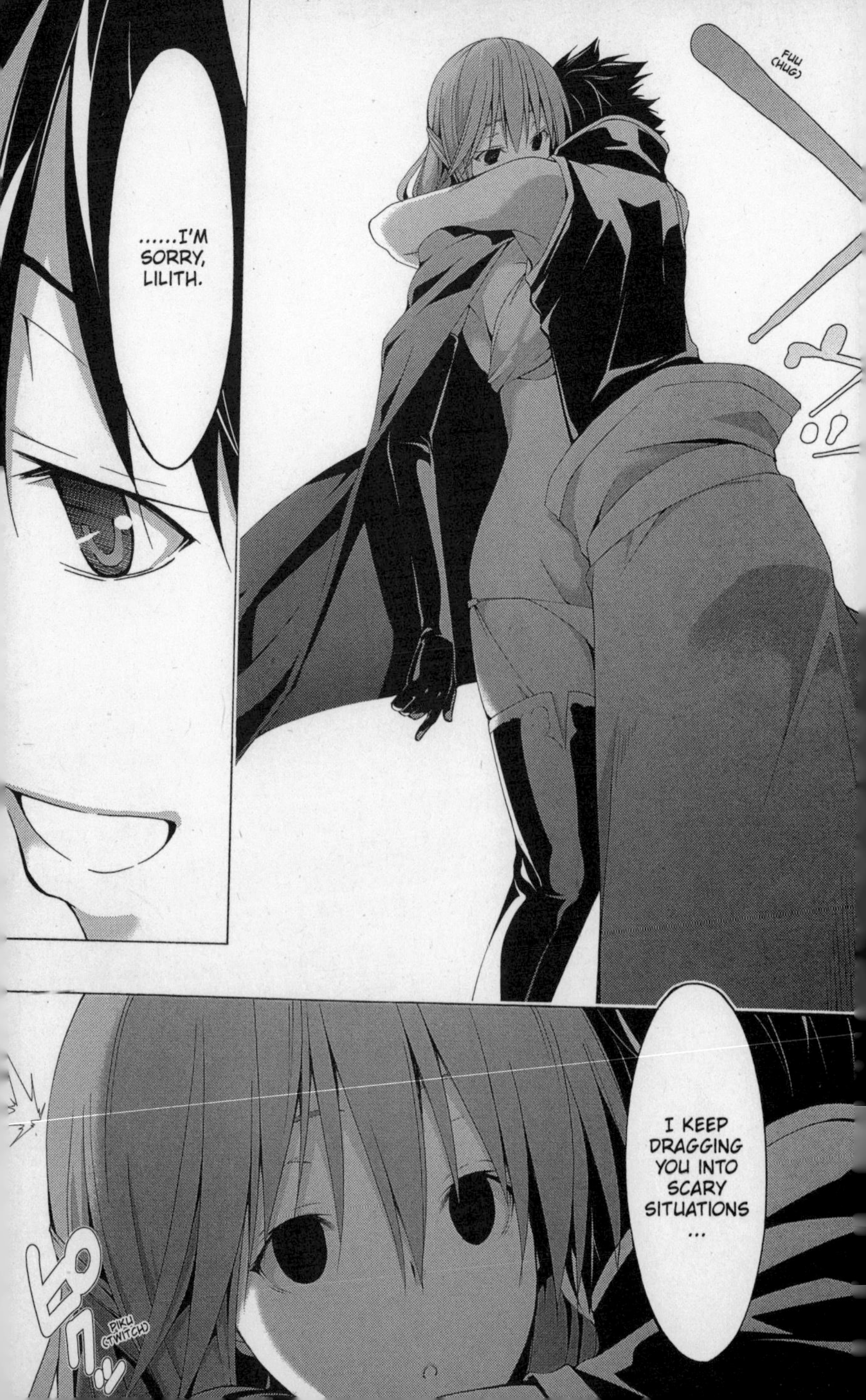
FUU (HUG)
......I'M SORRY, LILITH.
I KEEP DRAGGING YOU INTO SCARY SITUATIONS ...
PIKU (TWITCH)

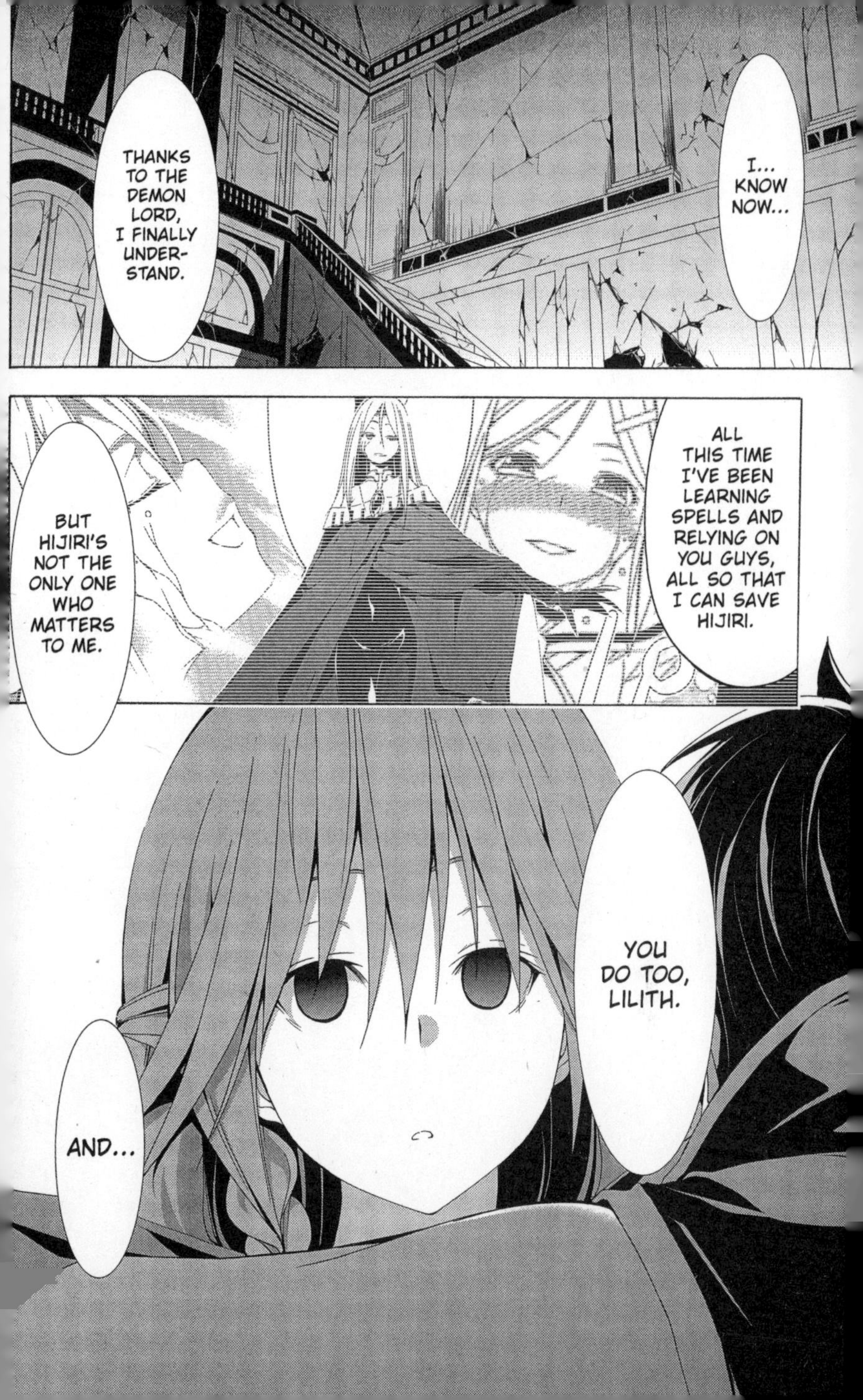
I... KNOW NOW...
THANKS TO THE DEMON LORD, I FINALLY UNDERSTAND.
ALL THIS TIME I'VE BEEN LEARNING SPELLS AND RELYING ON YOU GUYS, ALL SO THAT I CAN SAVE HIJIRI.
BUT HIJIRI'S NOT THE ONLY ONE WHO MATTERS TO ME.
YOU DO TOO, LILITH.
AND...

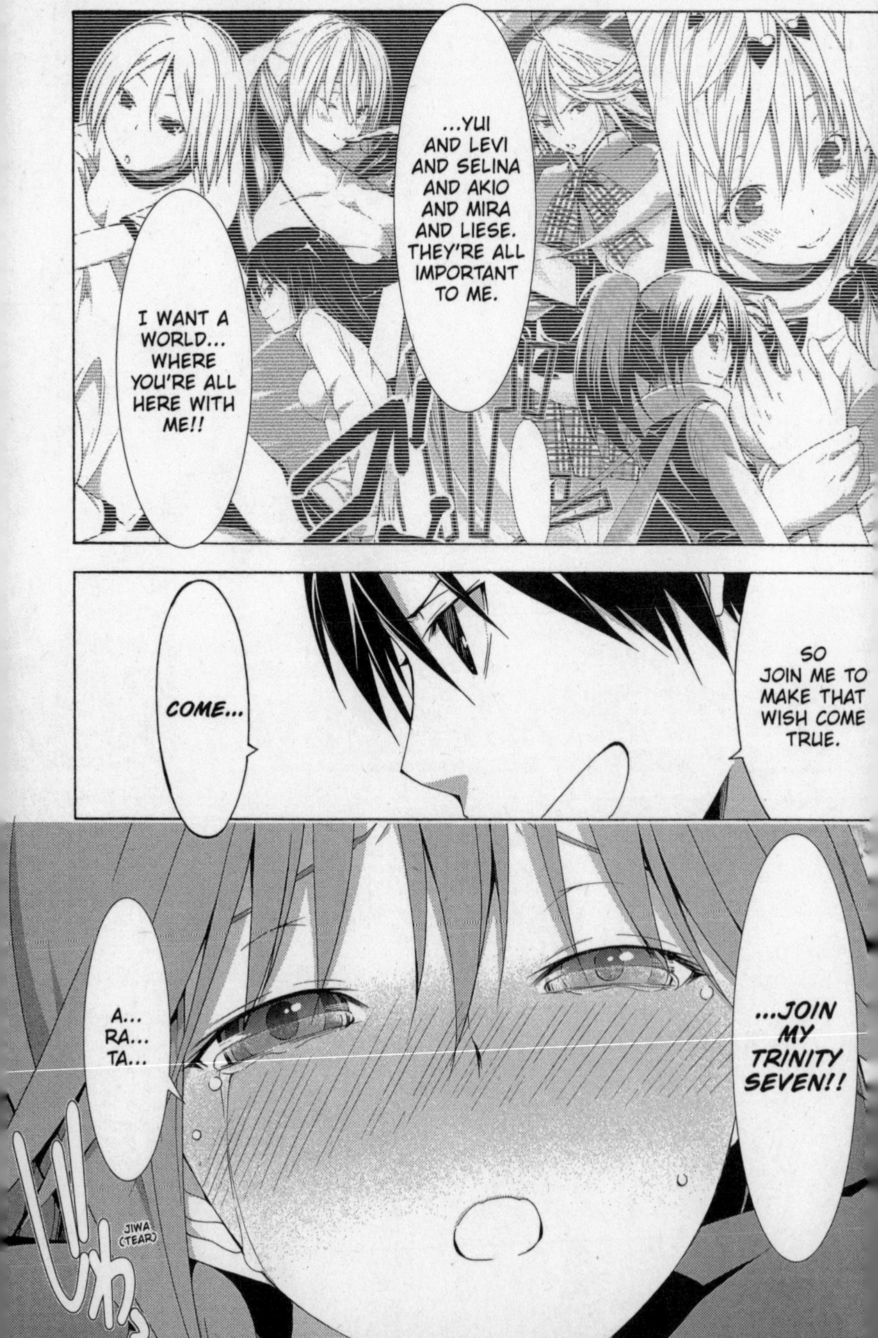
...YUI AND LEVI AND SELINA AND AKIO AND MIRA AND LIESE. THEY'RE ALL IMPORTANT TO ME.
I WANT A WORLD... WHERE YOU'RE ALL HERE WITH ME!!
SO JOIN ME TO MAKE THAT WISH COME TRUE.
COME...
...JOIN MY TRINITY SEVEN!!
A... RA... TA...
JIWA (TEAR)

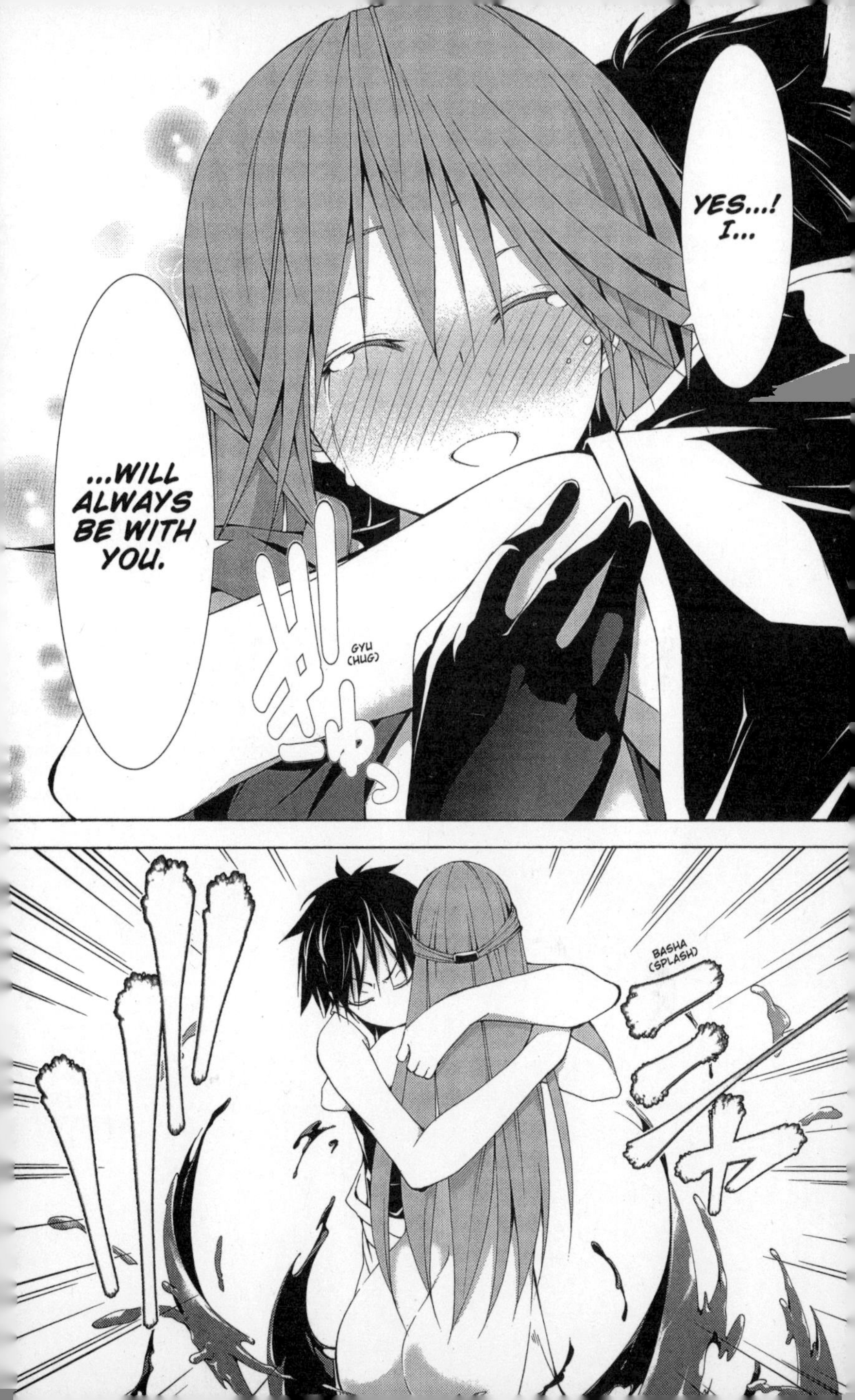
YES...! I...
...WILL ALWAYS BE WITH YOU.
GYU (HUG)
BASHA (SPLASH)

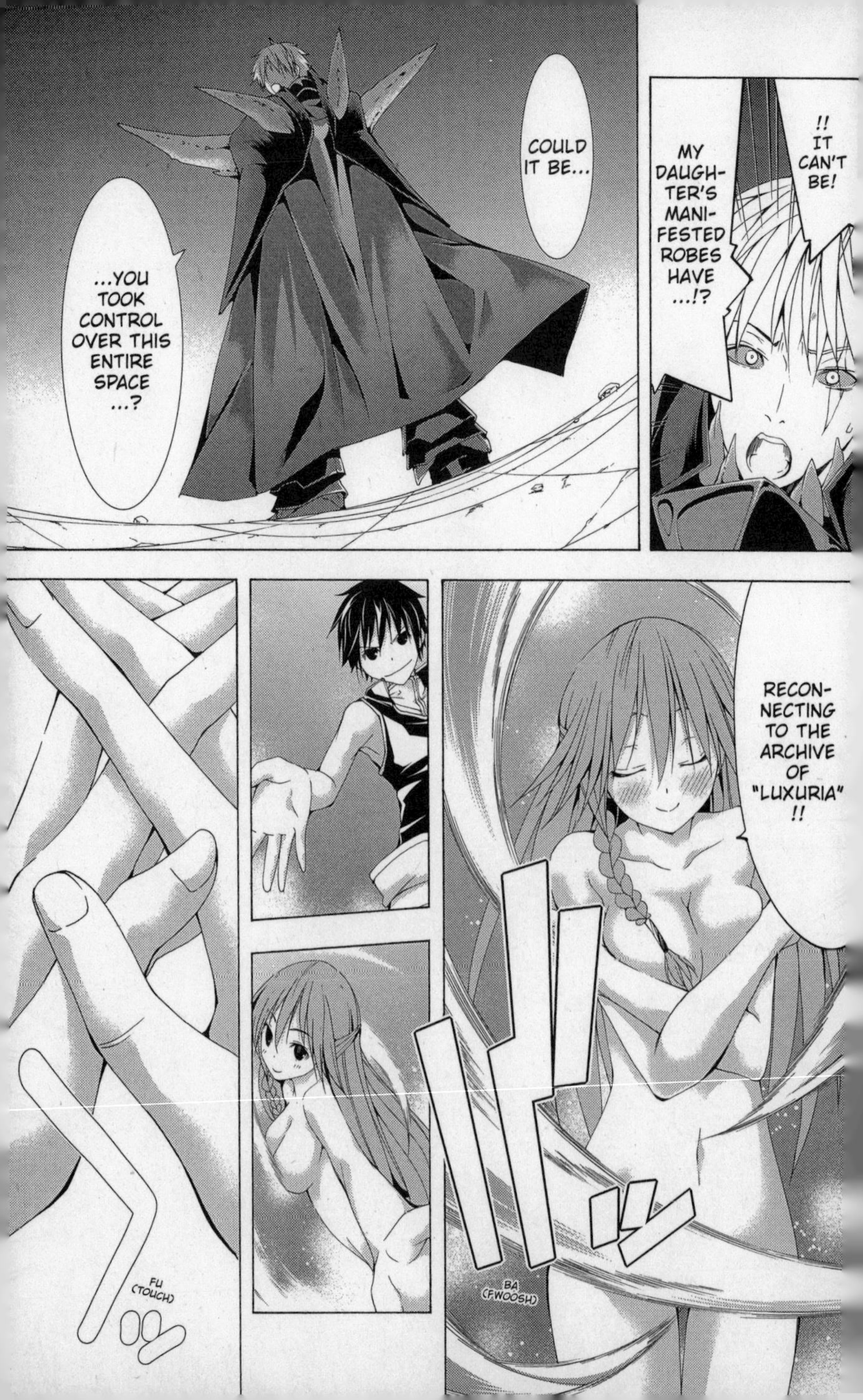
!! IT CAN'T BE!
MY DAUGHTER'S MANIFESTED ROBES HAVE ...!?
COULD IT BE...
...YOU TOOK CONTROL OVER THIS ENTIRE SPACE ...?
RECONNECTING TO THE ARCHIVE OF "LUXURIA" !!
BA (FWOOSH)
FU (TOUCH)

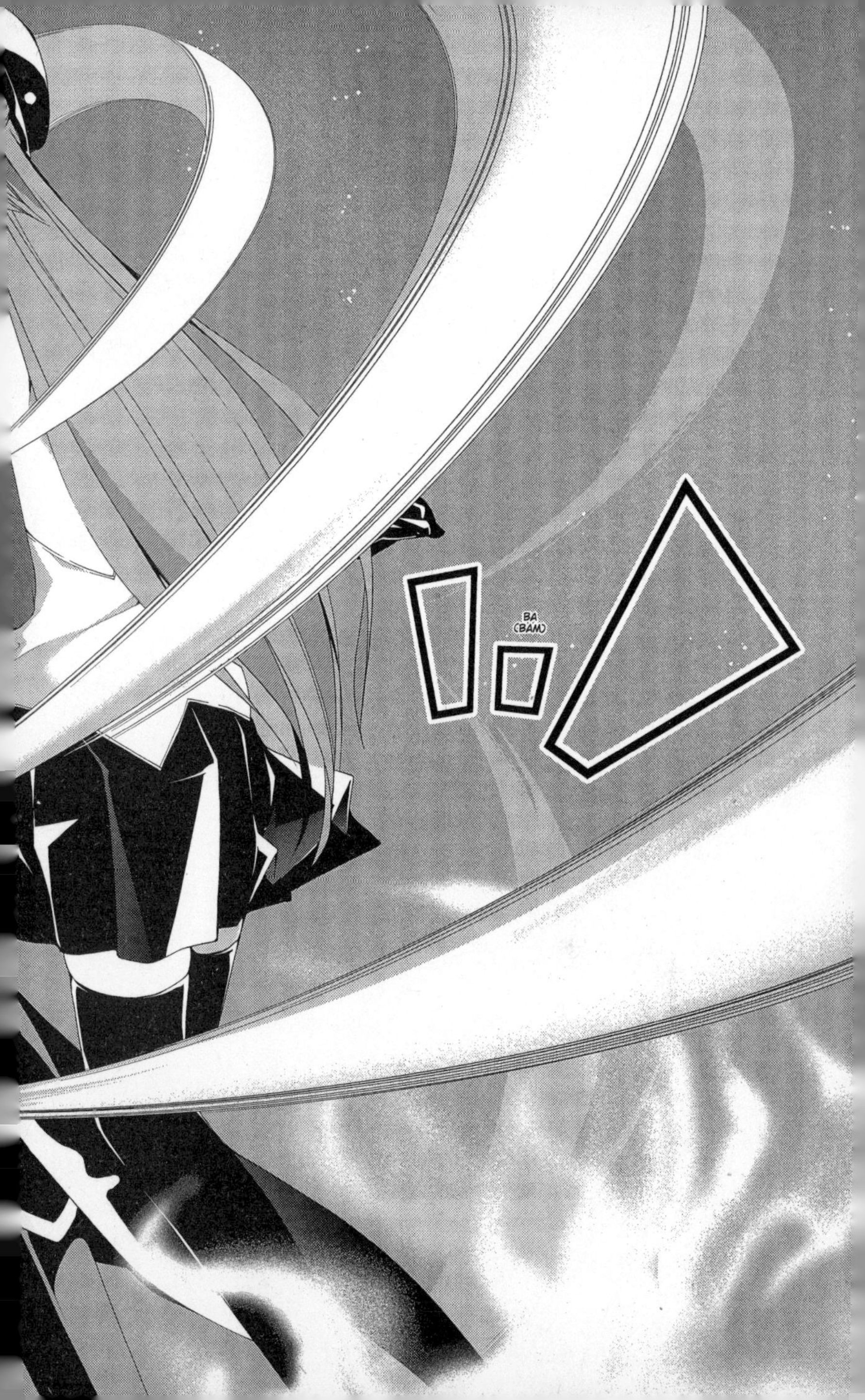
BA
(BAM)

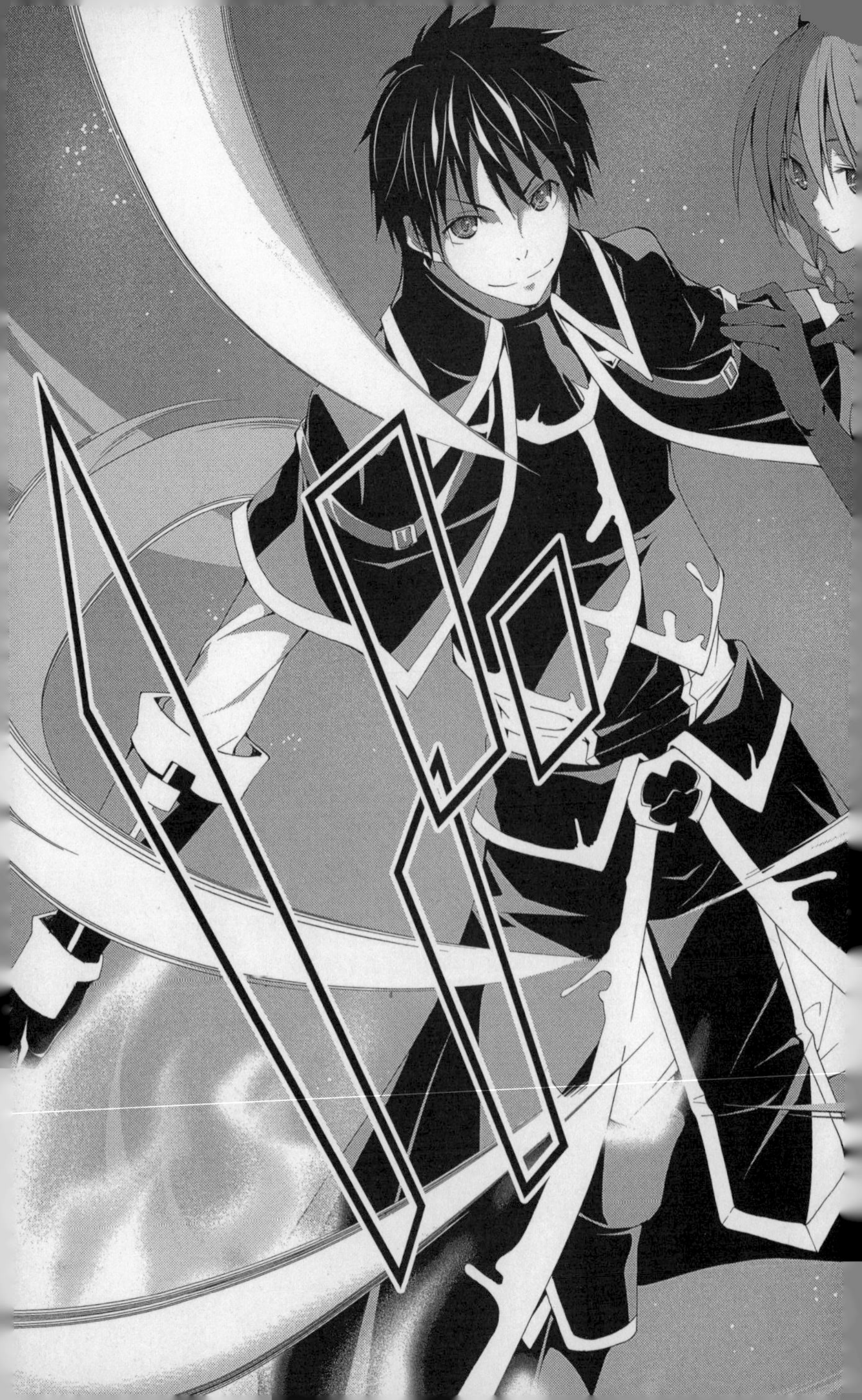

IMPOSSIBLE... DOES THIS MEAN...

...YOU CAN SURPASS TRINITY ...?

THIS IS MY FOURTH "ARCHIVE."

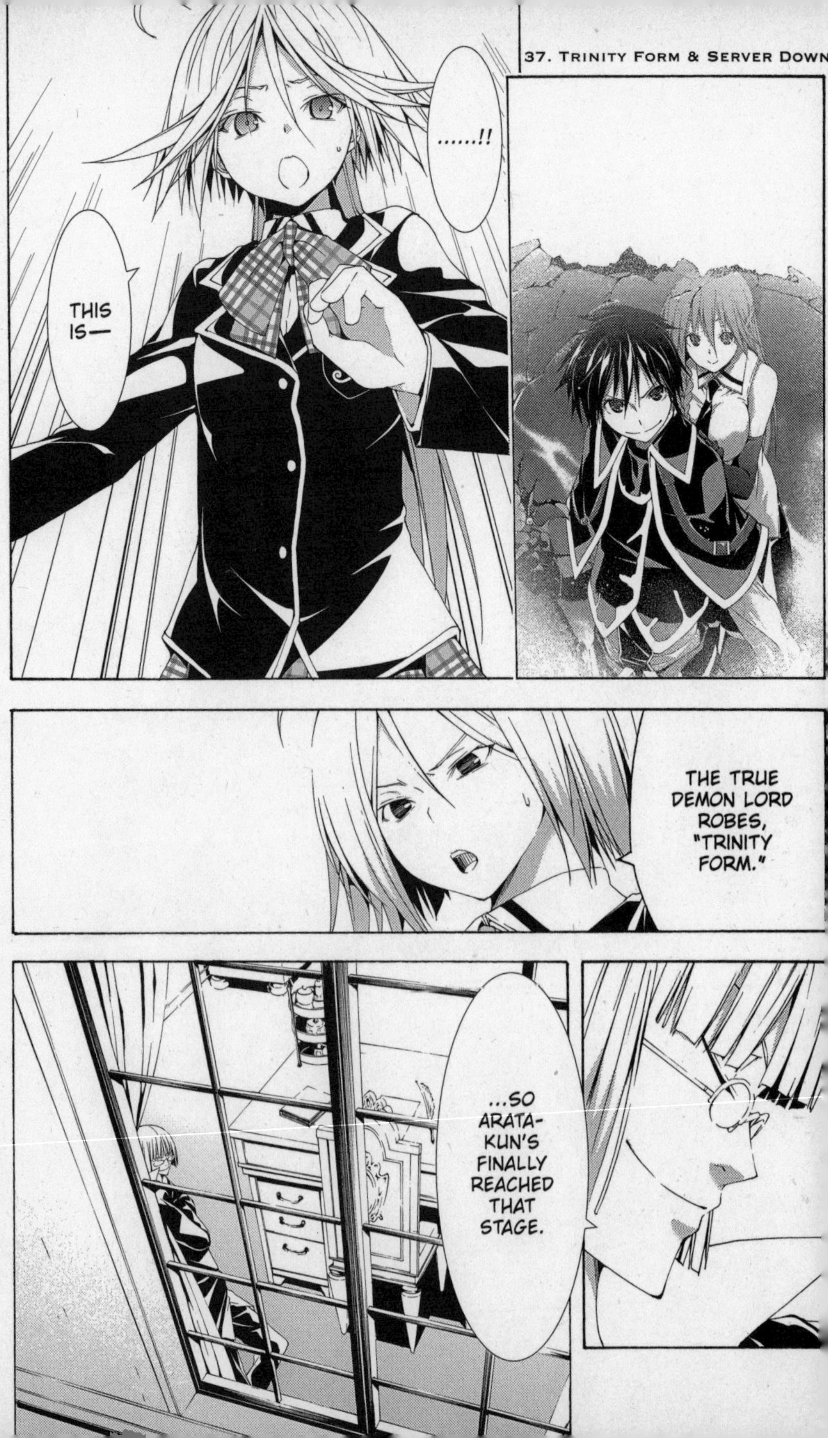
......!!
THIS IS—
THE TRUE DEMON LORD ROBES, "TRINITY FORM."
...SO ARATA-KUN'S FINALLY REACHED THAT STAGE.

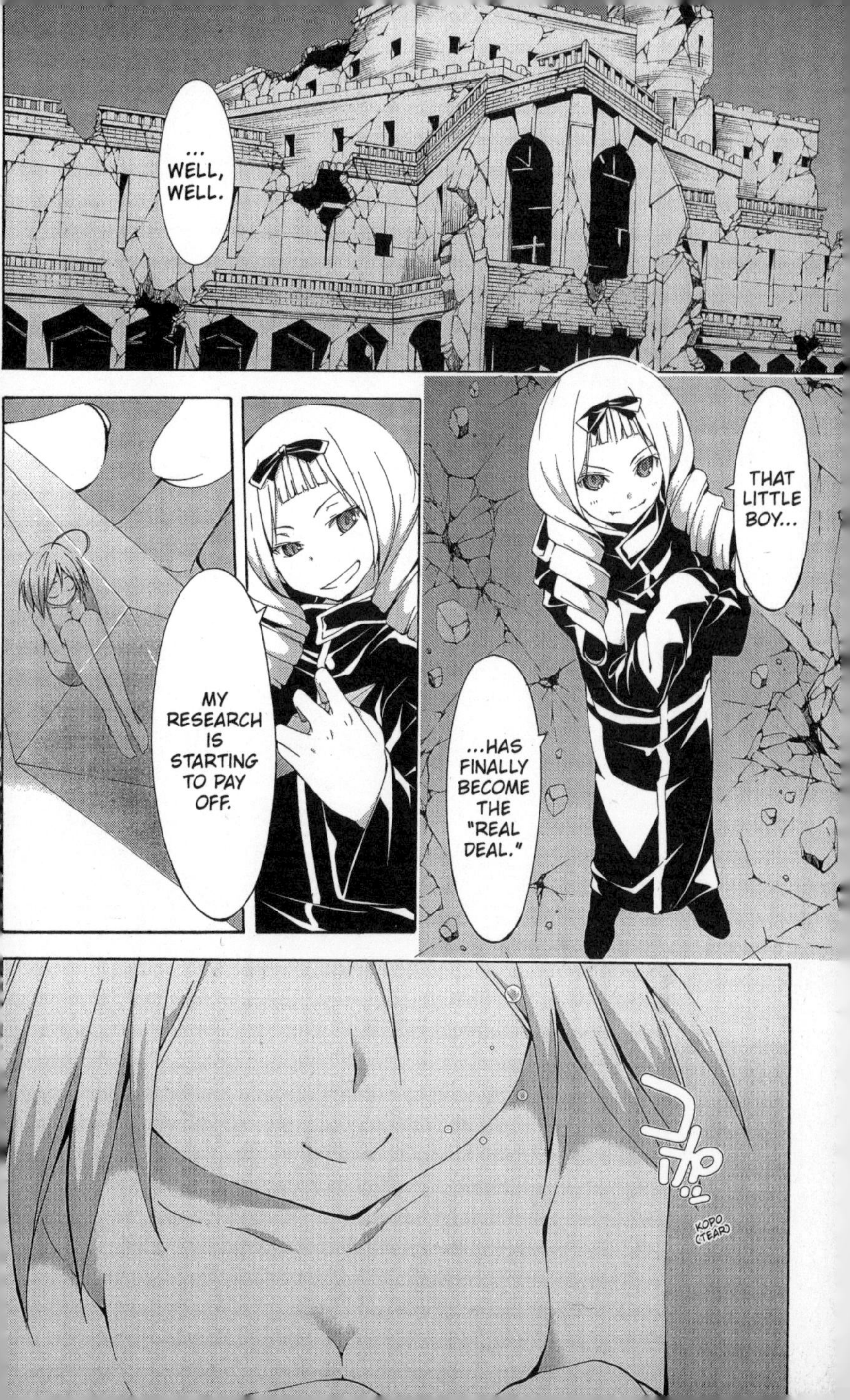
...WELL, WELL.
THAT LITTLE BOY...
...HAS FINALLY BECOME THE "REAL DEAL."
MY RESEARCH IS STARTING TO PAY OFF.
KOPO (TEAR)

37. Trinity Form & Server Down

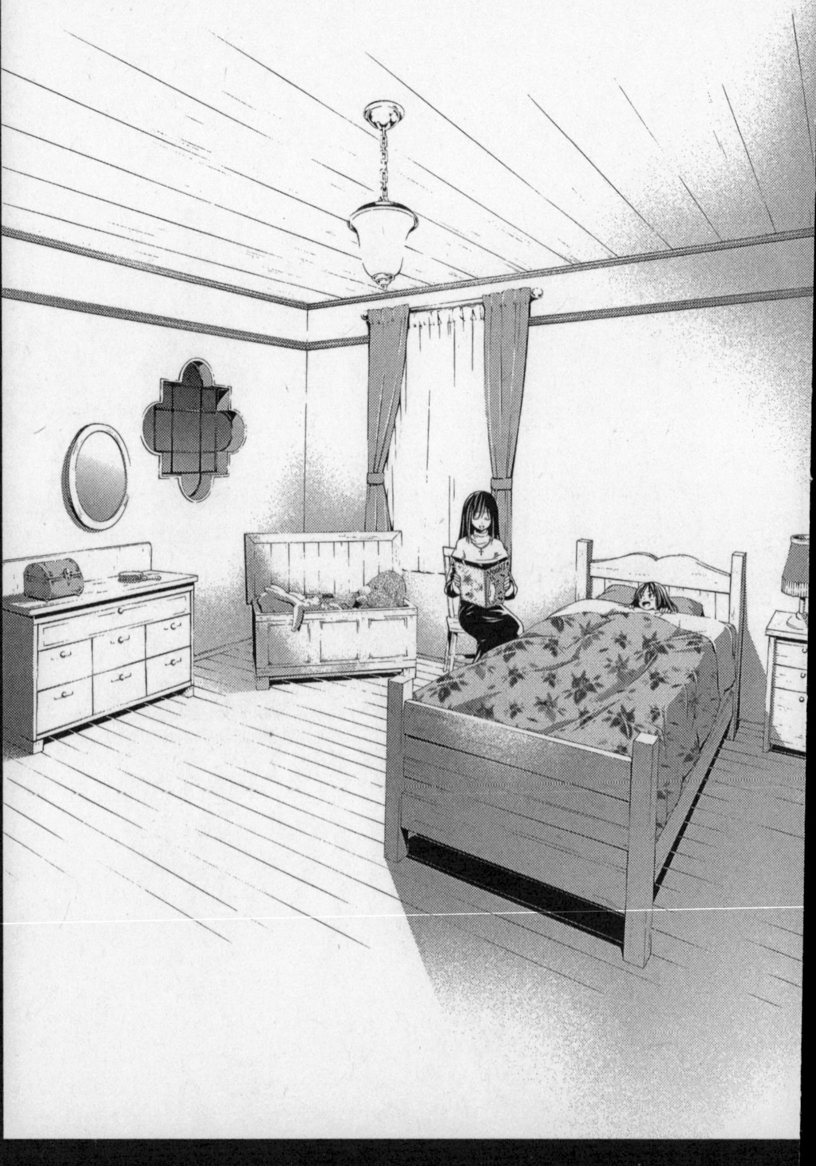

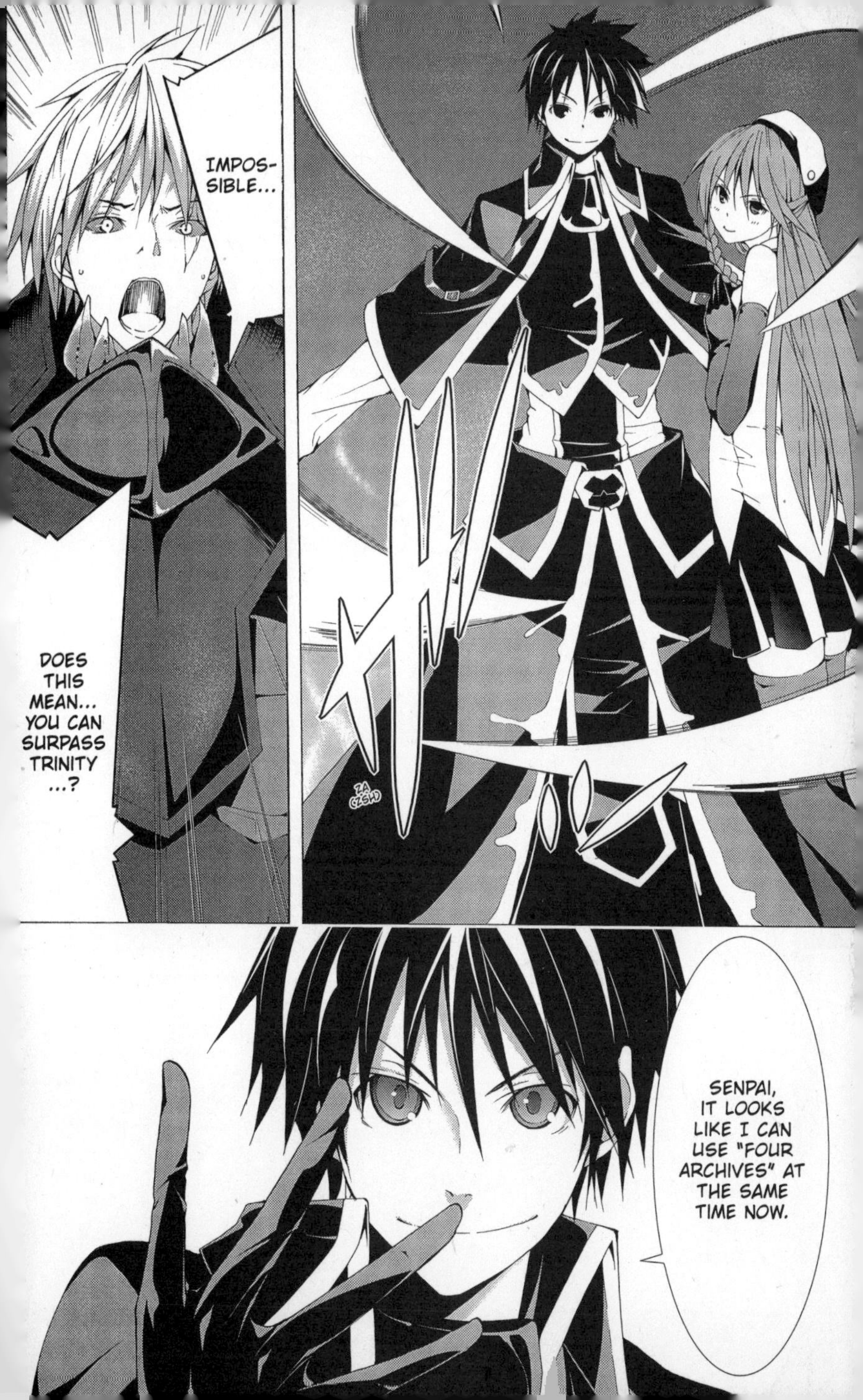
ZA (ZSH)
IMPOSSIBLE...
DOES THIS MEAN... YOU CAN SURPASS TRINITY ...?
SENPAI, IT LOOKS LIKE I CAN USE "FOUR ARCHIVES" AT THE SAME TIME NOW.

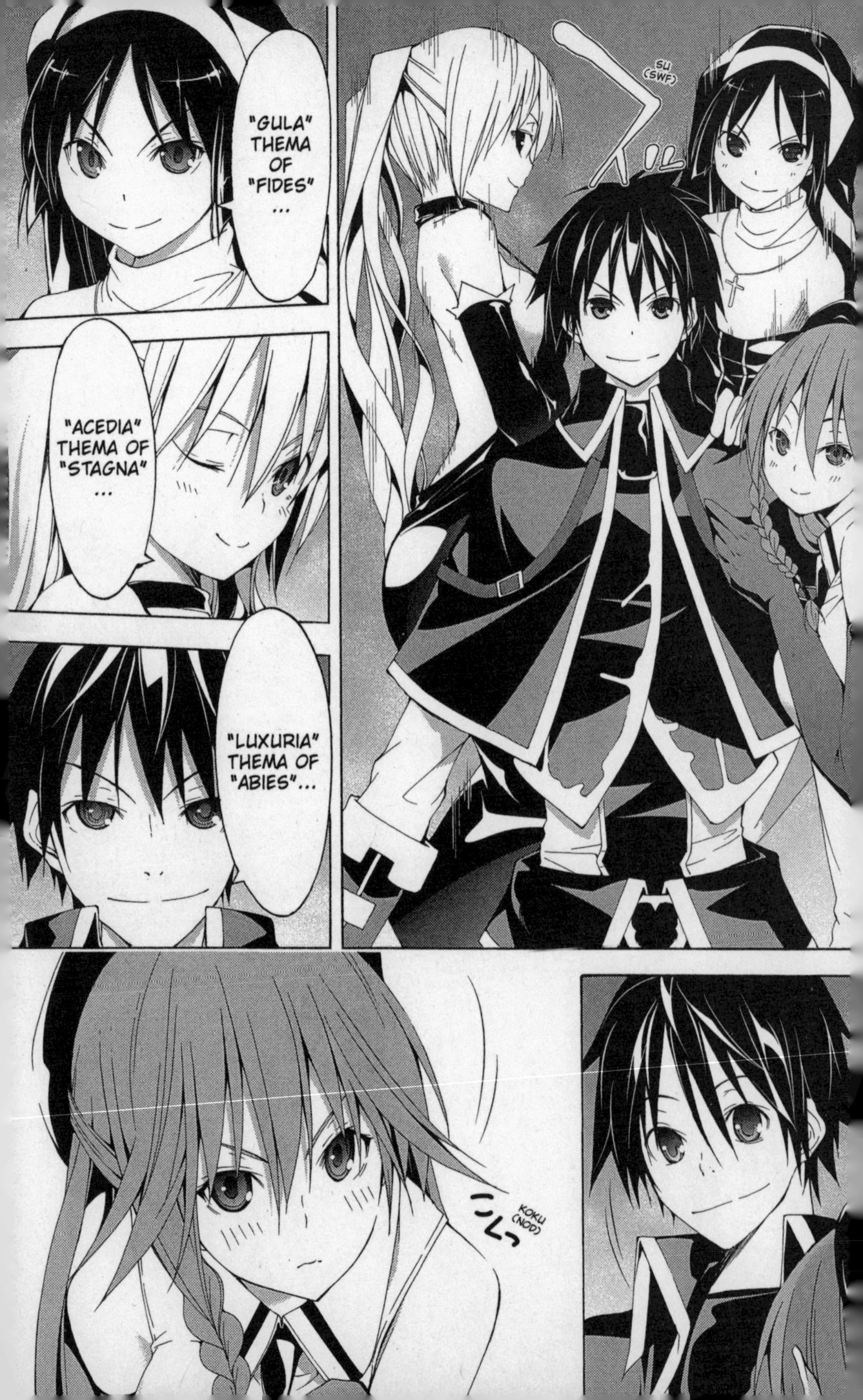
SU (SWF)
"GULA" THEMA OF "FIDES" ...
"ACEDIA" THEMA OF "STAGNA" ...
"LUXURIA" THEMA OF "ABIES"...
KOKU (NOD)

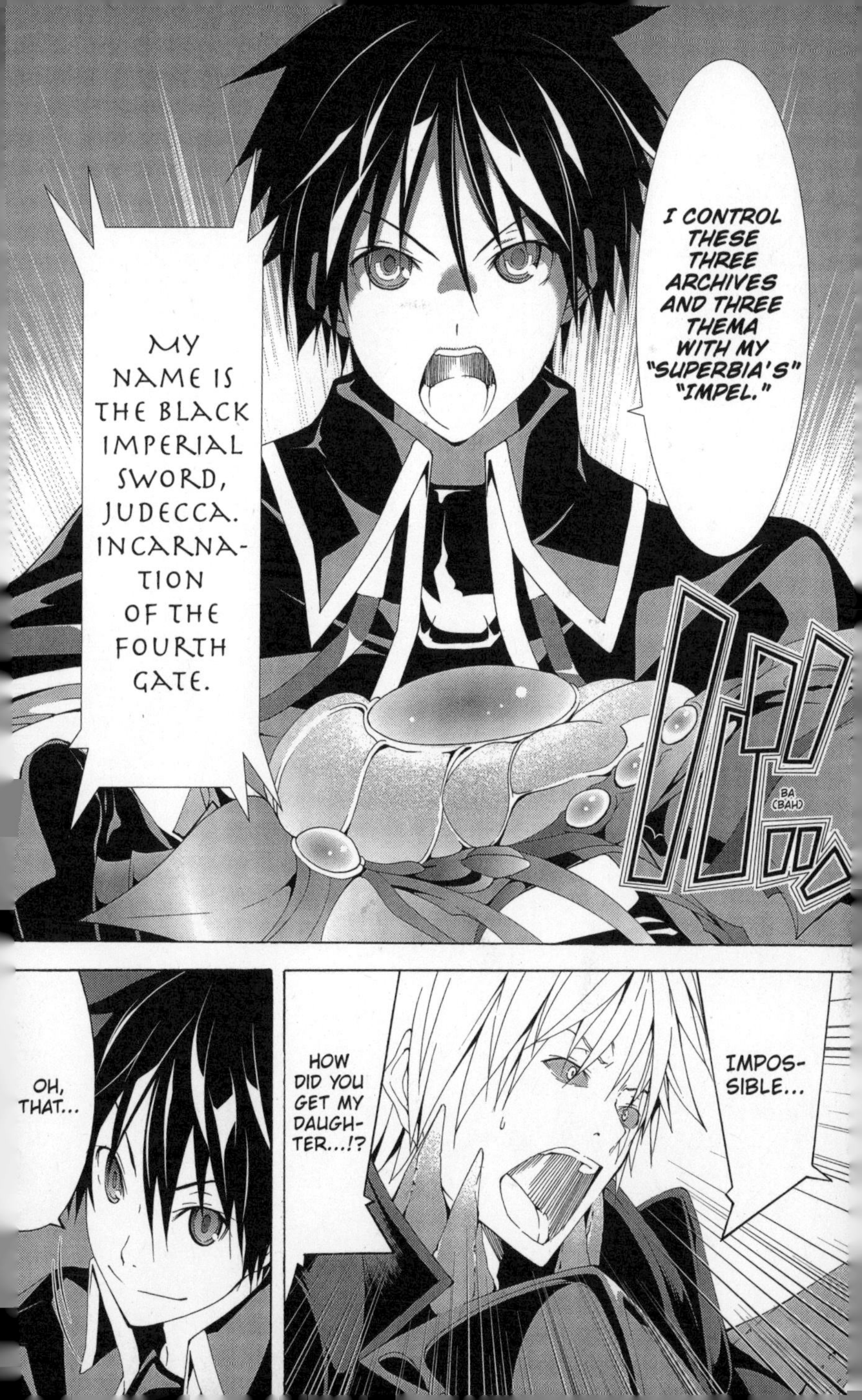
I CONTROL THESE THREE ARCHIVES AND THREE THEMA WITH MY "SUPERBIA'S" "IMPEL."
MY NAME IS THE BLACK IMPERIAL SWORD, JUDECCA. INCARNATION OF THE FOURTH GATE.
BA (BAH)
IMPOSSIBLE...
HOW DID YOU GET MY DAUGHTER...!?
OH, THAT...

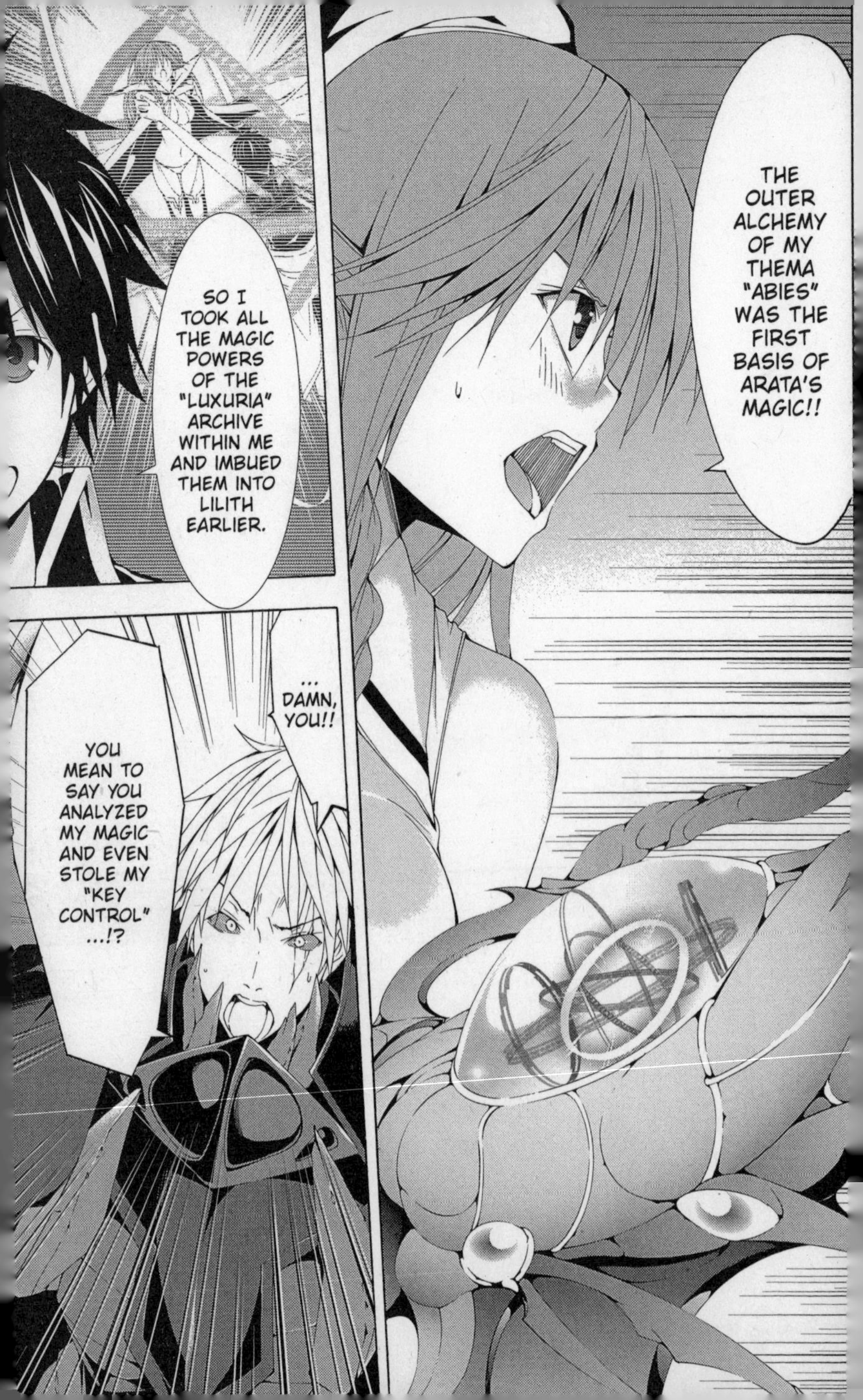
THE OUTER ALCHEMY OF MY THEMA "ABIES" WAS THE FIRST BASIS OF ARATA'S MAGIC!!
SO I TOOK ALL THE MAGIC POWERS OF THE "LUXURIA" ARCHIVE WITHIN ME AND IMBUED THEM INTO LILITH EARLIER.
... DAMN, YOU!!
YOU MEAN TO SAY YOU ANALYZED MY MAGIC AND EVEN STOLE MY "KEY CONTROL" ...!?

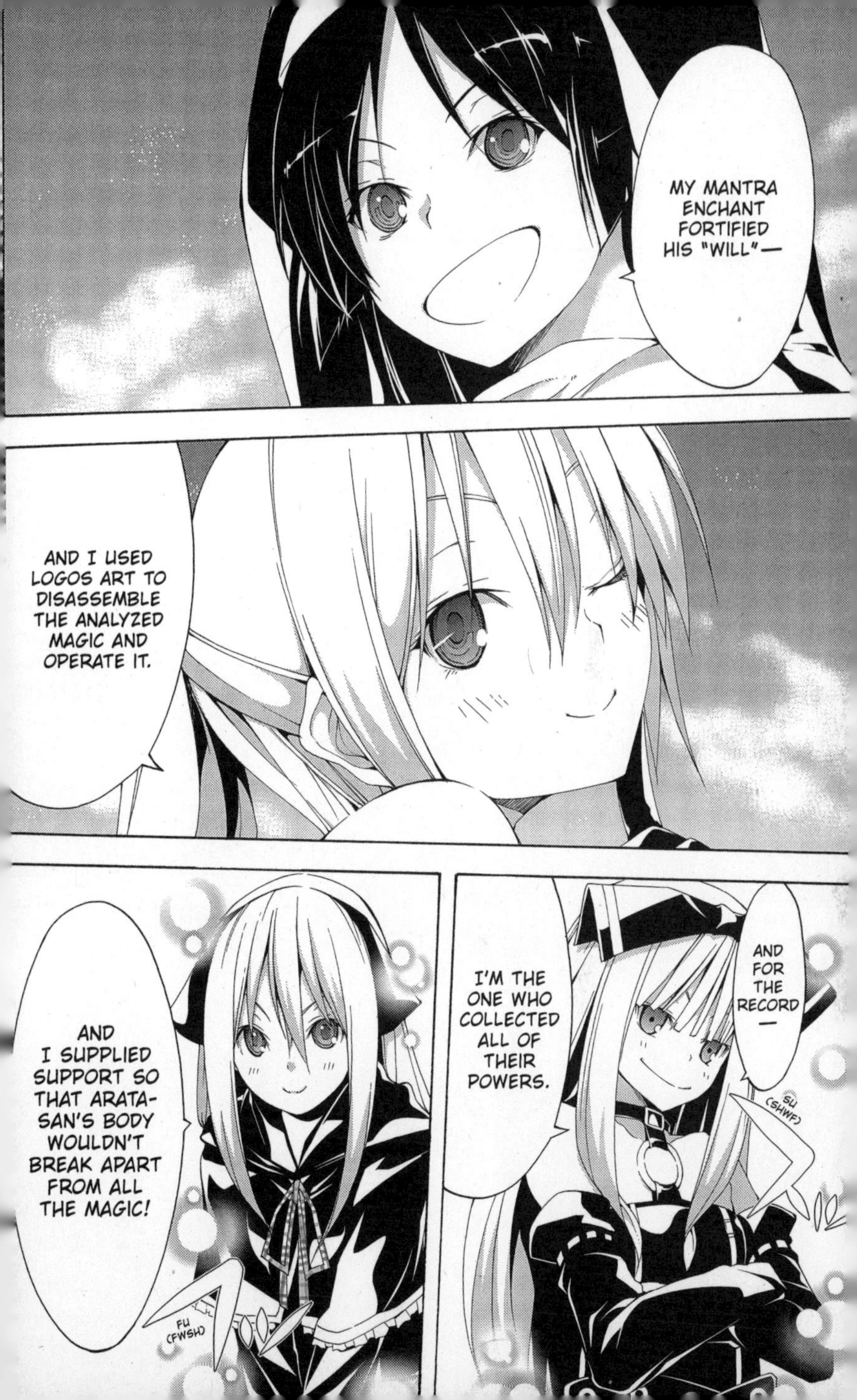
MY MANTRA ENCHANT FORTIFIED HIS "WILL"—
AND I USED LOGOS ART TO DISASSEMBLE THE ANALYZED MAGIC AND OPERATE IT.
AND FOR THE RECORD—
I'M THE ONE WHO COLLECTED ALL OF THEIR POWERS.
SU (SHWF)
AND I SUPPLIED SUPPORT SO THAT ARATA-SAN'S BODY WOULDN'T BREAK APART FROM ALL THE MAGIC!
FU (FWSH)

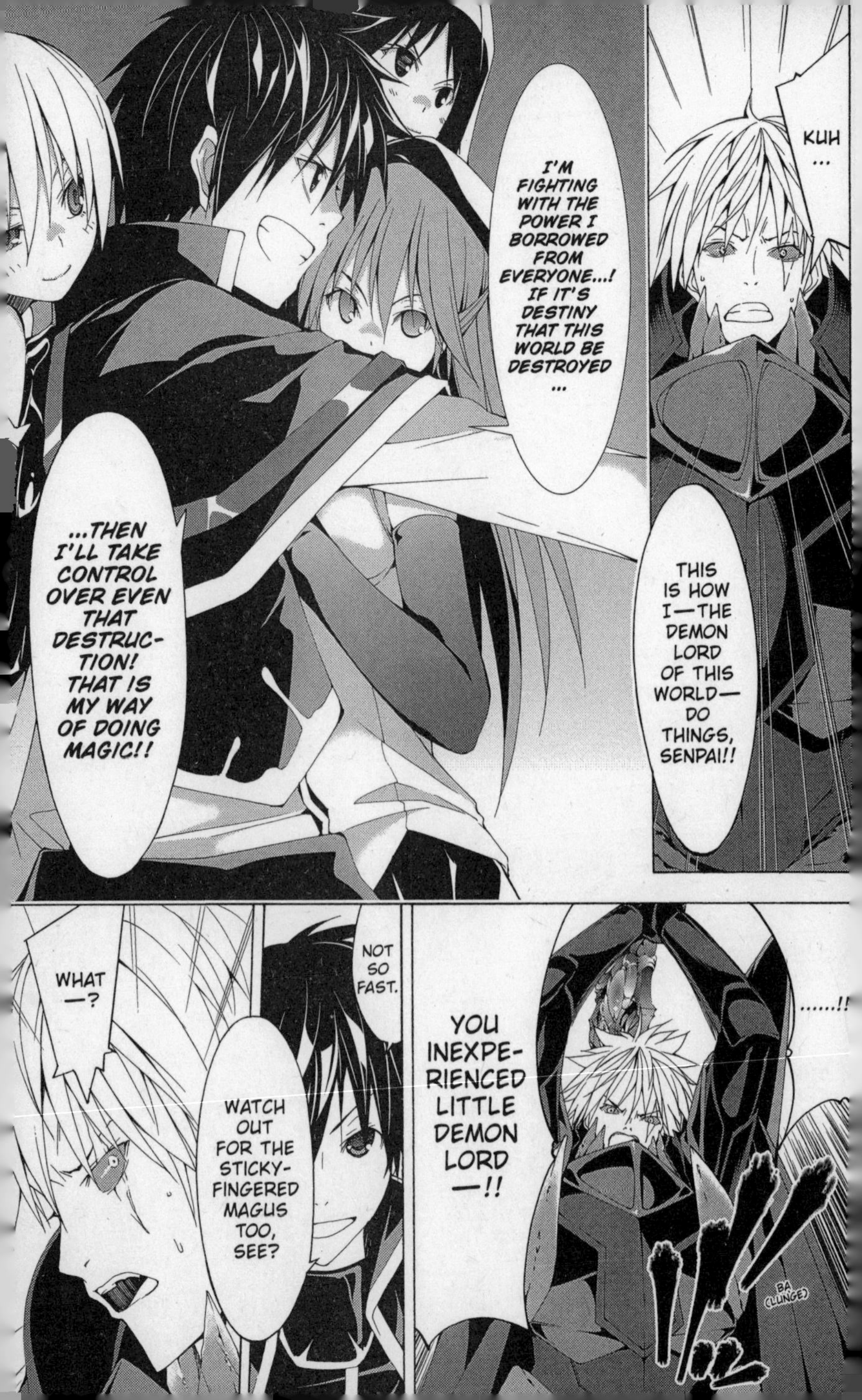
KUH ...
THIS IS HOW I—THE DEMON LORD OF THIS WORLD—DO THINGS, SENPAI!!
I'M FIGHTING WITH THE POWER I BORROWED FROM EVERYONE...! IF IT'S DESTINY THAT THIS WORLD BE DESTROYED ...
...THEN I'LL TAKE CONTROL OVER EVEN THAT DESTRUC-TION! THAT IS MY WAY OF DOING MAGIC!!
......!!
YOU INEXPE-RIENCED LITTLE DEMON LORD —!!
BA (LUNGE)
NOT SO FAST.
WHAT —?
WATCH OUT FOR THE STICKY-FINGERED MAGUS TOO, SEE?

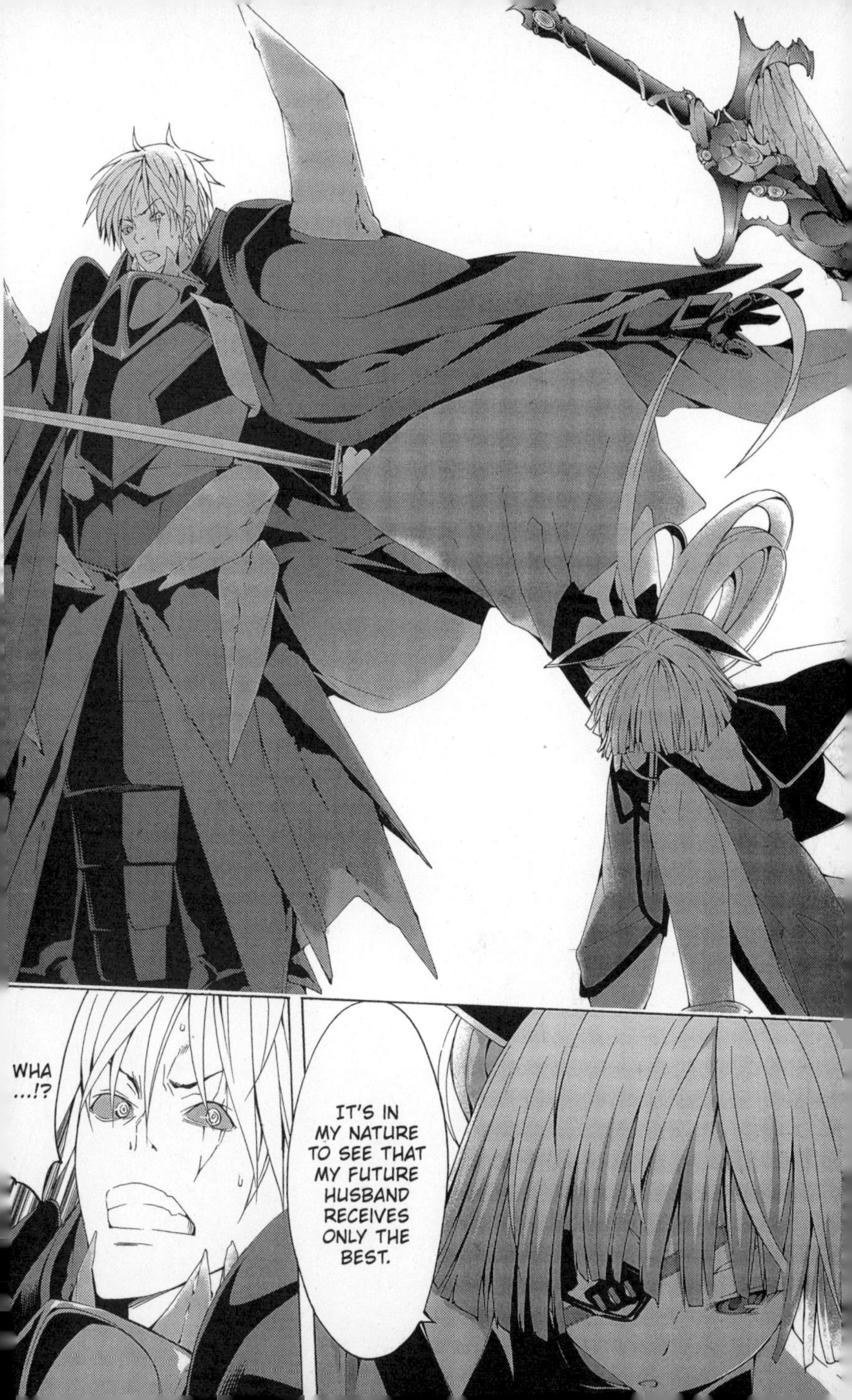
IT'S IN MY NATURE TO SEE THAT MY FUTURE HUSBAND RECEIVES ONLY THE BEST.
WHA ...!?

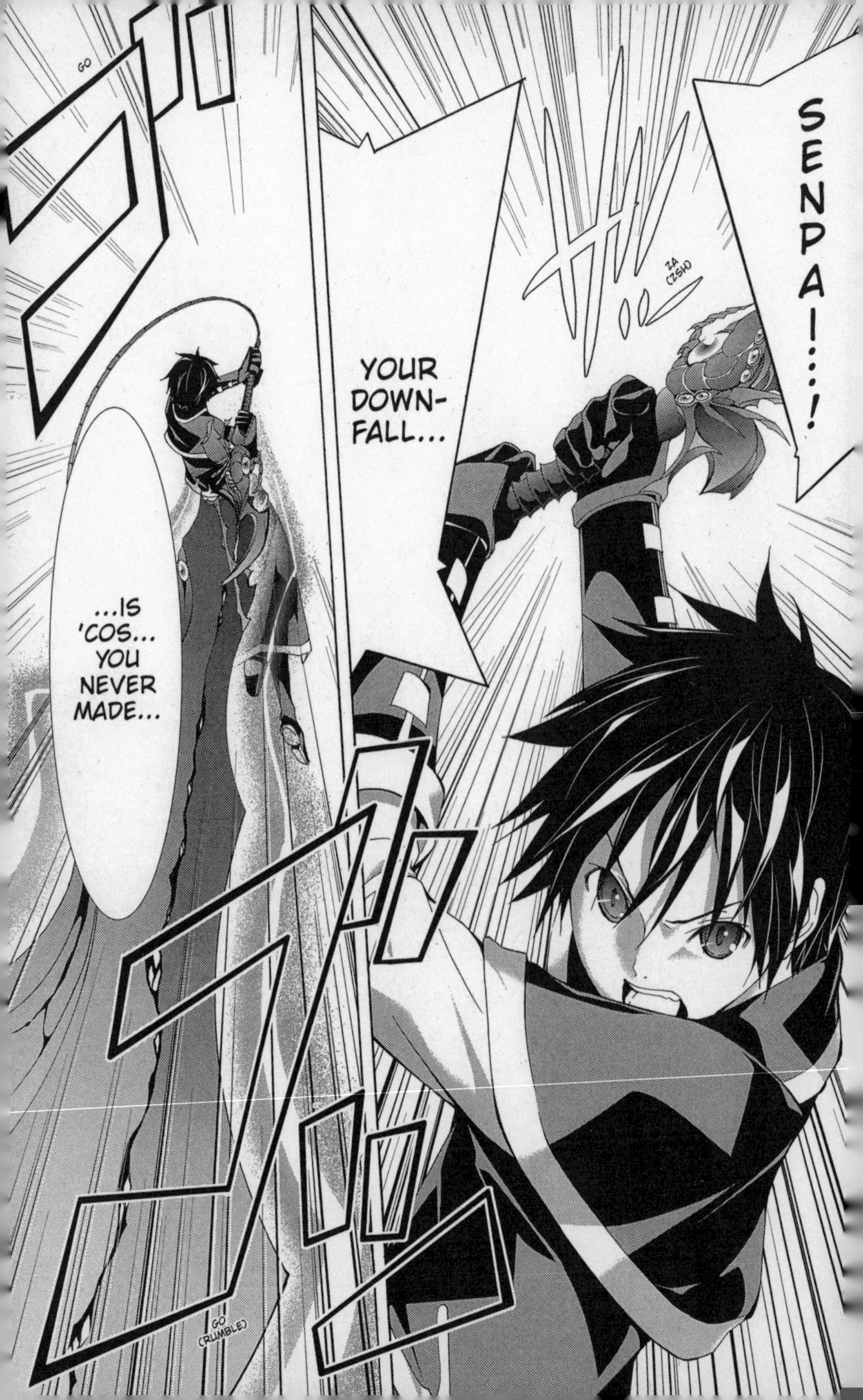
SENPAI...!
ZA (ZSH)
YOUR DOWN-FALL...
GO
...IS 'COS... YOU NEVER MADE...
GO (RUMBLE)

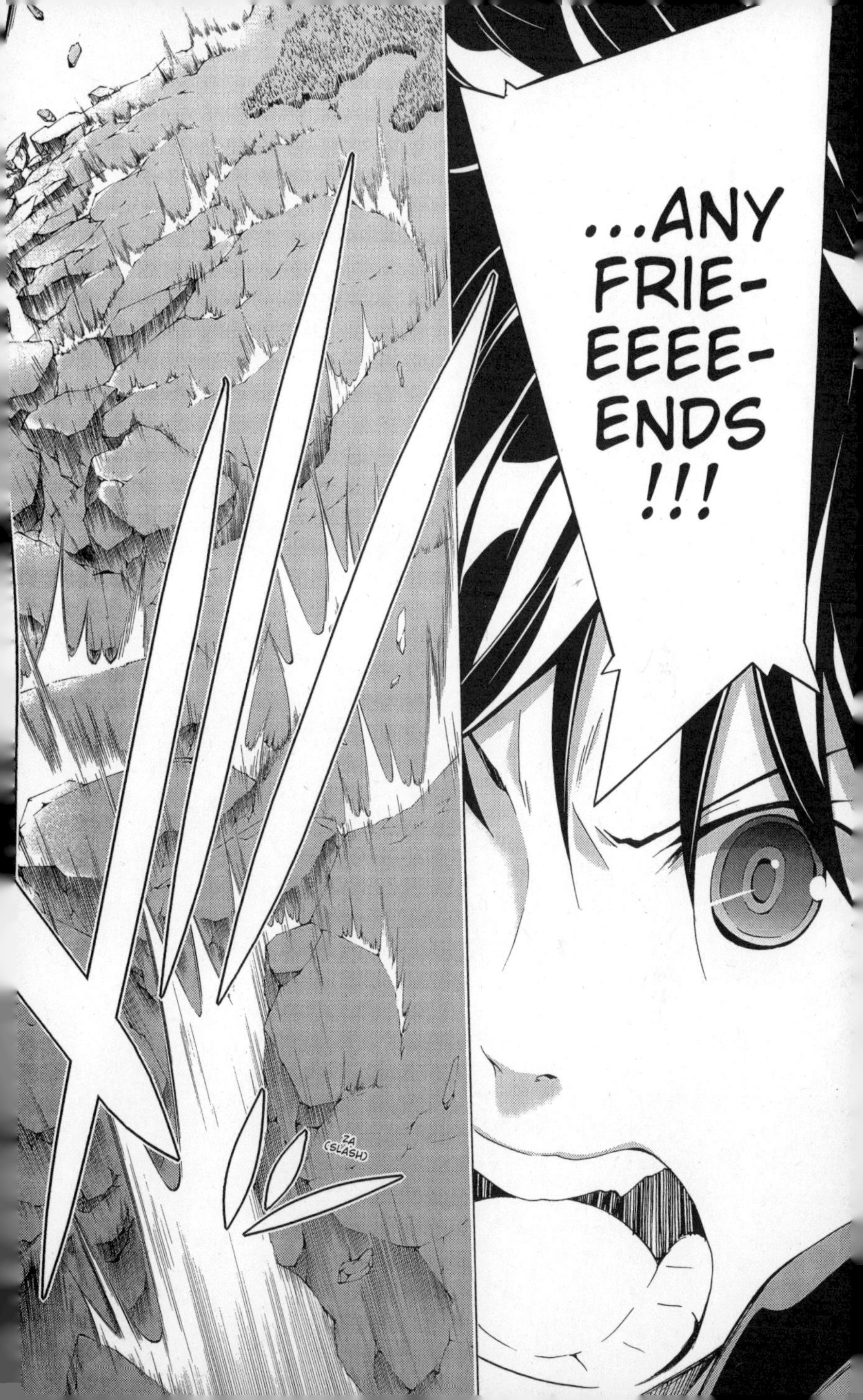
...ANY FRIE-EEEE-ENDS !!!
ZA (SLASH)

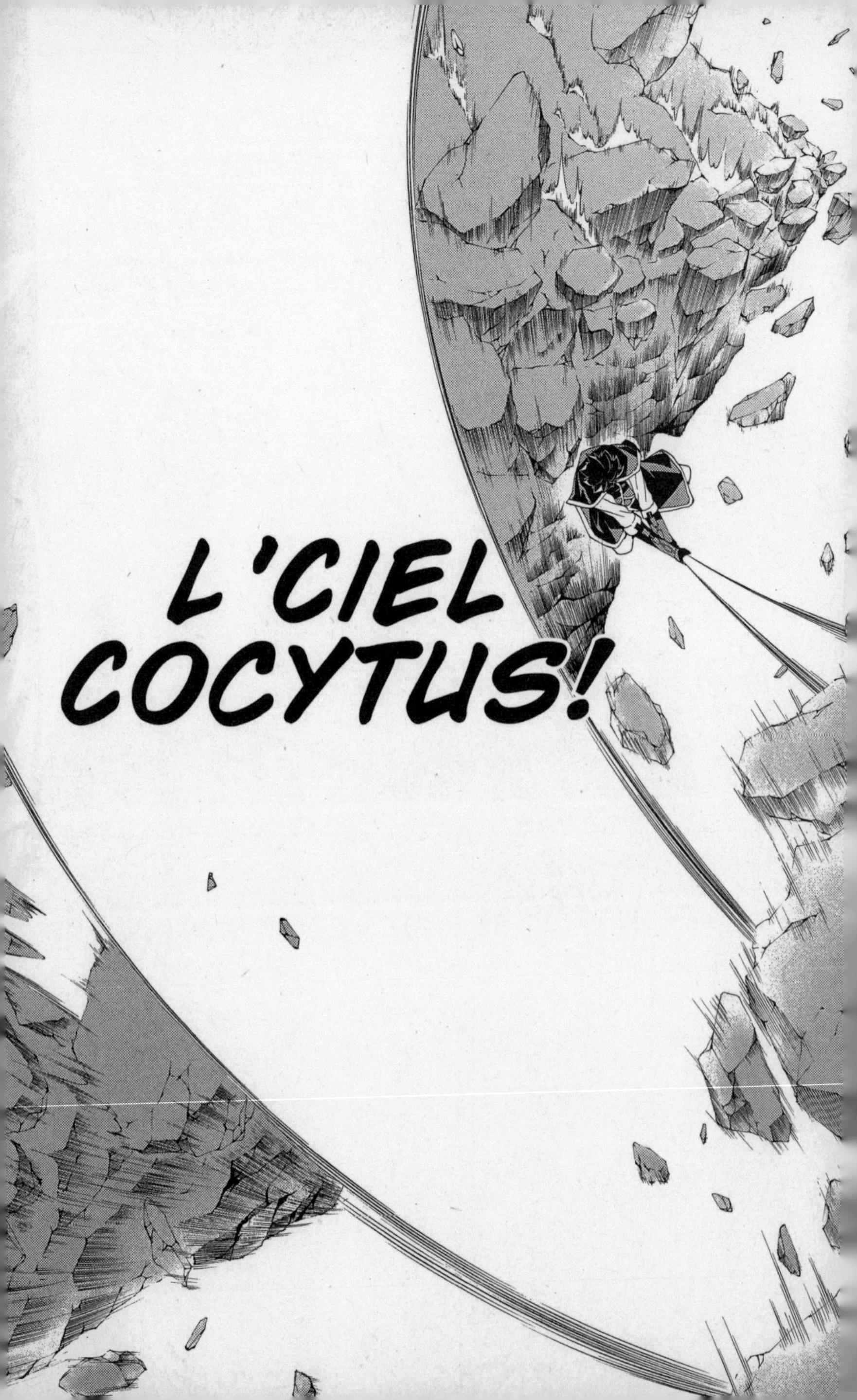
L'CIEL COCYTUS!

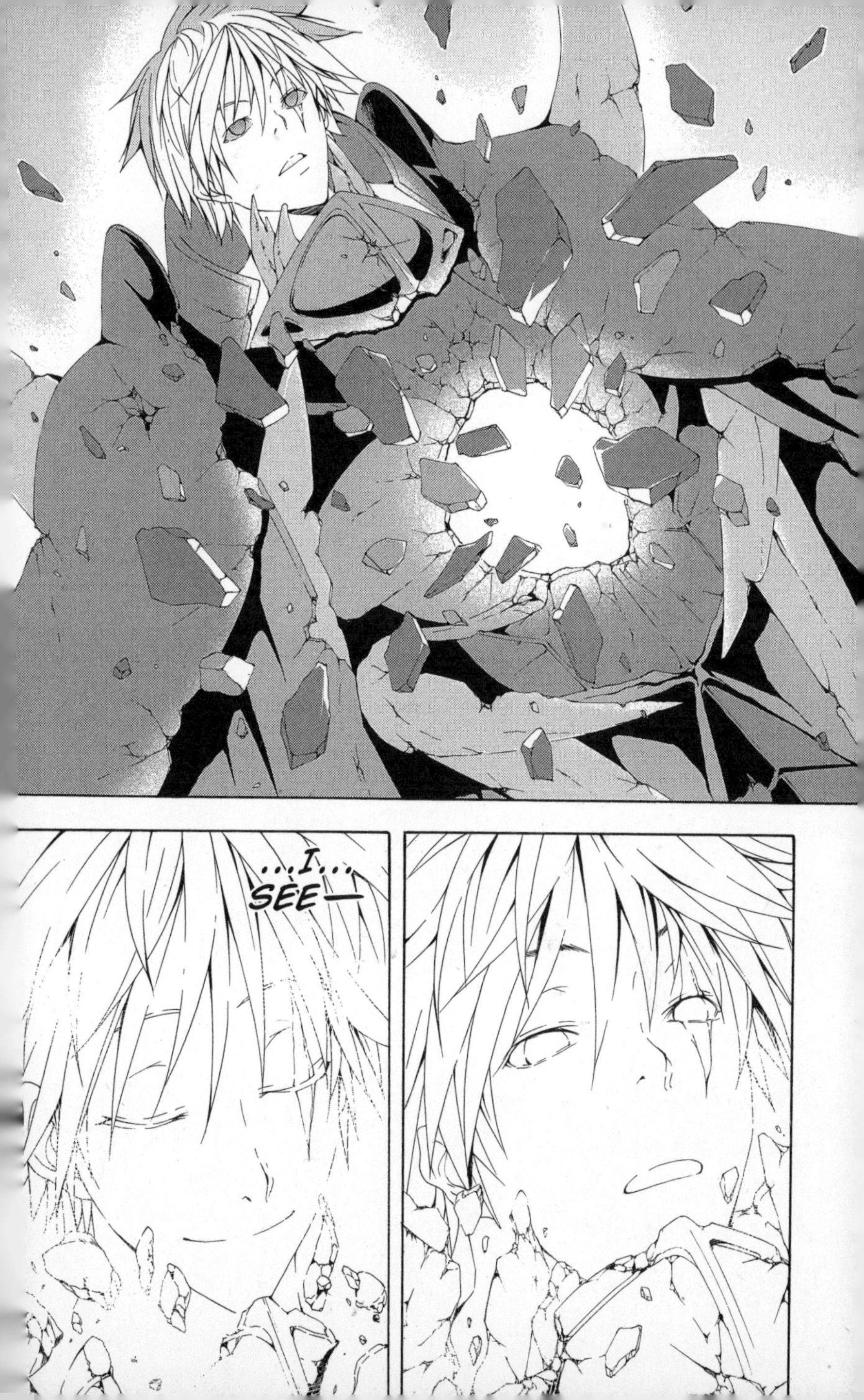
...I... SEE—

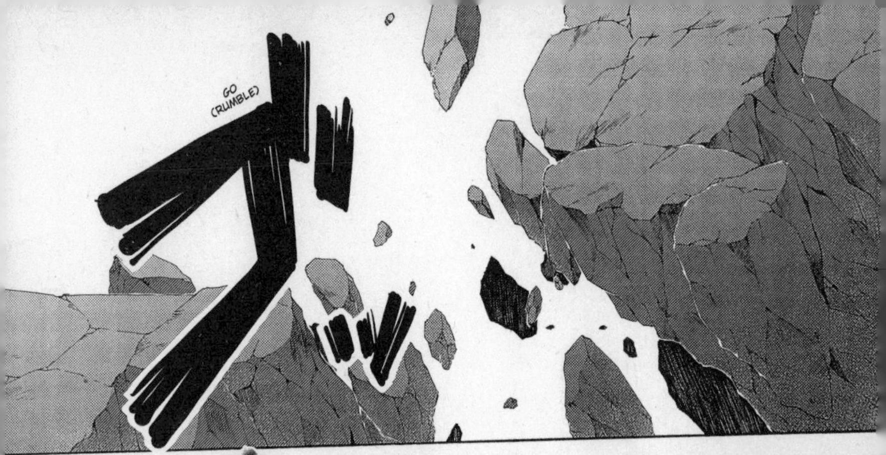
GO
(RUMBLE)
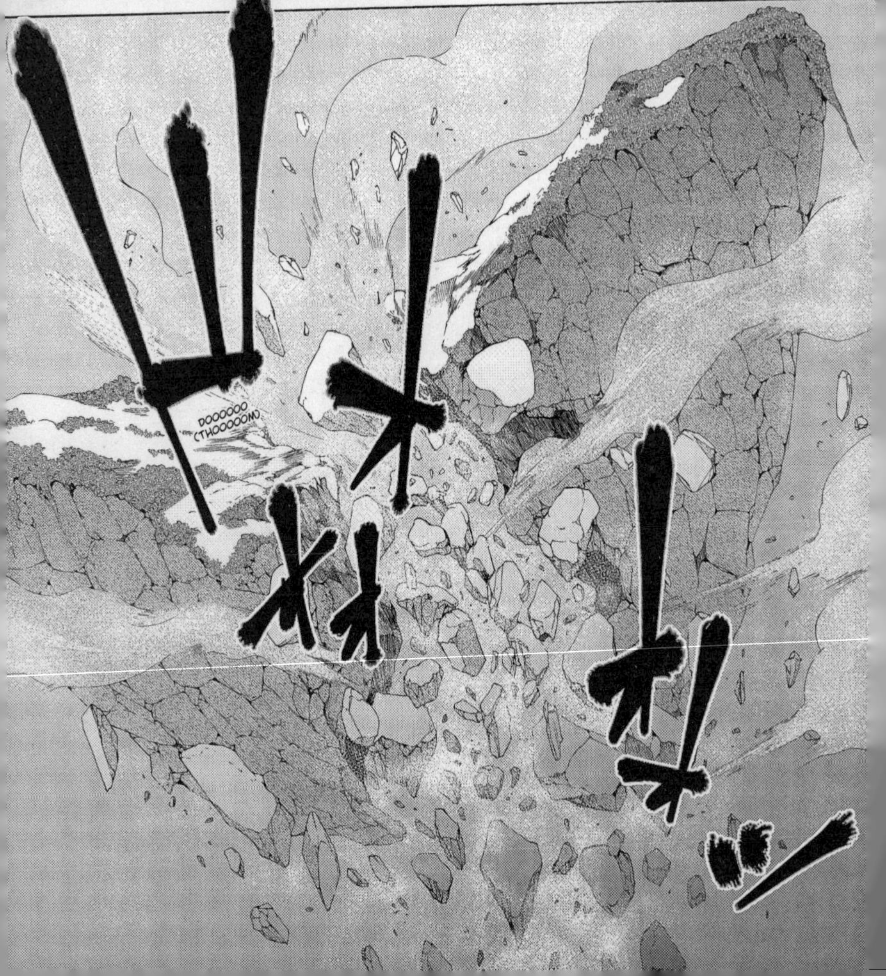
DOOOOOO
(THOOOOOM)

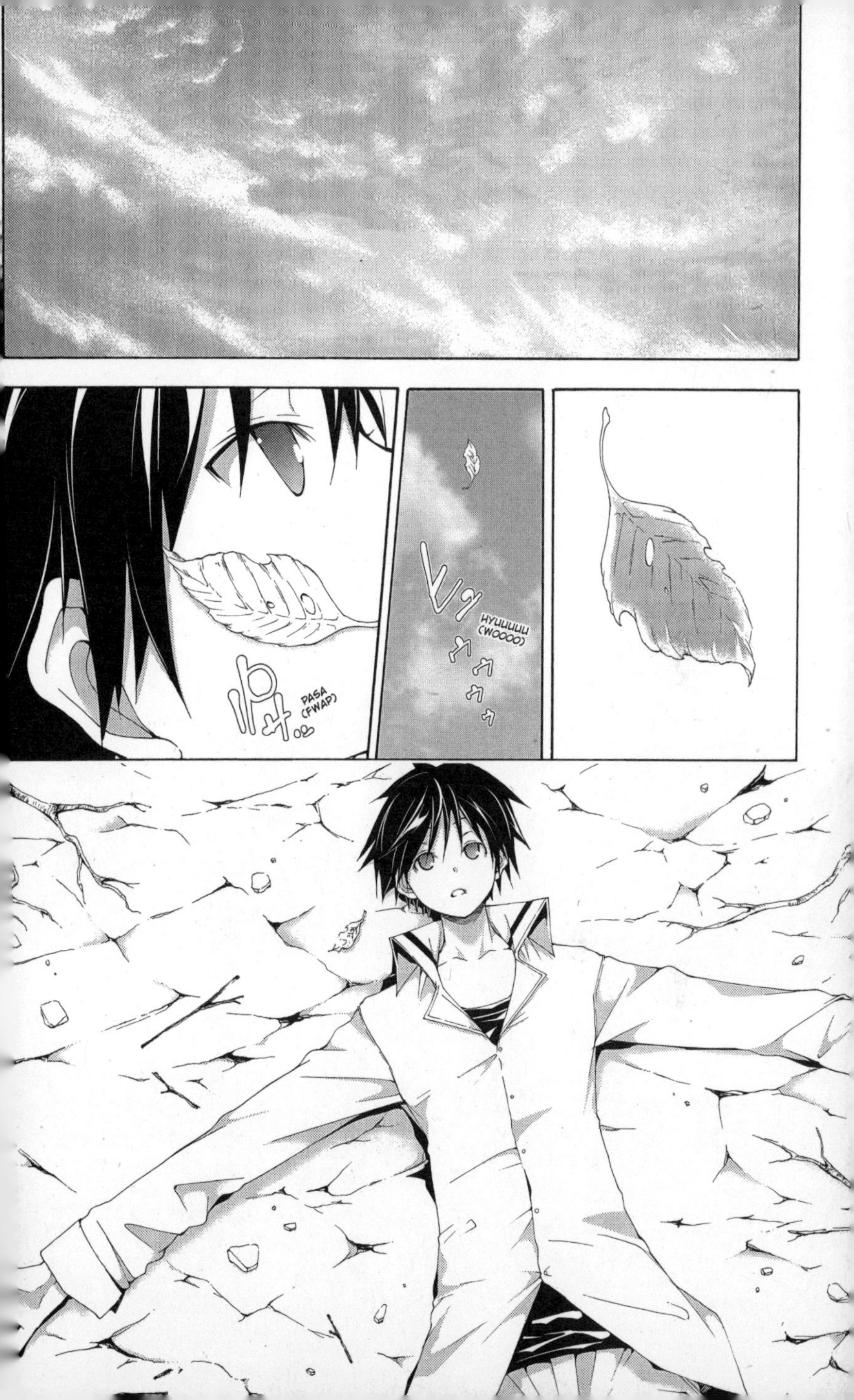
HYUUUUU (WOOOO)
PASA (FWAP)

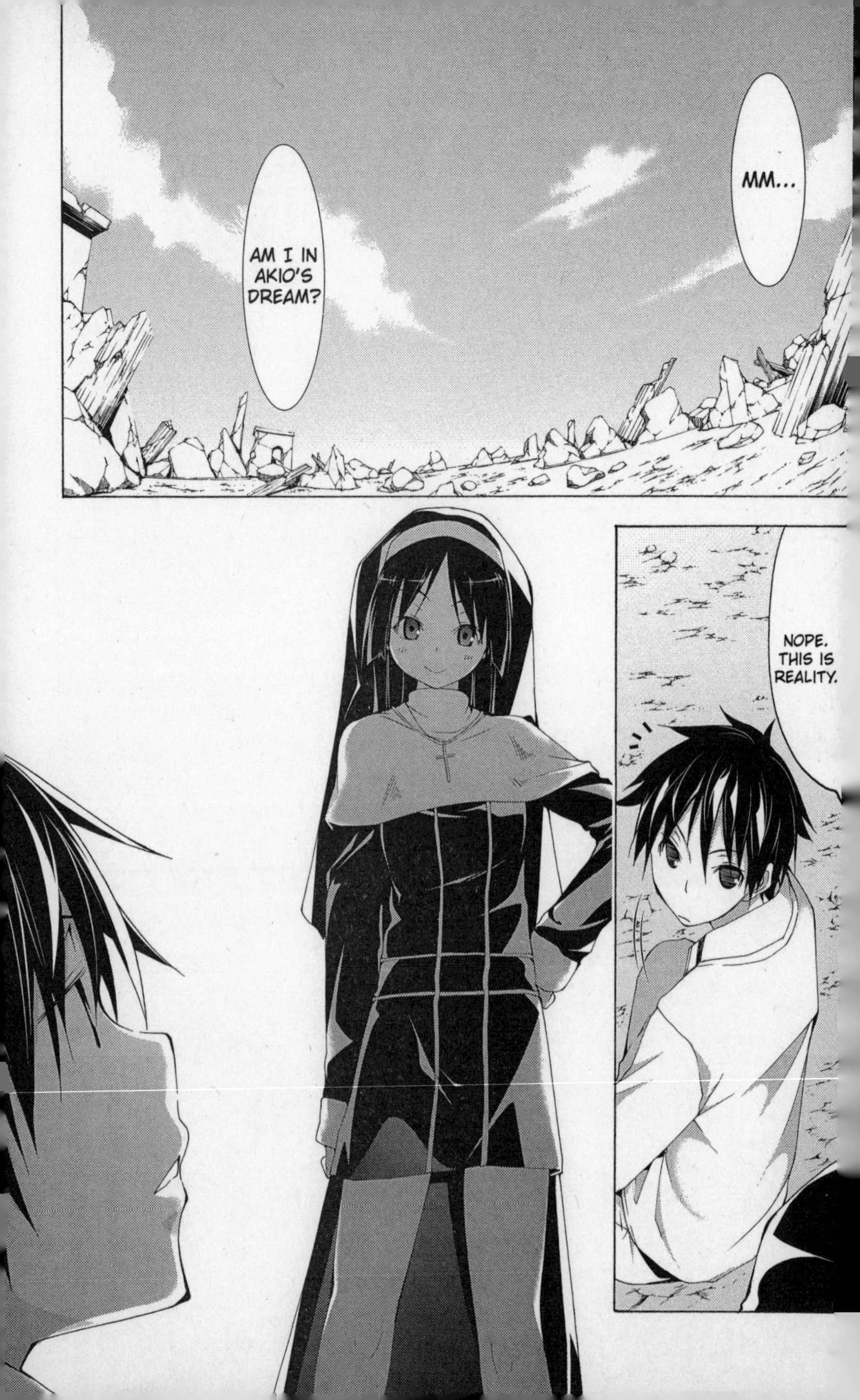
MM...
AM I IN AKIO'S DREAM?
NOPE. THIS IS REALITY.

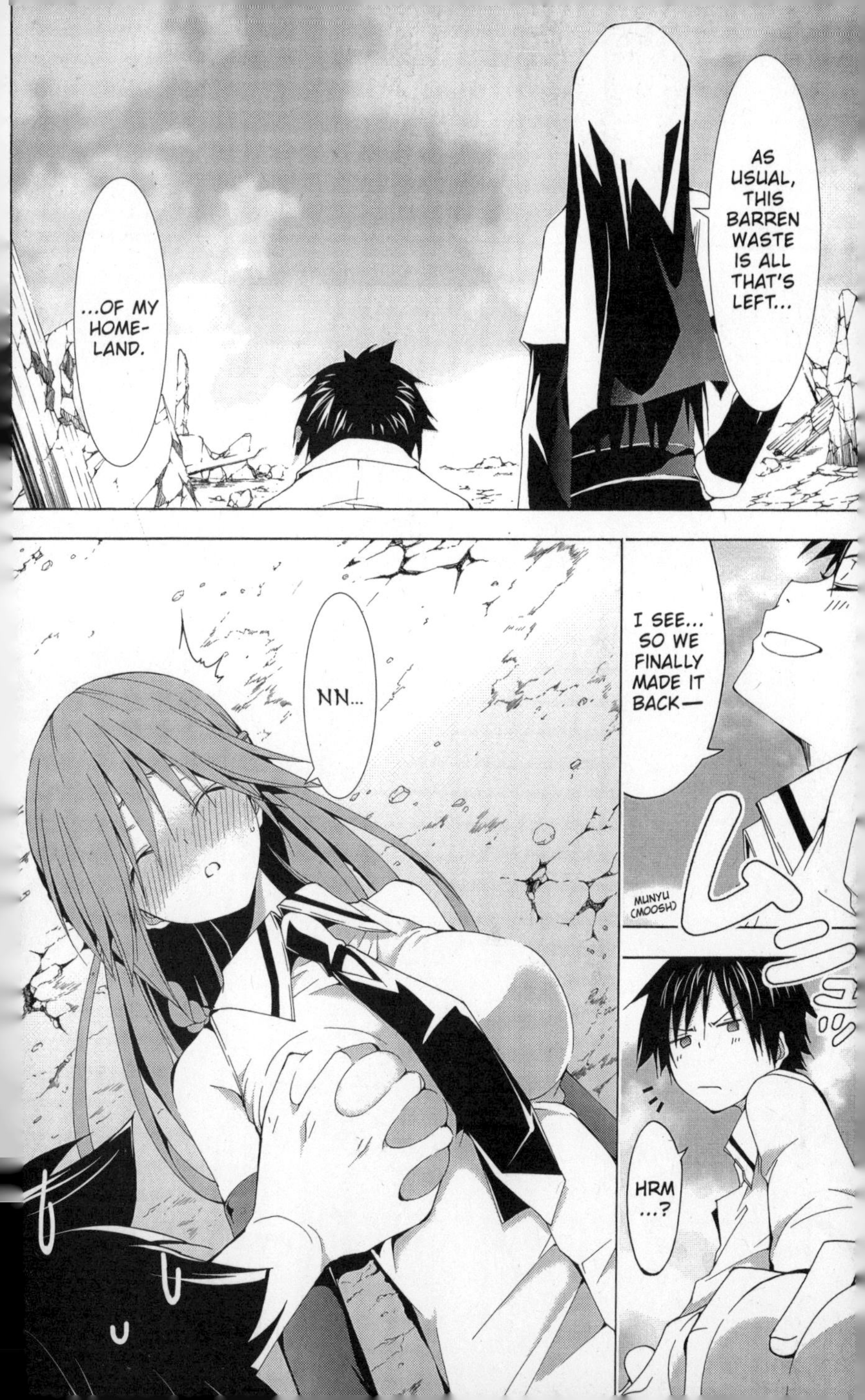
AS USUAL, THIS BARREN WASTE IS ALL THAT'S LEFT...
...OF MY HOME-LAND.
I SEE... SO WE FINALLY MADE IT BACK—
MUNYU (MOOSH)
HRM ...?
NN...

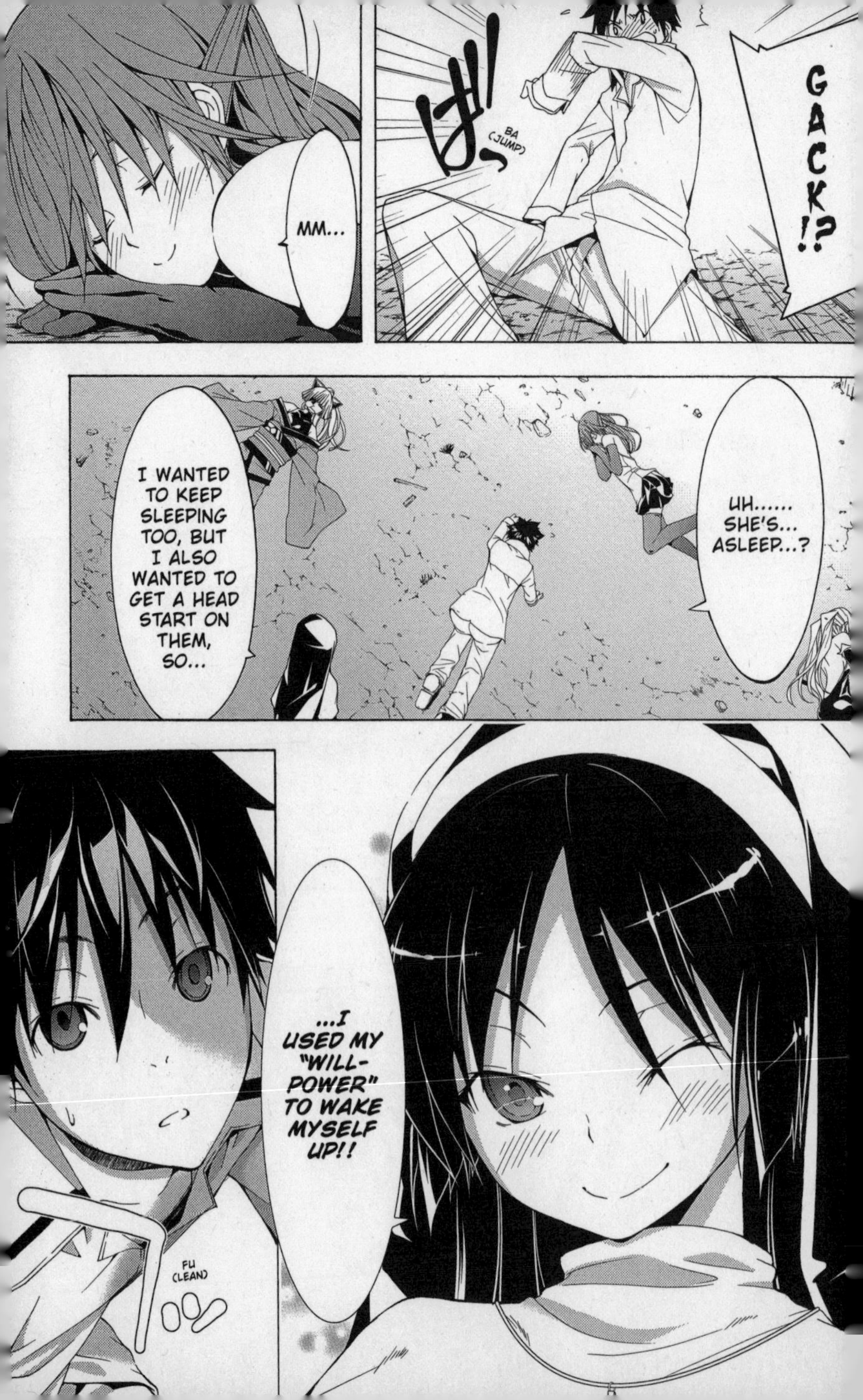
GACK!?
BA (JUMP)
MM...
UH...... SHE'S... ASLEEP...?
I WANTED TO KEEP SLEEPING TOO, BUT I ALSO WANTED TO GET A HEAD START ON THEM, SO...
...I USED MY "WILL-POWER" TO WAKE MYSELF UP!!
FU (LEAN)

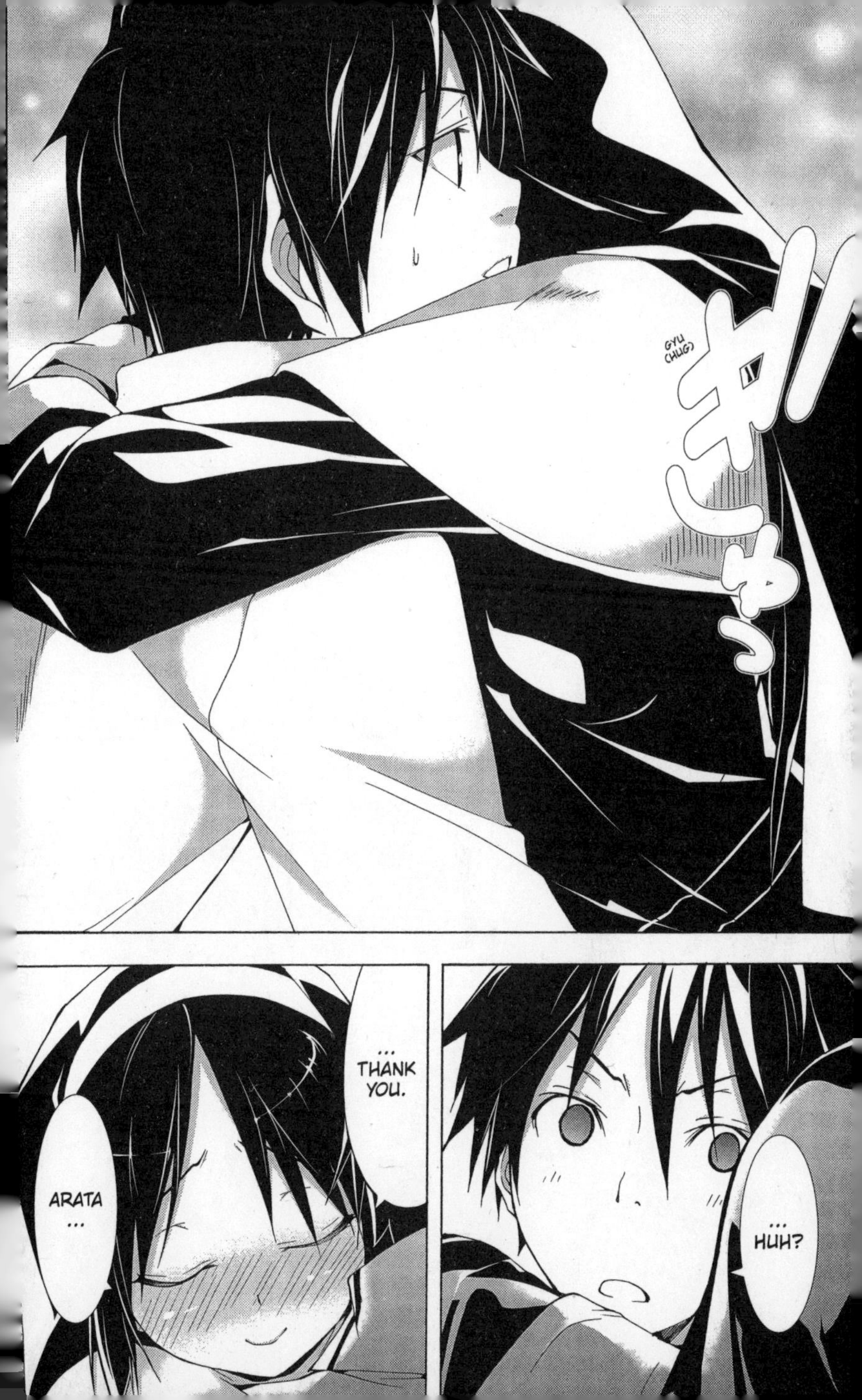
ぎゅっ
GYU (HUG)
... HUH?
... THANK YOU.
ARATA ...

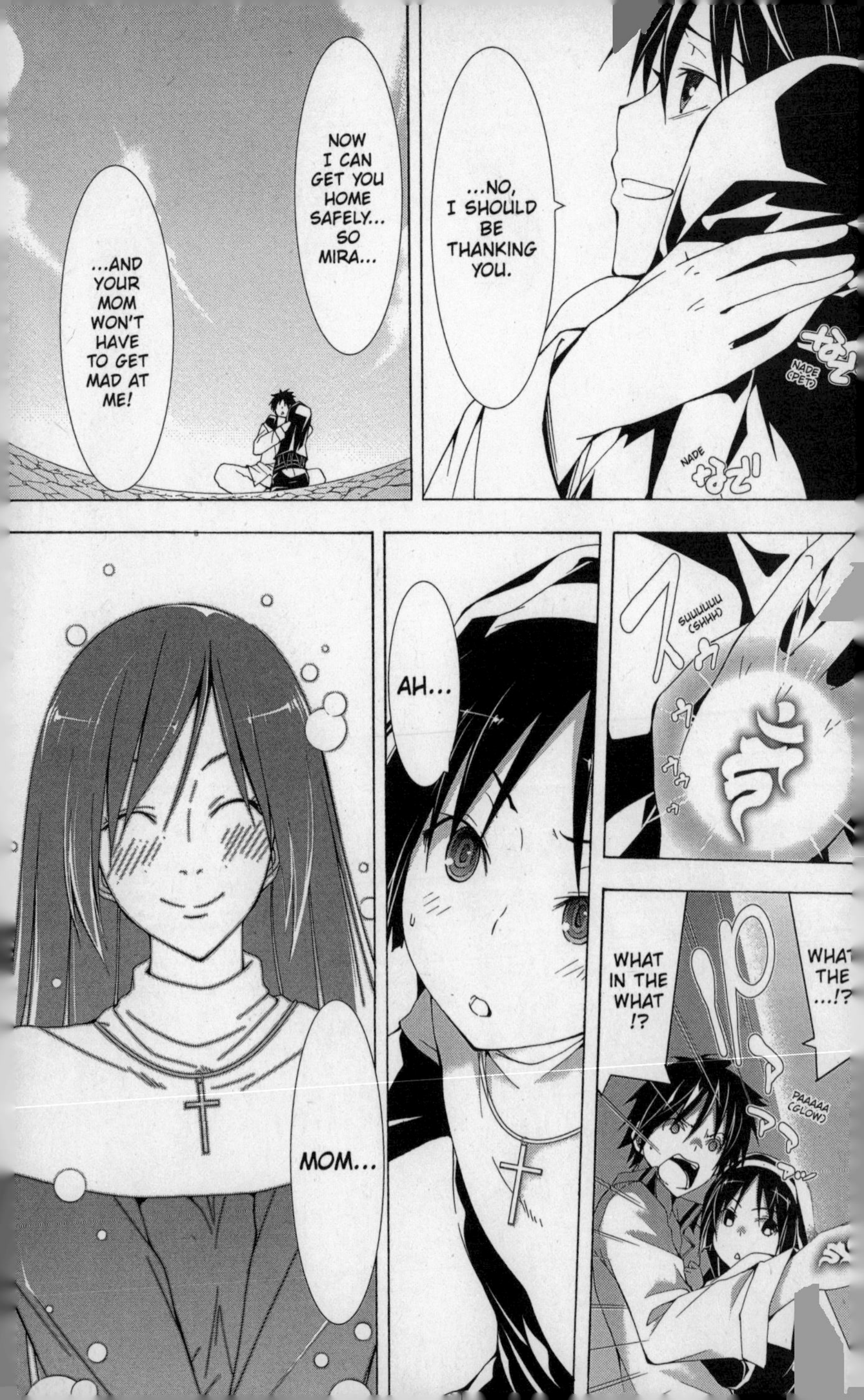
...NO, I SHOULD BE THANKING YOU.
NADE (PET)
NADE
NOW I CAN GET YOU HOME SAFELY... SO MIRA...
...AND YOUR MOM WON'T HAVE TO GET MAD AT ME!
SUUUUUUU (SHHH)
WHAT THE ...!?
WHAT IN THE WHAT !?
PAAAAA (GLOW)
AH...
MOM...

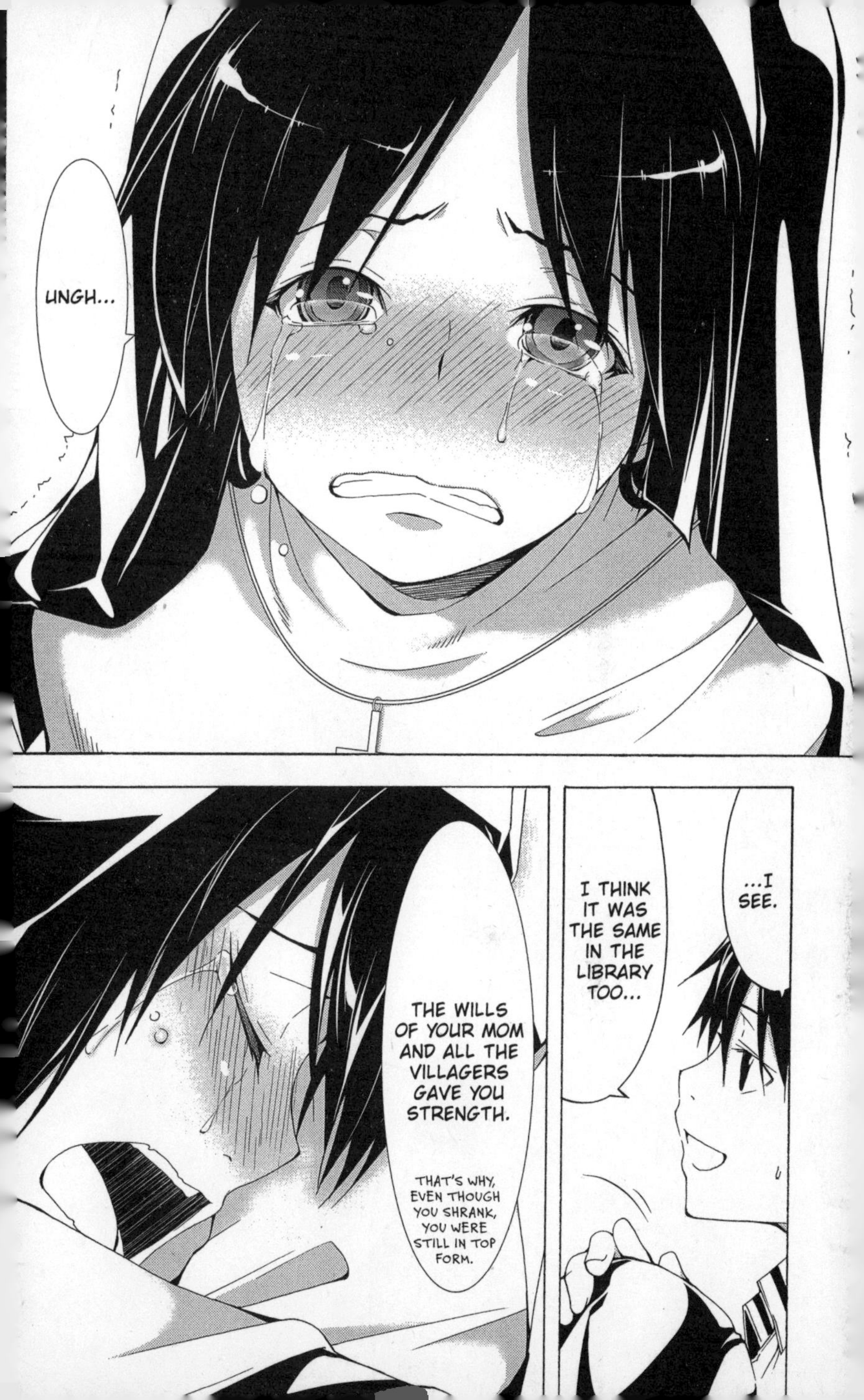
UNGH...
...I SEE.
I THINK IT WAS THE SAME IN THE LIBRARY TOO...
THE WILLS OF YOUR MOM AND ALL THE VILLAGERS GAVE YOU STRENGTH.
THAT'S WHY, EVEN THOUGH YOU SHRANK, YOU WERE STILL IN TOP FORM.

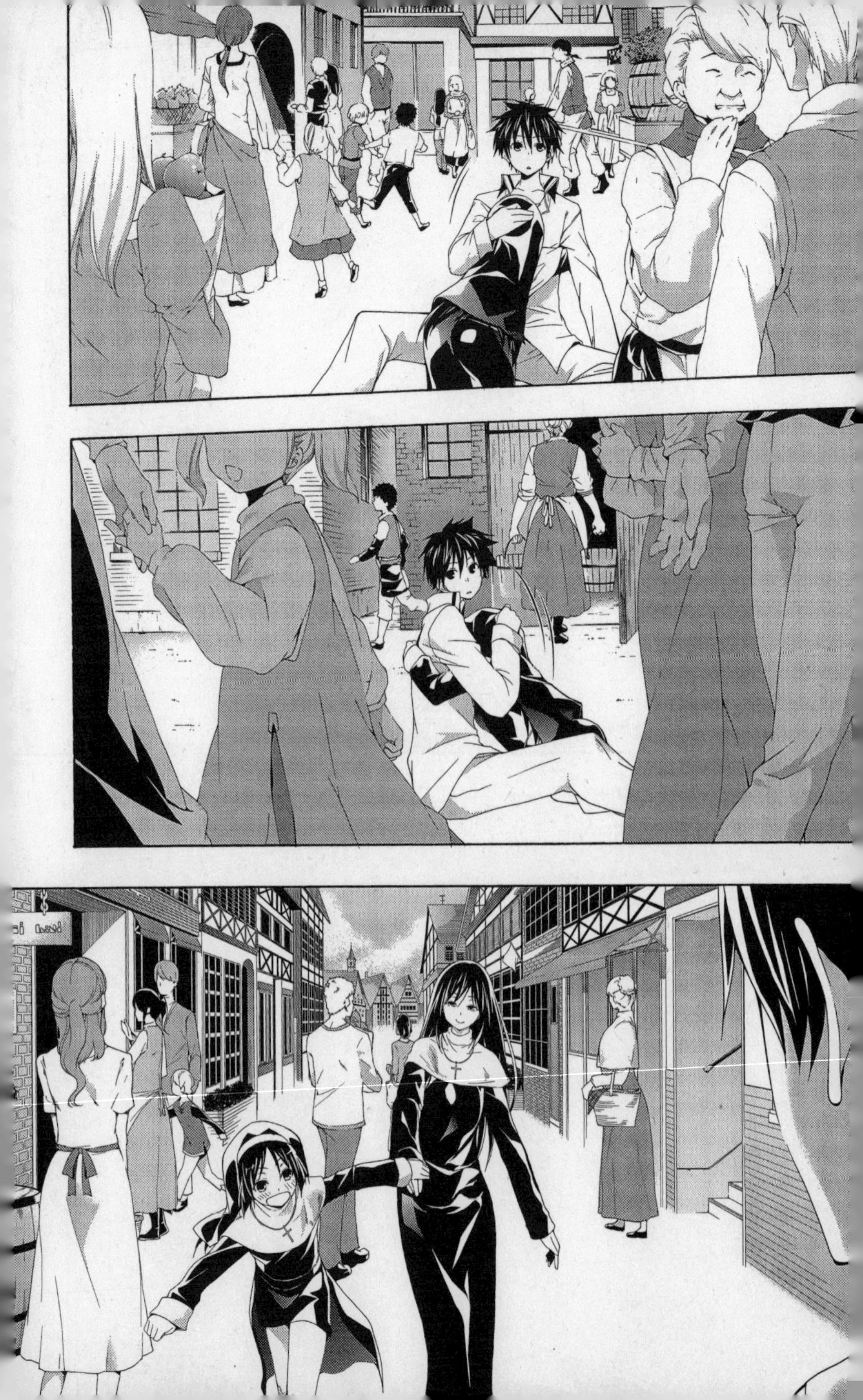

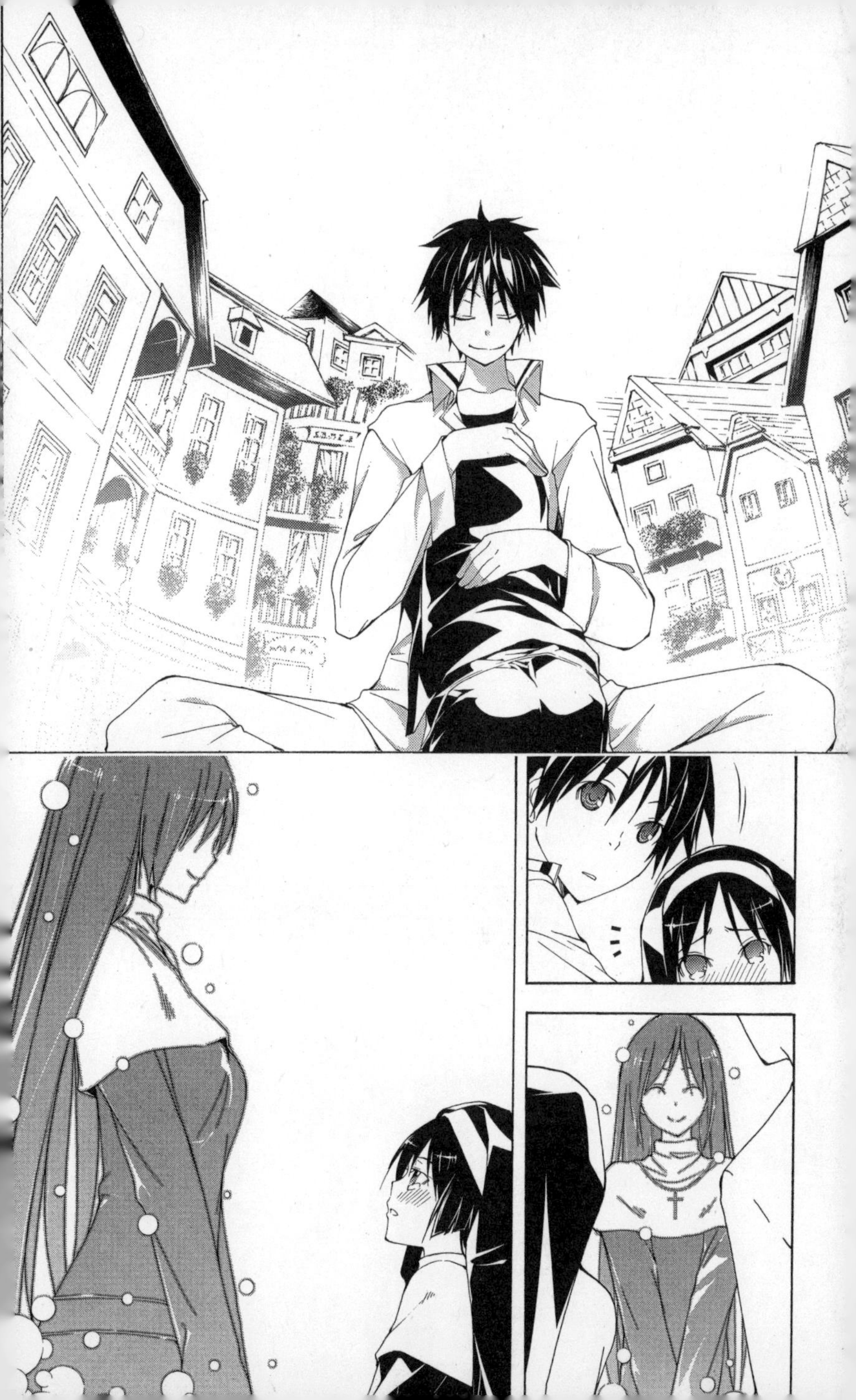

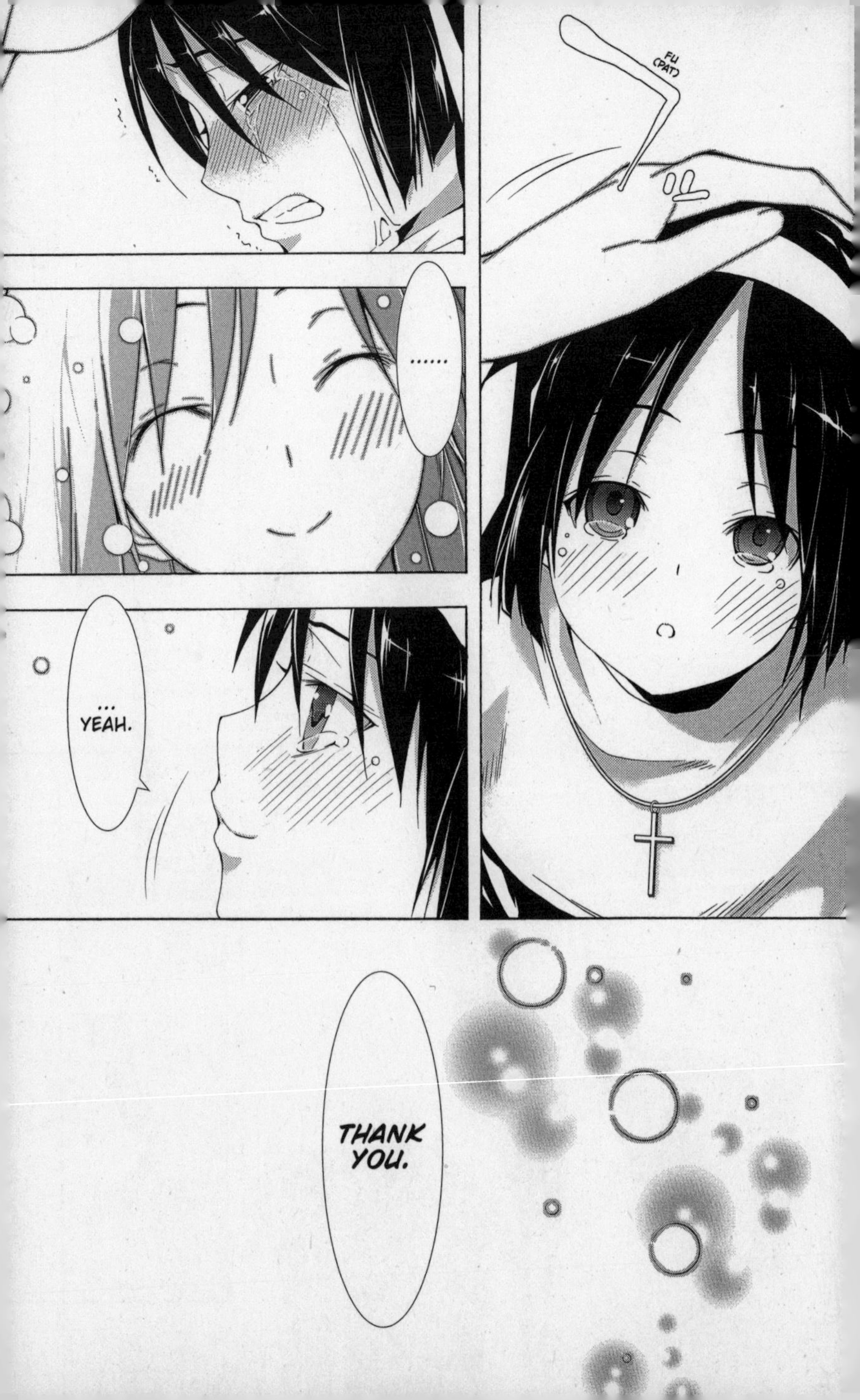
FU (PAT)
......
... YEAH.
THANK YOU.

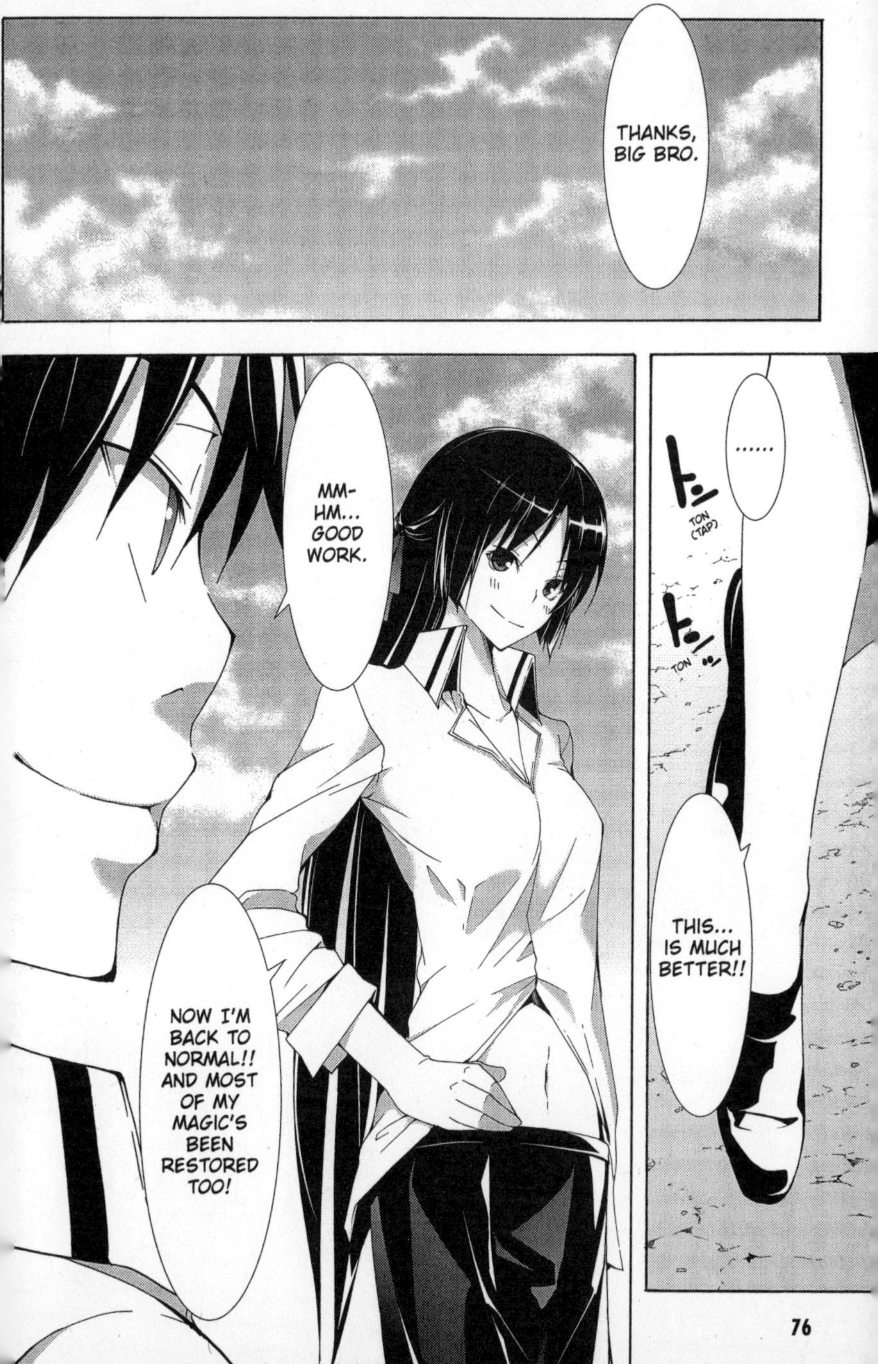
THANKS, BIG BRO.
......
TON (TAP)
TON
THIS... IS MUCH BETTER!!
MM-HM... GOOD WORK.
NOW I'M BACK TO NORMAL!! AND MOST OF MY MAGIC'S BEEN RESTORED TOO!

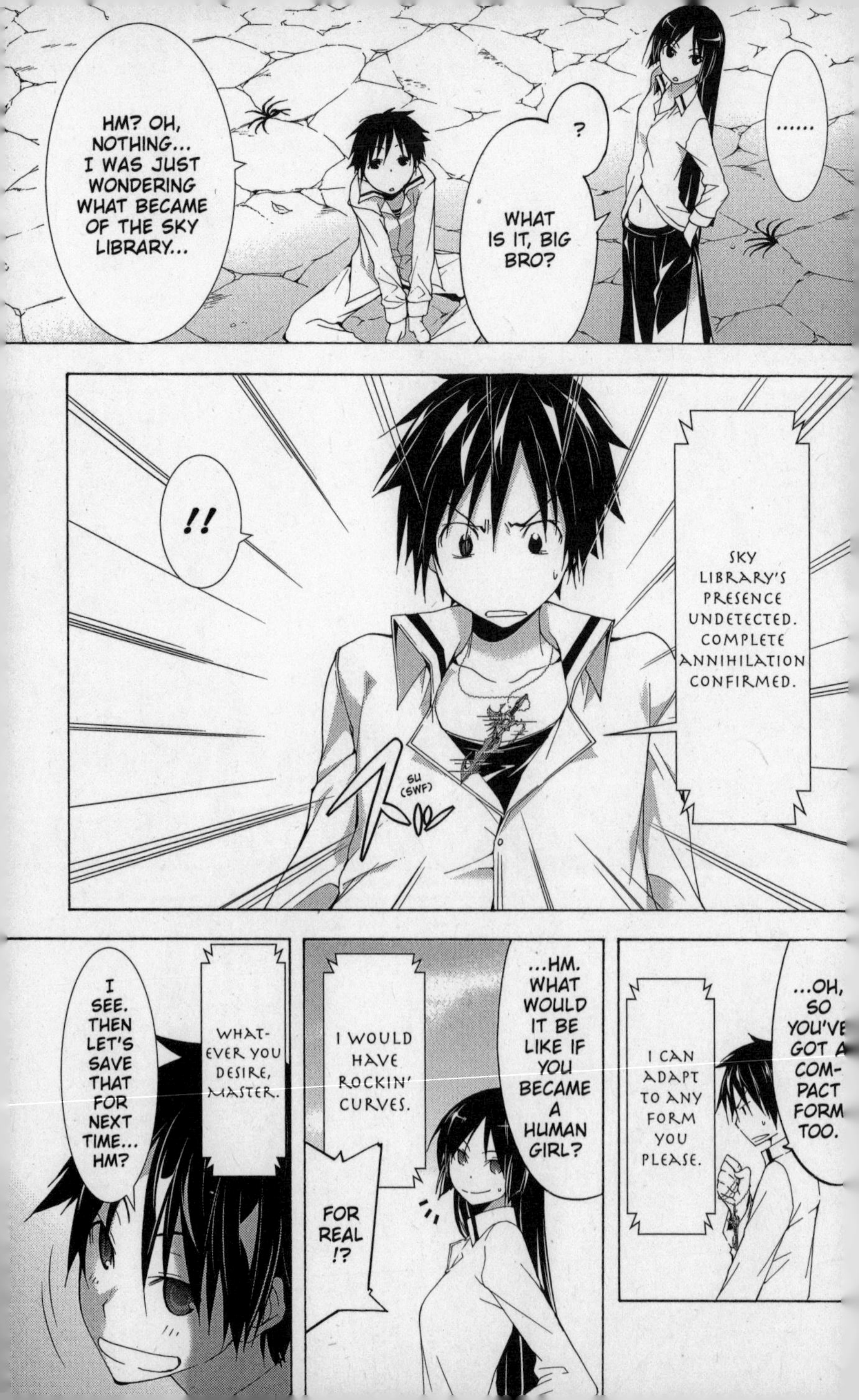
......
?
WHAT IS IT, BIG BRO?
HM? OH, NOTHING... I WAS JUST WONDERING WHAT BECAME OF THE SKY LIBRARY...
SKY LIBRARY'S PRESENCE UNDETECTED. COMPLETE ANNIHILATION CONFIRMED.
!!
SU (SWF)
...OH, SO YOU'VE GOT A COMPACT FORM TOO.
I CAN ADAPT TO ANY FORM YOU PLEASE.
...HM. WHAT WOULD IT BE LIKE IF YOU BECAME A HUMAN GIRL?
I WOULD HAVE ROCKIN' CURVES.
FOR REAL!?
WHATEVER YOU DESIRE, MASTER.
I SEE. THEN LET'S SAVE THAT FOR NEXT TIME... HM?

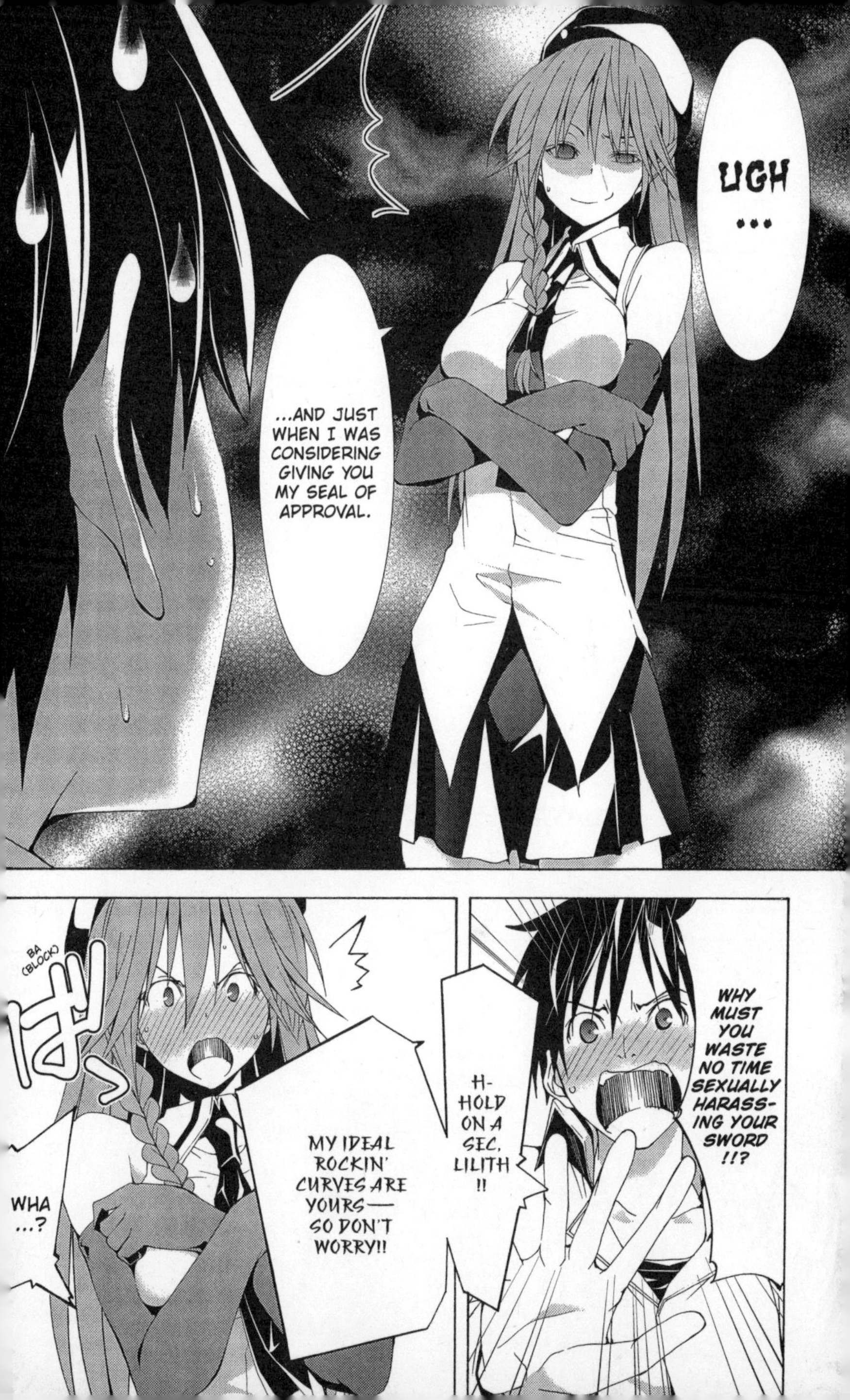
UGH ...
...AND JUST WHEN I WAS CONSIDERING GIVING YOU MY SEAL OF APPROVAL.
WHY MUST YOU WASTE NO TIME SEXUALLY HARASS-ING YOUR SWORD !!?
H-HOLD ON A SEC, LILITH !!
MY IDEAL ROCKIN' CURVES ARE YOURS— SO DON'T WORRY!!
BA (BLOCK)
WHA ...?

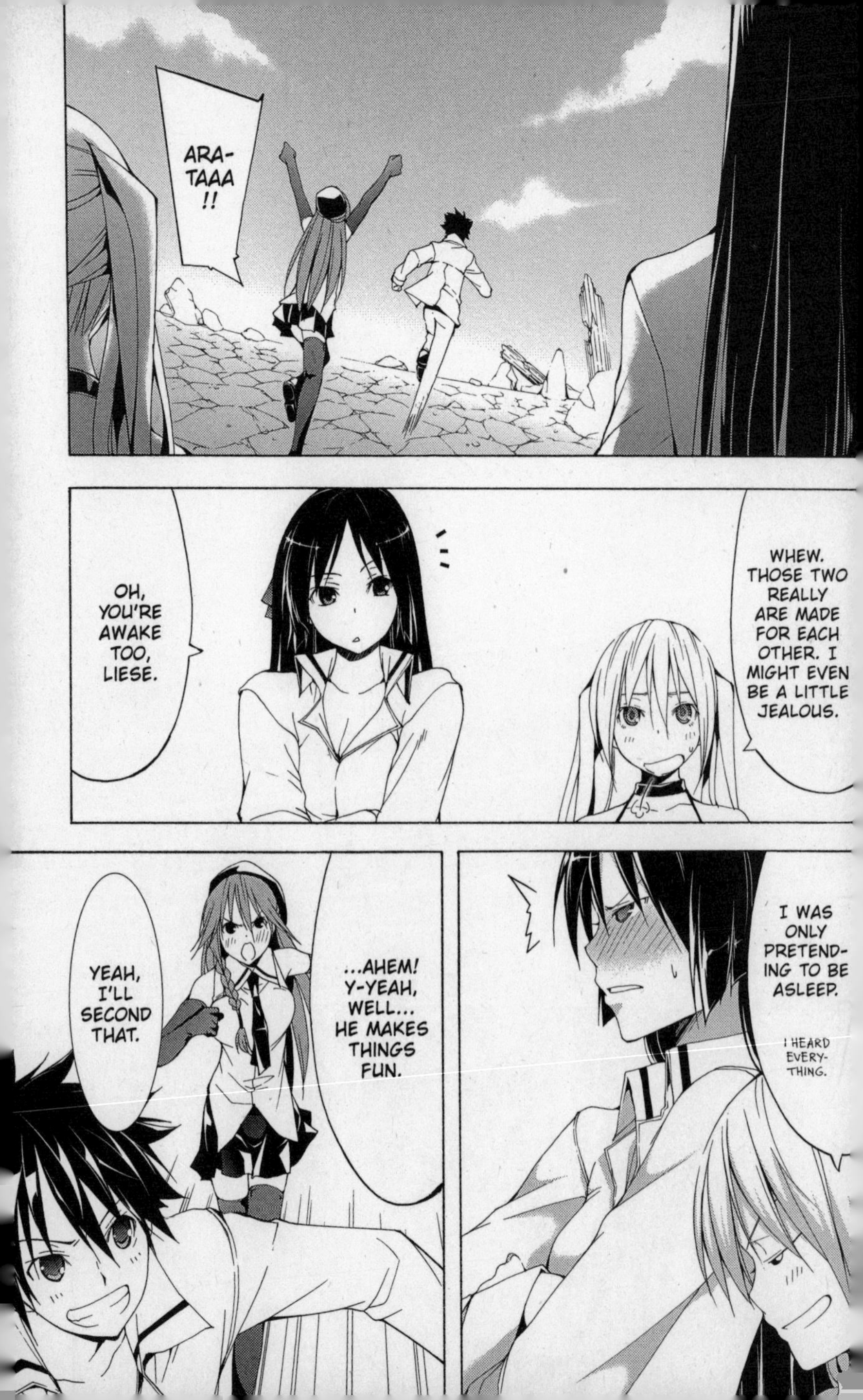
ARA-TAAA!!
WHEW. THOSE TWO REALLY ARE MADE FOR EACH OTHER. I MIGHT EVEN BE A LITTLE JEALOUS.
OH, YOU'RE AWAKE TOO, LIESE.
I WAS ONLY PRETENDING TO BE ASLEEP.
I HEARD EVERYTHING.
...AHEM! Y-YEAH, WELL... HE MAKES THINGS FUN.
YEAH, I'LL SECOND THAT.

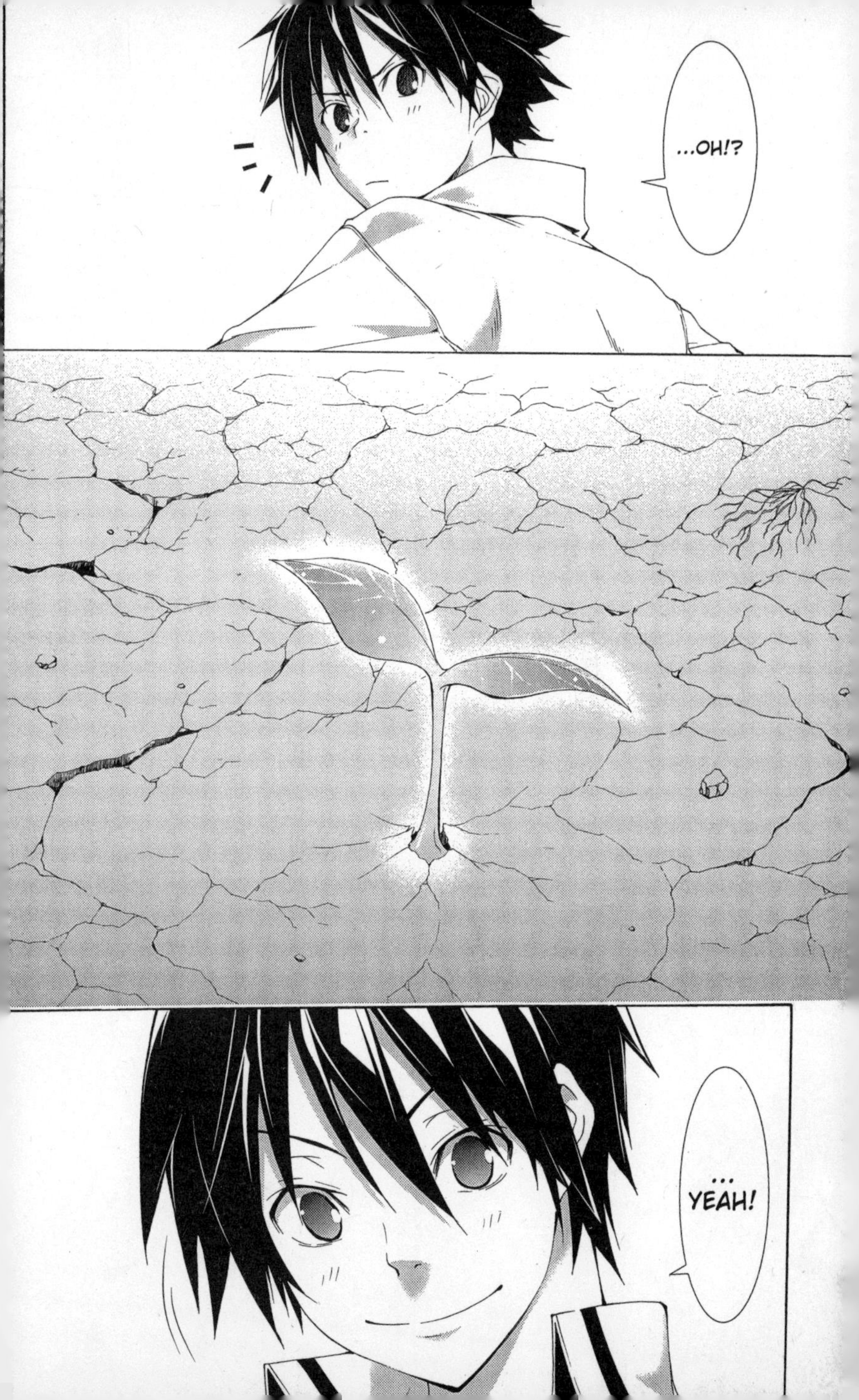
...OH!?
...
YEAH!

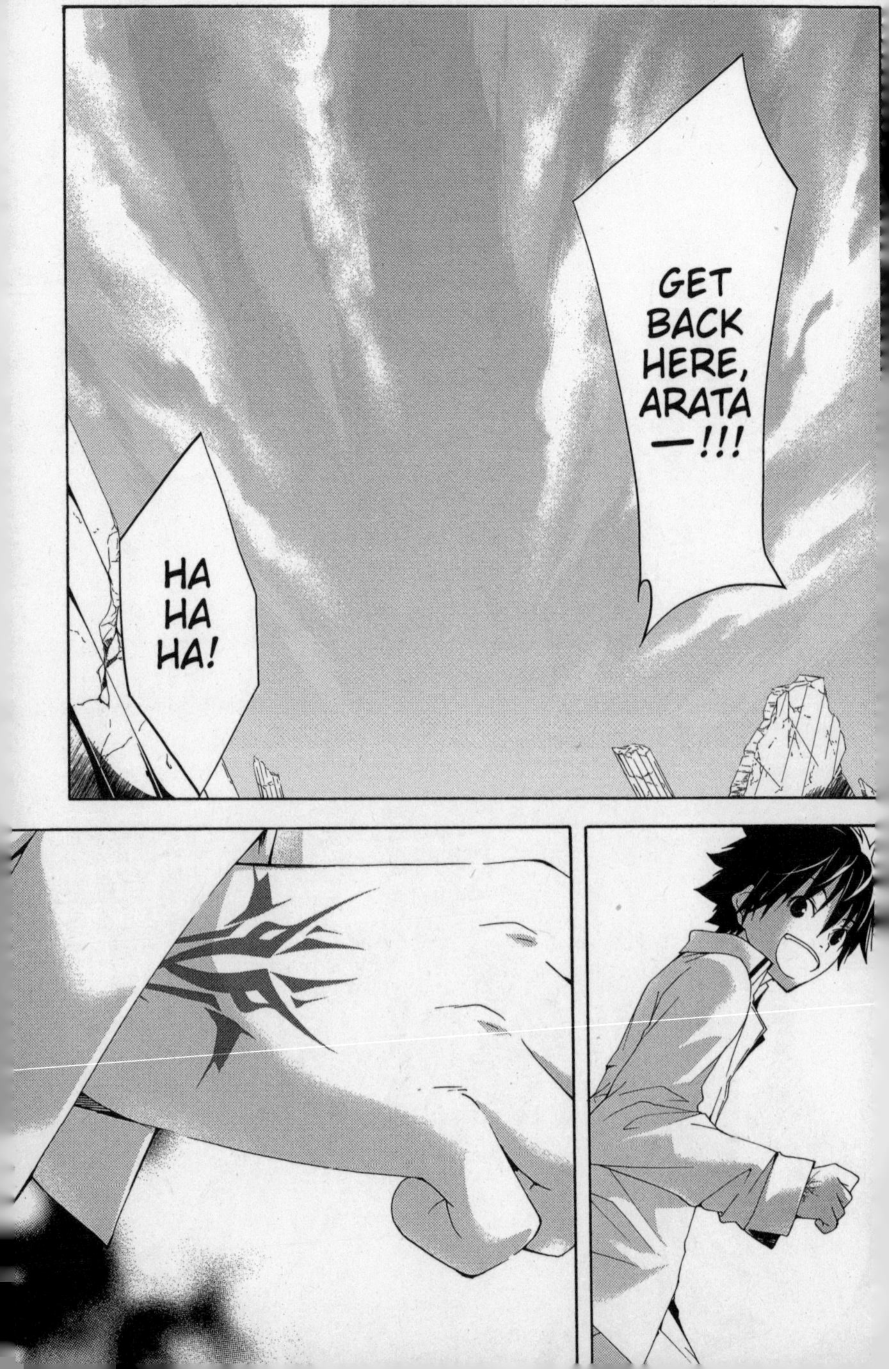
GET BACK HERE, ARATA—!!!
HA HA HA!

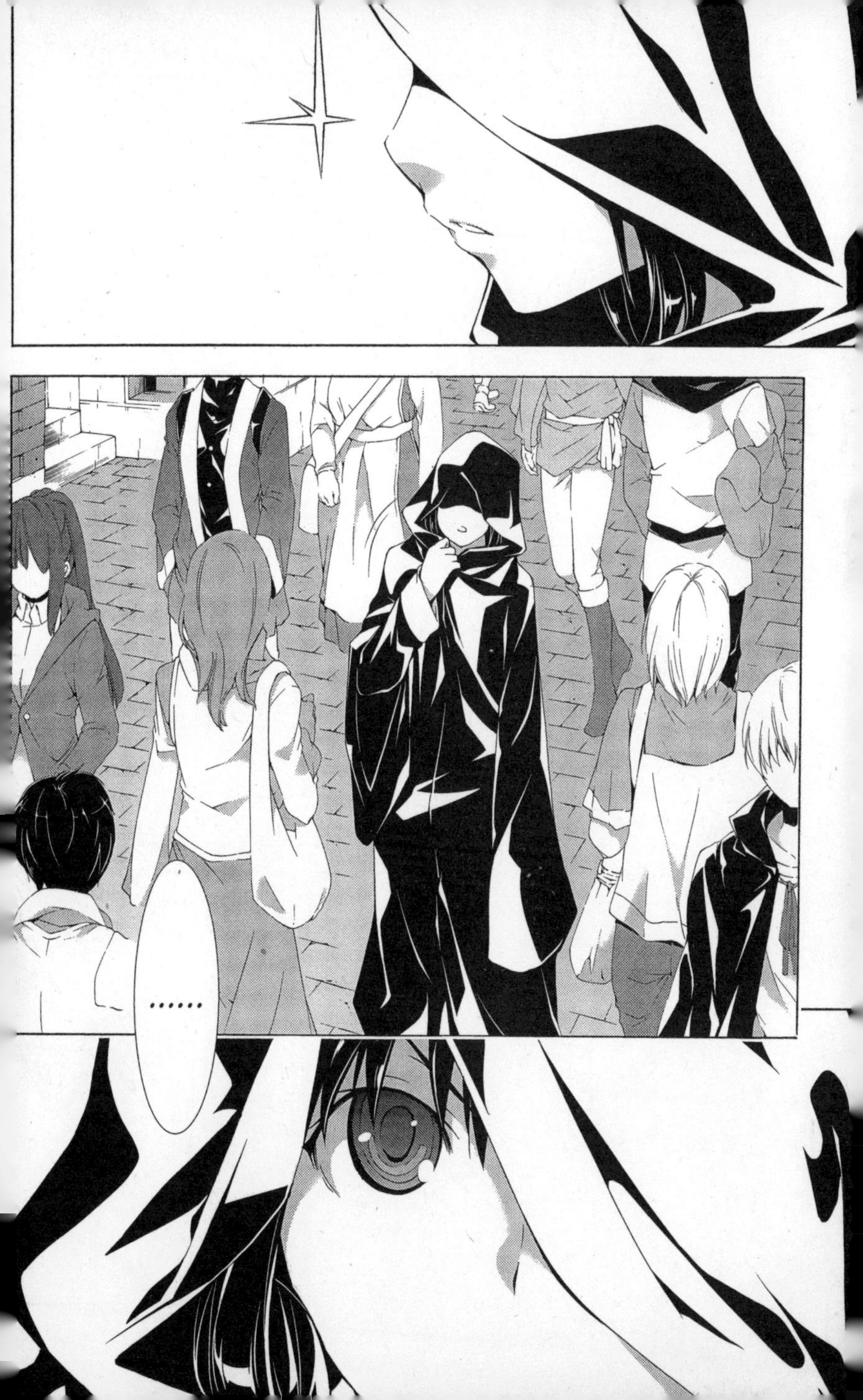
......

38. Manhunt & Eve of the Party

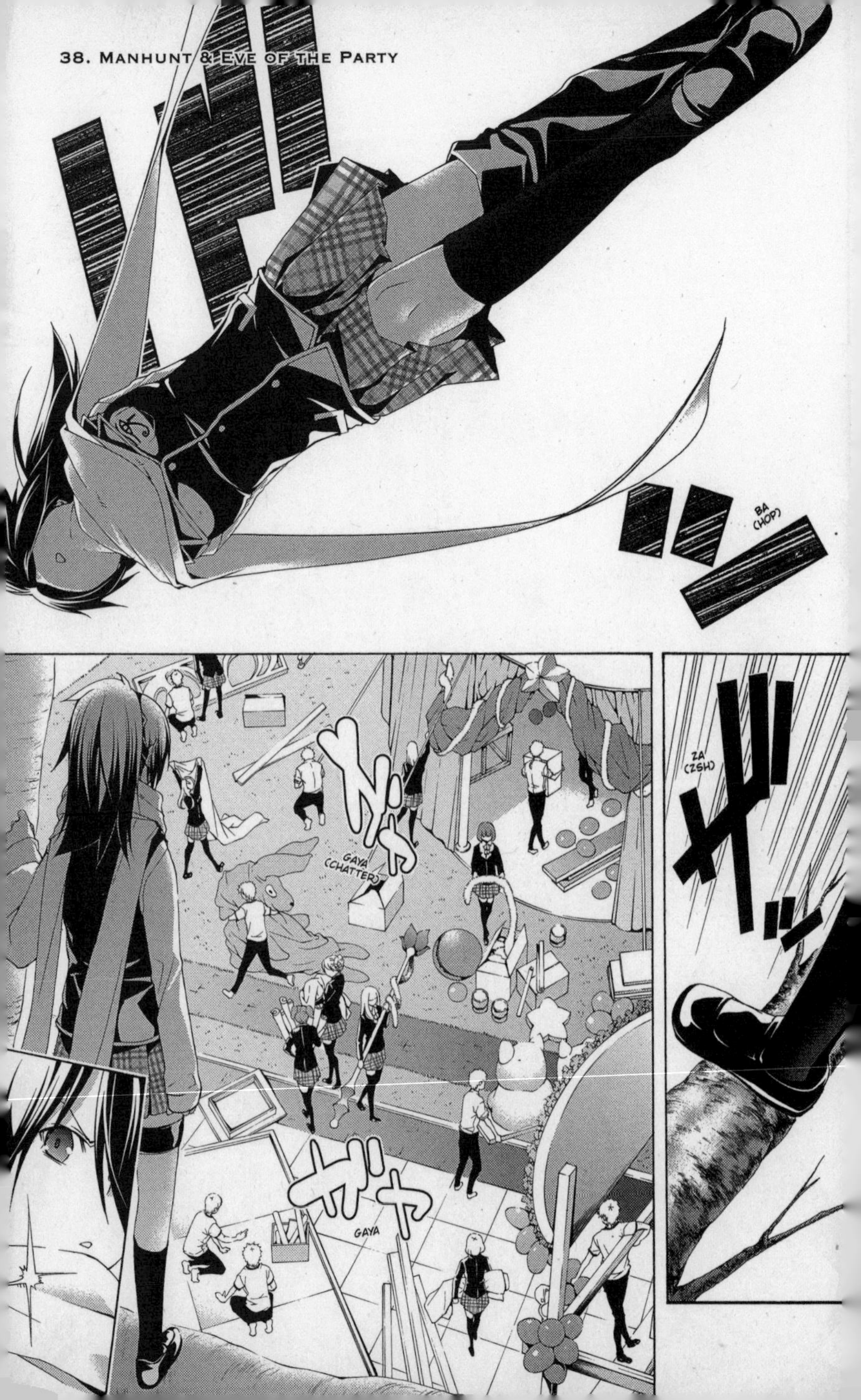
BA
(HOP)
ZA
(ZSH)
GAYA
(CHATTER)
GAYA

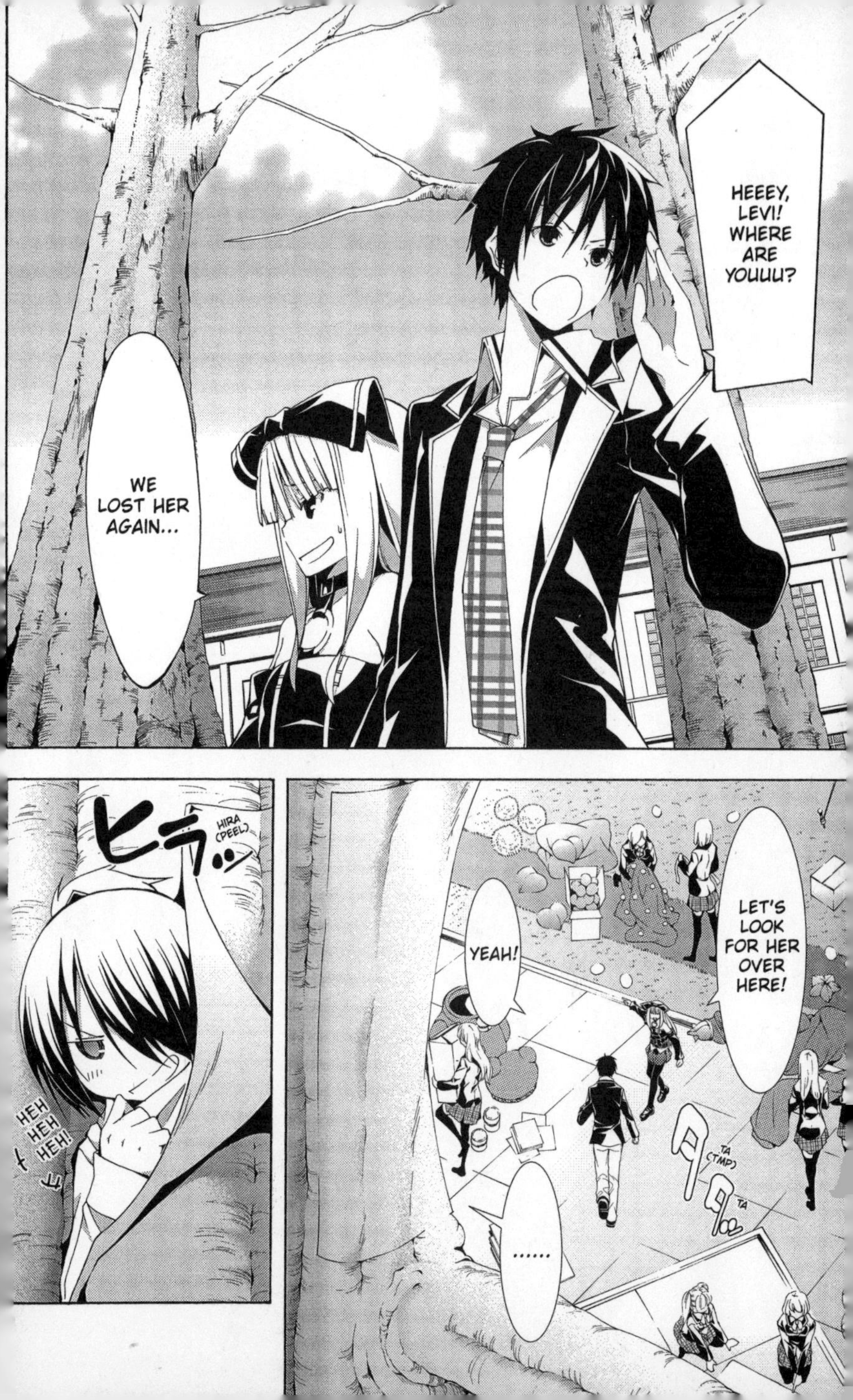
HEEEY, LEVI! WHERE ARE YOUUU?
WE LOST HER AGAIN...
LET'S LOOK FOR HER OVER HERE!
YEAH!
TA (TMP)
TA
......
HIRA (PEEL)
HEH HEH HEH!

38. Manhunt & Eve of the Par

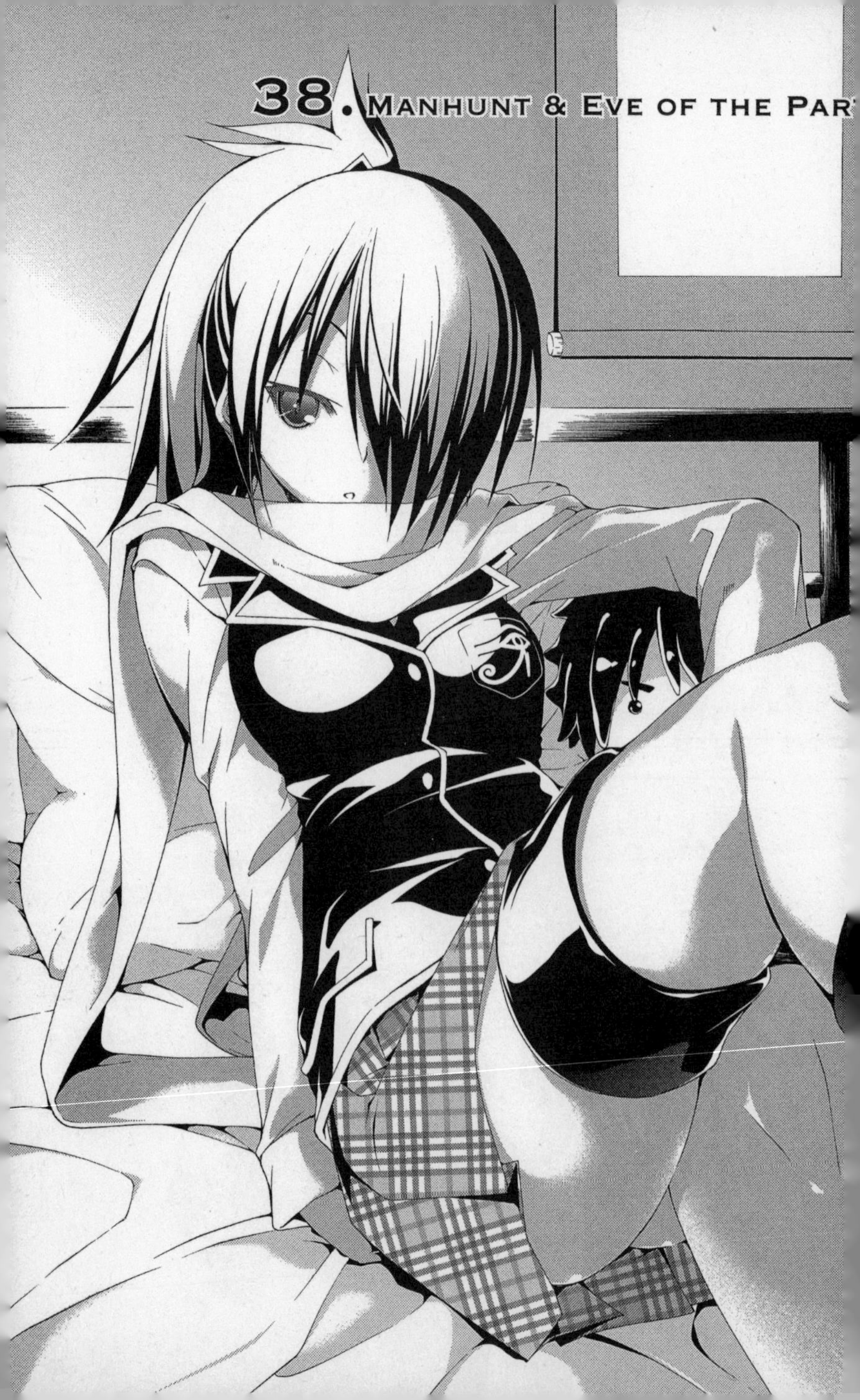

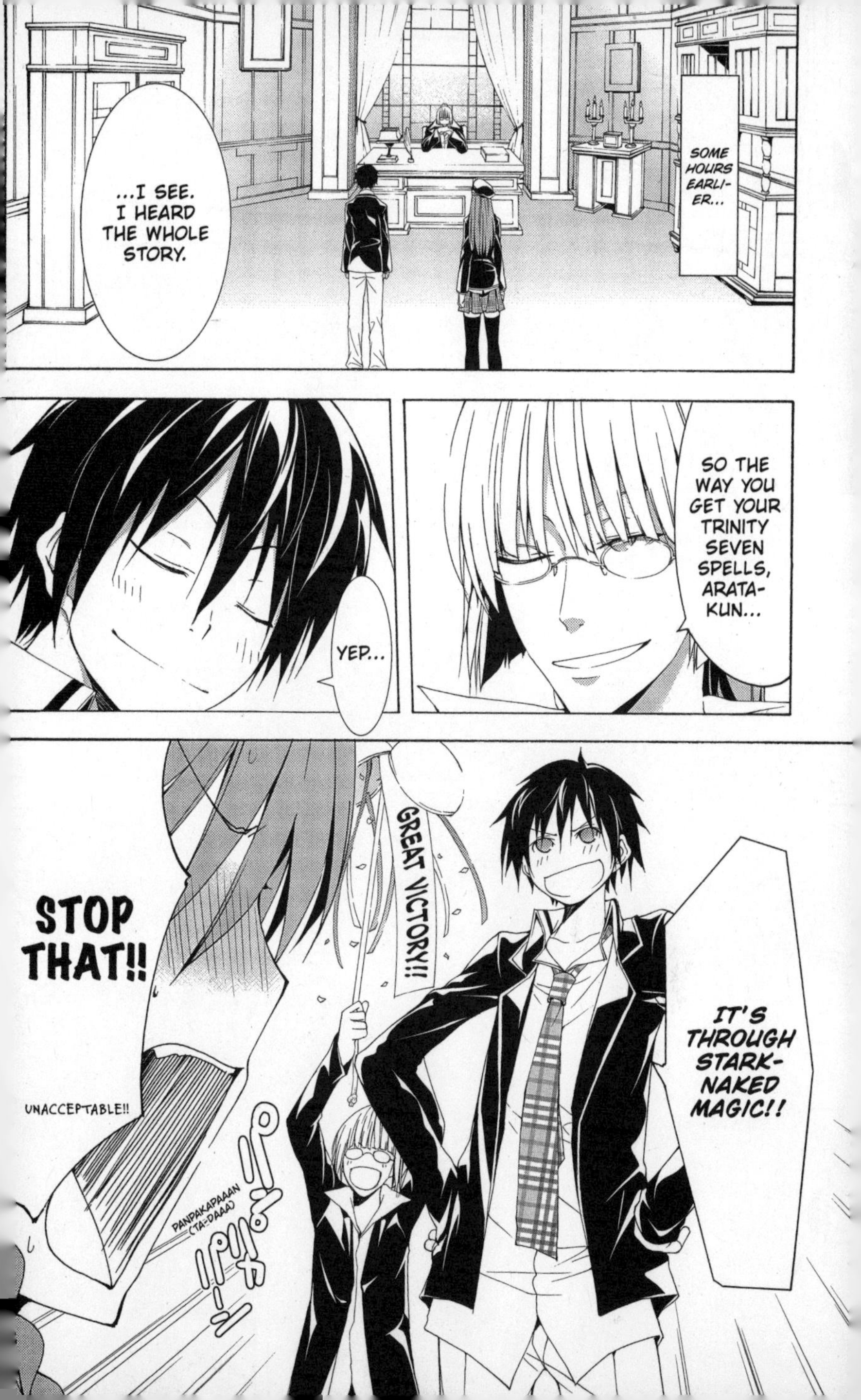
SOME HOURS EARLI-ER...
...I SEE. I HEARD THE WHOLE STORY.
SO THE WAY YOU GET YOUR TRINITY SEVEN SPELLS, ARATA-KUN...
YEP...
IT'S THROUGH STARK-NAKED MAGIC!!
GREAT VICTORY!!
STOP THAT!!
UNACCEPTABLE!!
PANPAKAPAAAN (TA-DAAA)

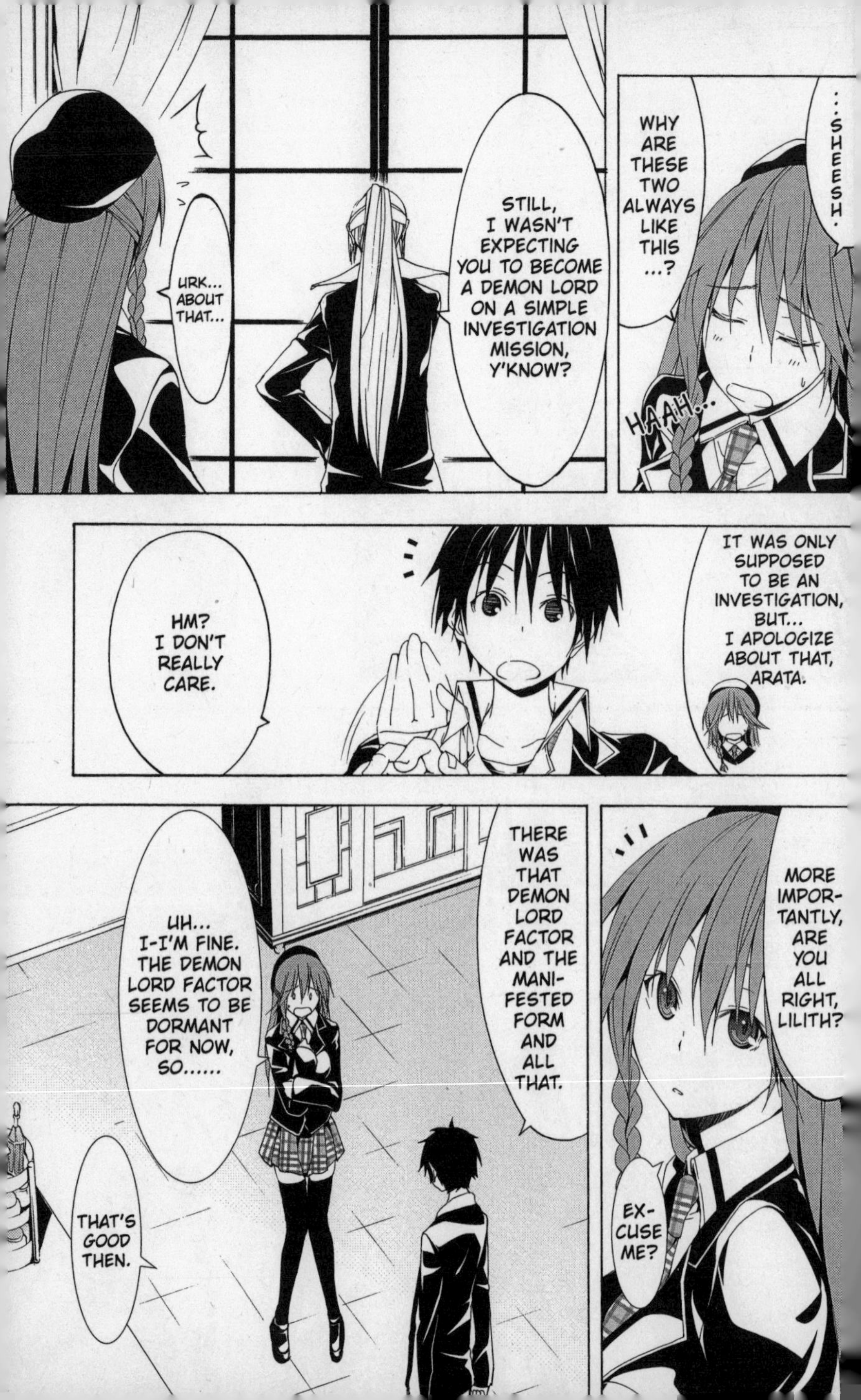
...SHEESH.
WHY ARE THESE TWO ALWAYS LIKE THIS ...?
HAAAH...
STILL, I WASN'T EXPECTING YOU TO BECOME A DEMON LORD ON A SIMPLE INVESTIGATION MISSION, Y'KNOW?
URK... ABOUT THAT...
IT WAS ONLY SUPPOSED TO BE AN INVESTIGATION, BUT... I APOLOGIZE ABOUT THAT, ARATA.
HM? I DON'T REALLY CARE.
MORE IMPOR-TANTLY, ARE YOU ALL RIGHT, LILITH?
EX-CUSE ME?
THERE WAS THAT DEMON LORD FACTOR AND THE MANI-FESTED FORM AND ALL THAT.
UH... I-I'M FINE. THE DEMON LORD FACTOR SEEMS TO BE DORMANT FOR NOW, SO......
THAT'S GOOD THEN.

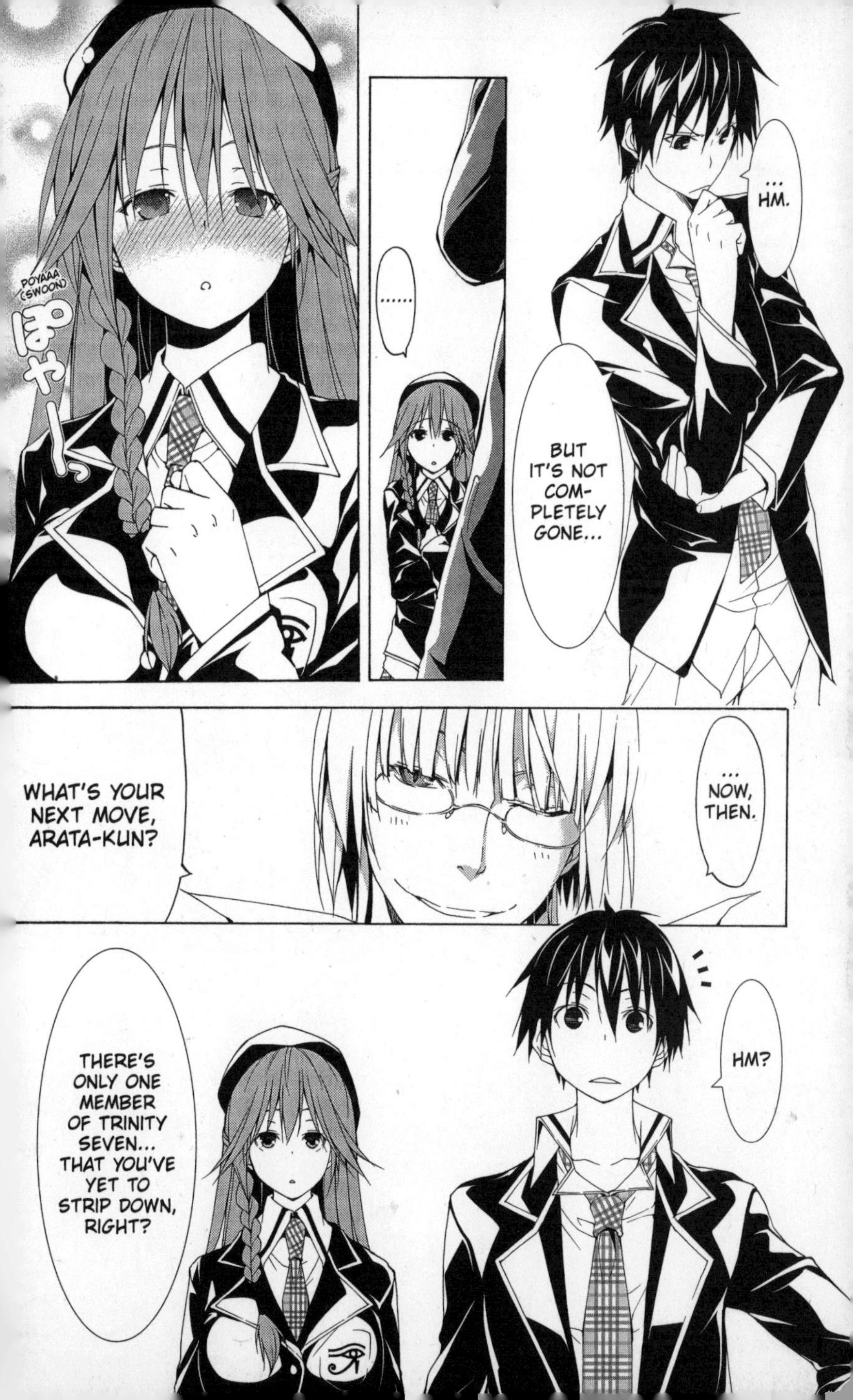
... HM.
BUT IT'S NOT COM-PLETELY GONE...
......
POYAAA (SWOON)
ぽやーっ
... NOW, THEN.
WHAT'S YOUR NEXT MOVE, ARATA-KUN?
HM?
THERE'S ONLY ONE MEMBER OF TRINITY SEVEN... THAT YOU'VE YET TO STRIP DOWN, RIGHT?

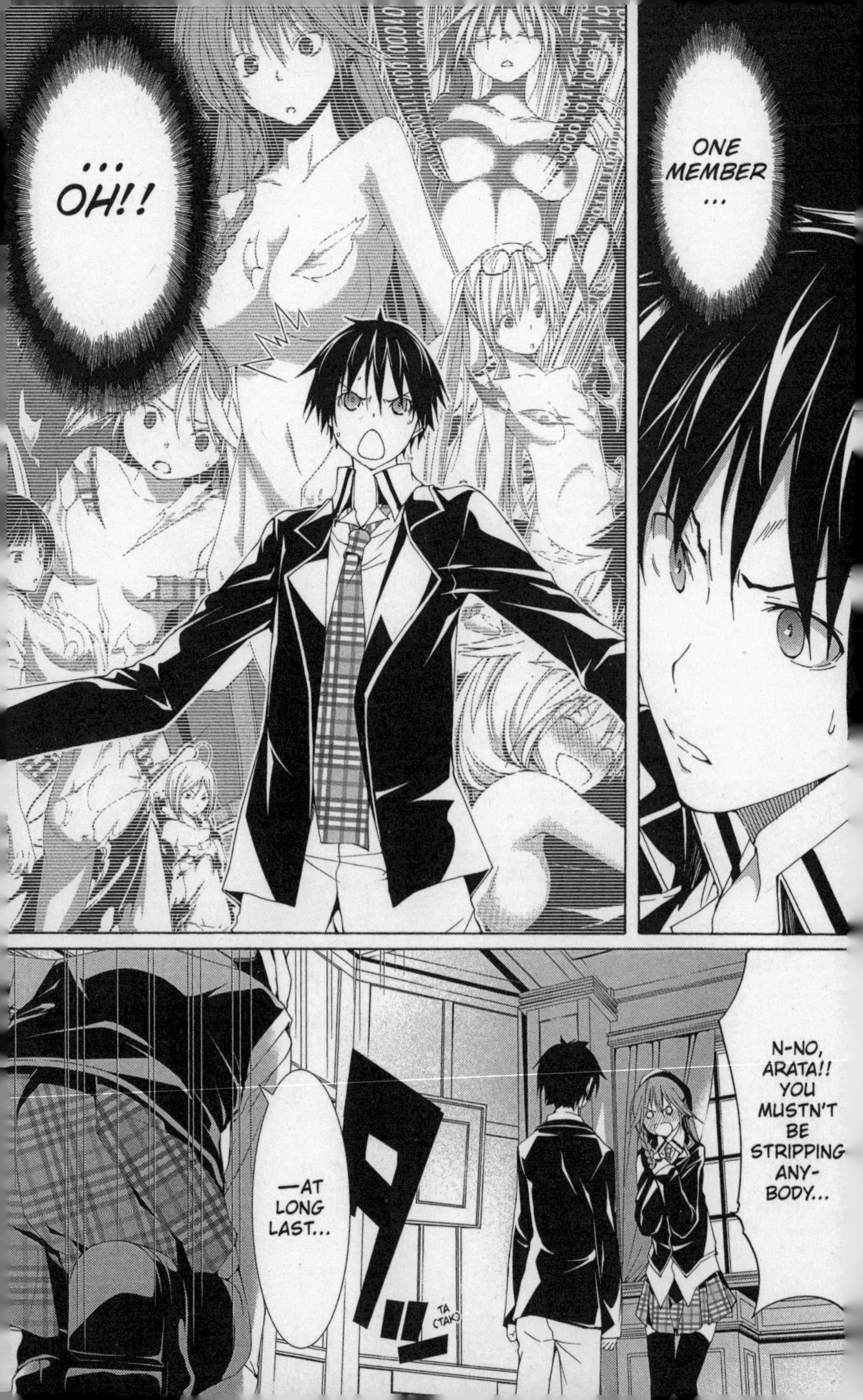
ONE MEMBER ...
... OH!!
N-NO, ARATA!! YOU MUSTN'T BE STRIPPING ANY-BODY...
TA (TAK)
—AT LONG LAST...

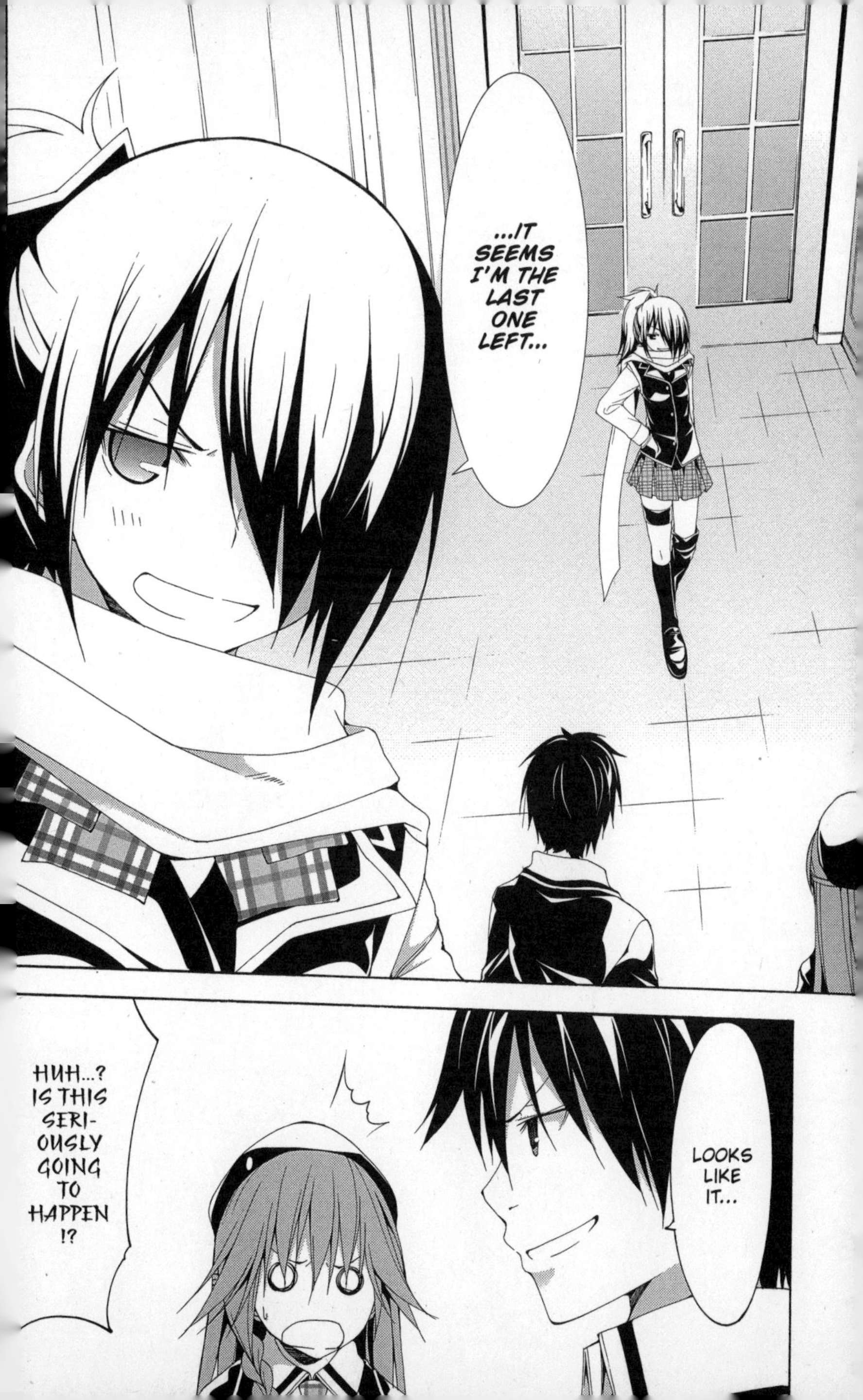
...IT SEEMS I'M THE LAST ONE LEFT...
LOOKS LIKE IT...
HUH...? IS THIS SERIOUSLY GOING TO HAPPEN!?

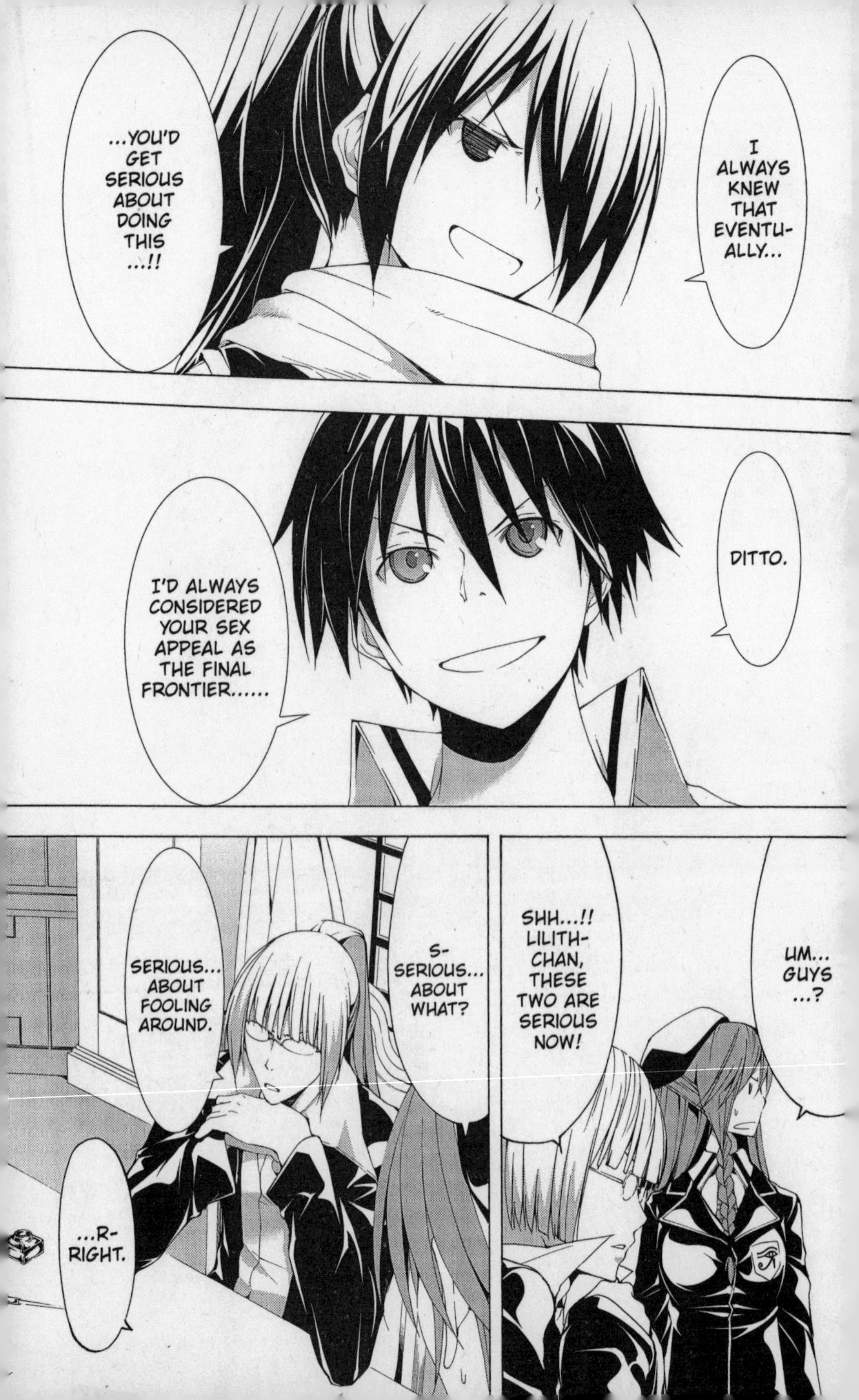
I ALWAYS KNEW THAT EVENTU-ALLY...
...YOU'D GET SERIOUS ABOUT DOING THIS ...!!
DITTO.
I'D ALWAYS CONSIDERED YOUR SEX APPEAL AS THE FINAL FRONTIER......
UM... GUYS ...?
SHH...!! LILITH-CHAN, THESE TWO ARE SERIOUS NOW!
S-SERIOUS... ABOUT WHAT?
SERIOUS... ABOUT FOOLING AROUND.
...R-RIGHT.

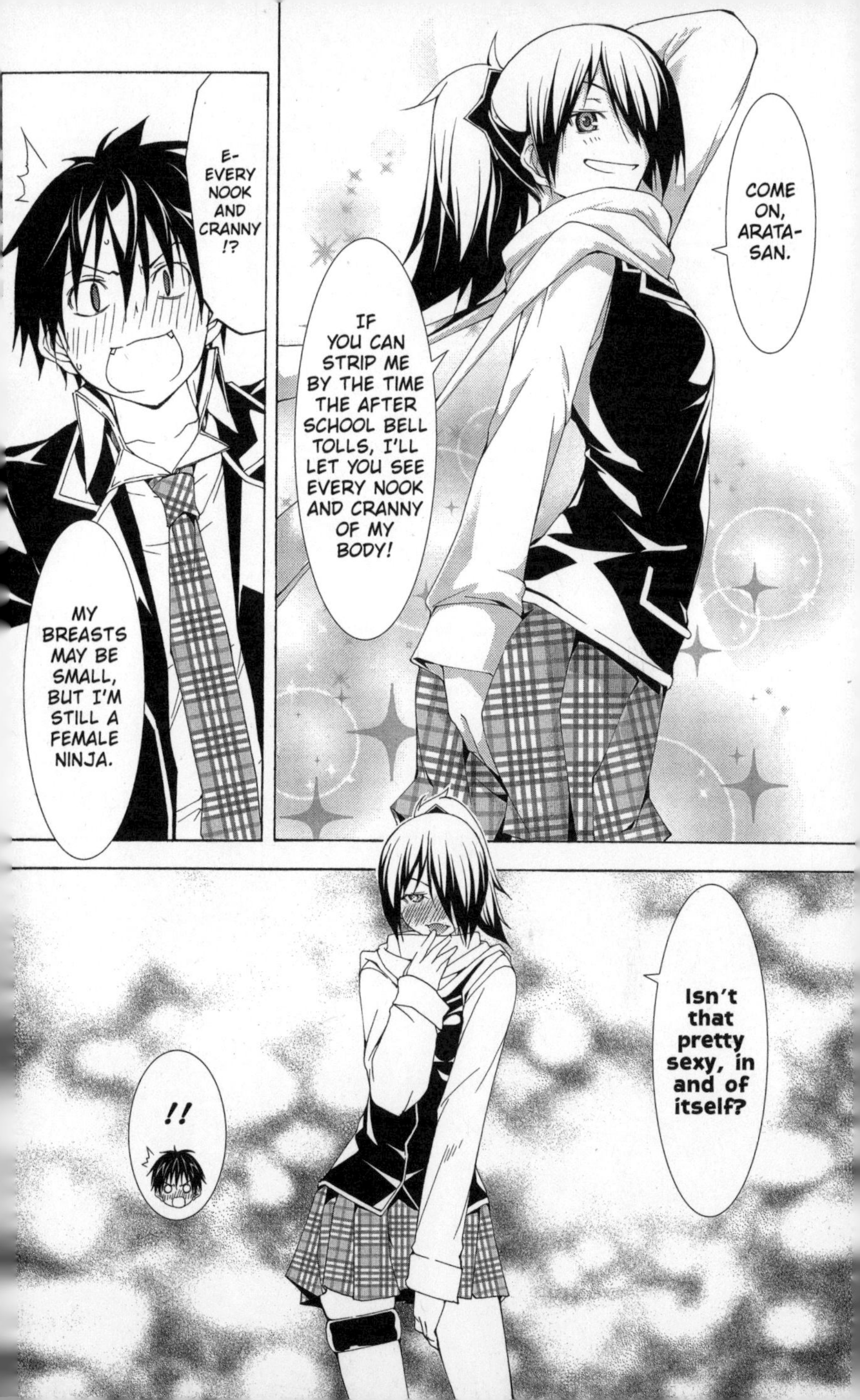
COME ON, ARATA-SAN.
IF YOU CAN STRIP ME BY THE TIME THE AFTER SCHOOL BELL TOLLS, I'LL LET YOU SEE EVERY NOOK AND CRANNY OF MY BODY!
E- EVERY NOOK AND CRANNY !?
MY BREASTS MAY BE SMALL, BUT I'M STILL A FEMALE NINJA.
Isn't that pretty sexy, in and of itself?
!!

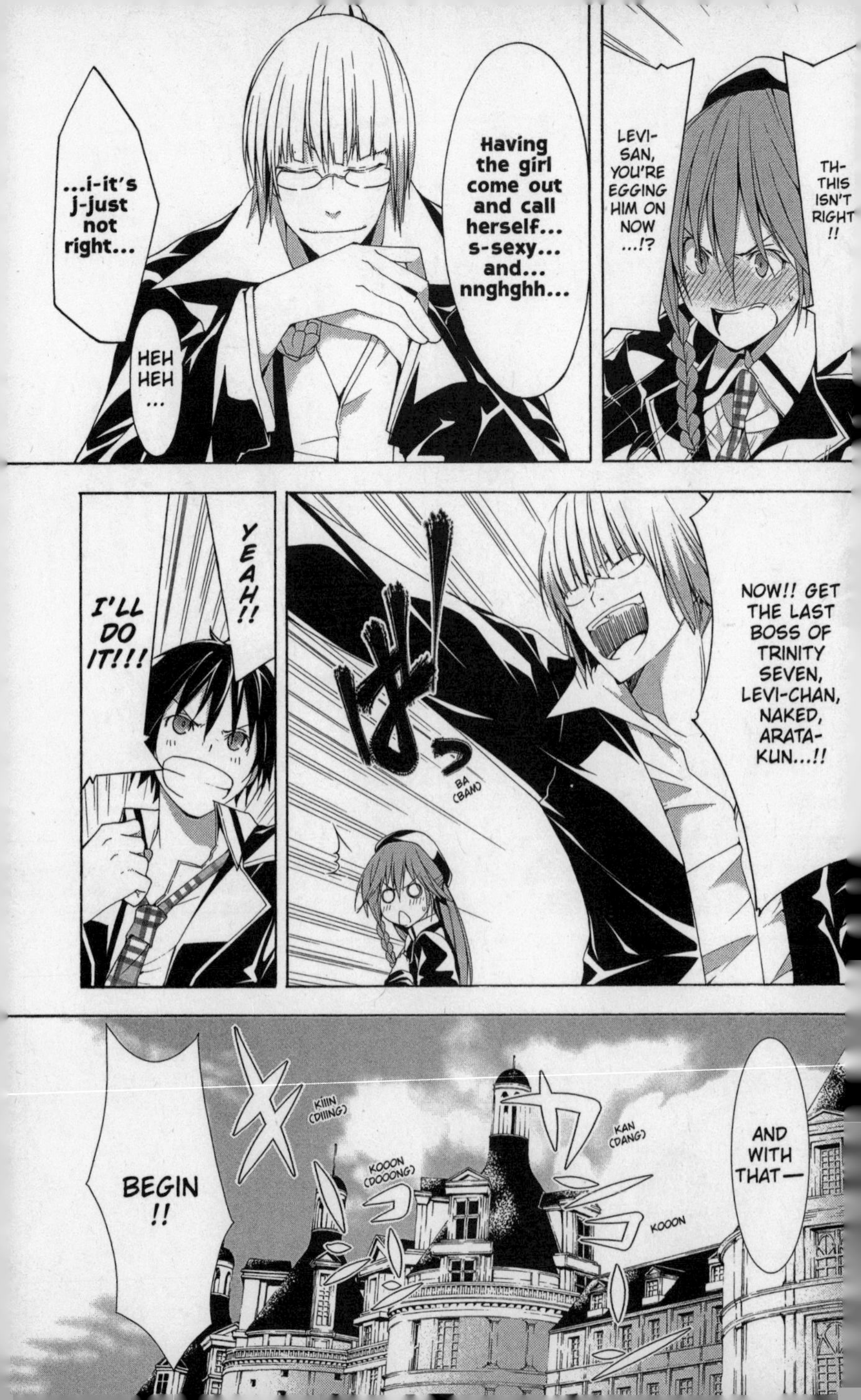
TH-THIS ISN'T RIGHT!!
LEVI-SAN, YOU'RE EGGING HIM ON NOW...!?
Having the girl come out and call herself... s-sexy... and... nnghghh...
...i-it's j-just not right...
HEH HEH ...
NOW!! GET THE LAST BOSS OF TRINITY SEVEN, LEVI-CHAN, NAKED, ARATA-KUN...!!
BA (BAM)
YEAH!!
I'LL DO IT!!!
AND WITH THAT—
KAN (DANG)
KOOON
KOOON (DOOONG)
KIIIN (DIIING)
BEGIN!!

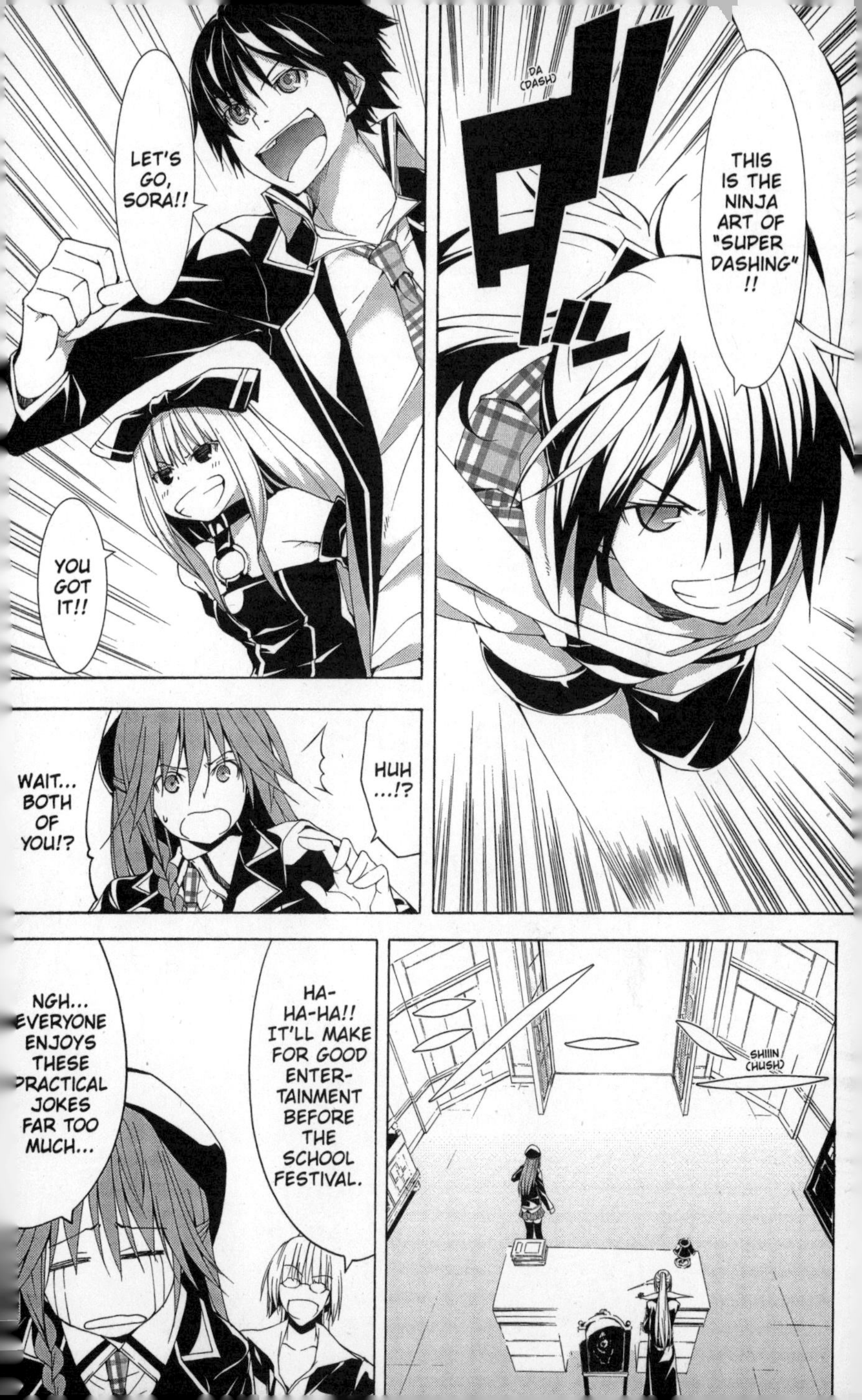
DA (DASH)
THIS IS THE NINJA ART OF "SUPER DASHING"!!
LET'S GO, SORA!!
YOU GOT IT!!
HUH ...!?
WAIT... BOTH OF YOU!?
SHIIIN (HUSH)
HA-HA-HA!! IT'LL MAKE FOR GOOD ENTERTAINMENT BEFORE THE SCHOOL FESTIVAL.
NGH... EVERYONE ENJOYS THESE PRACTICAL JOKES FAR TOO MUCH...

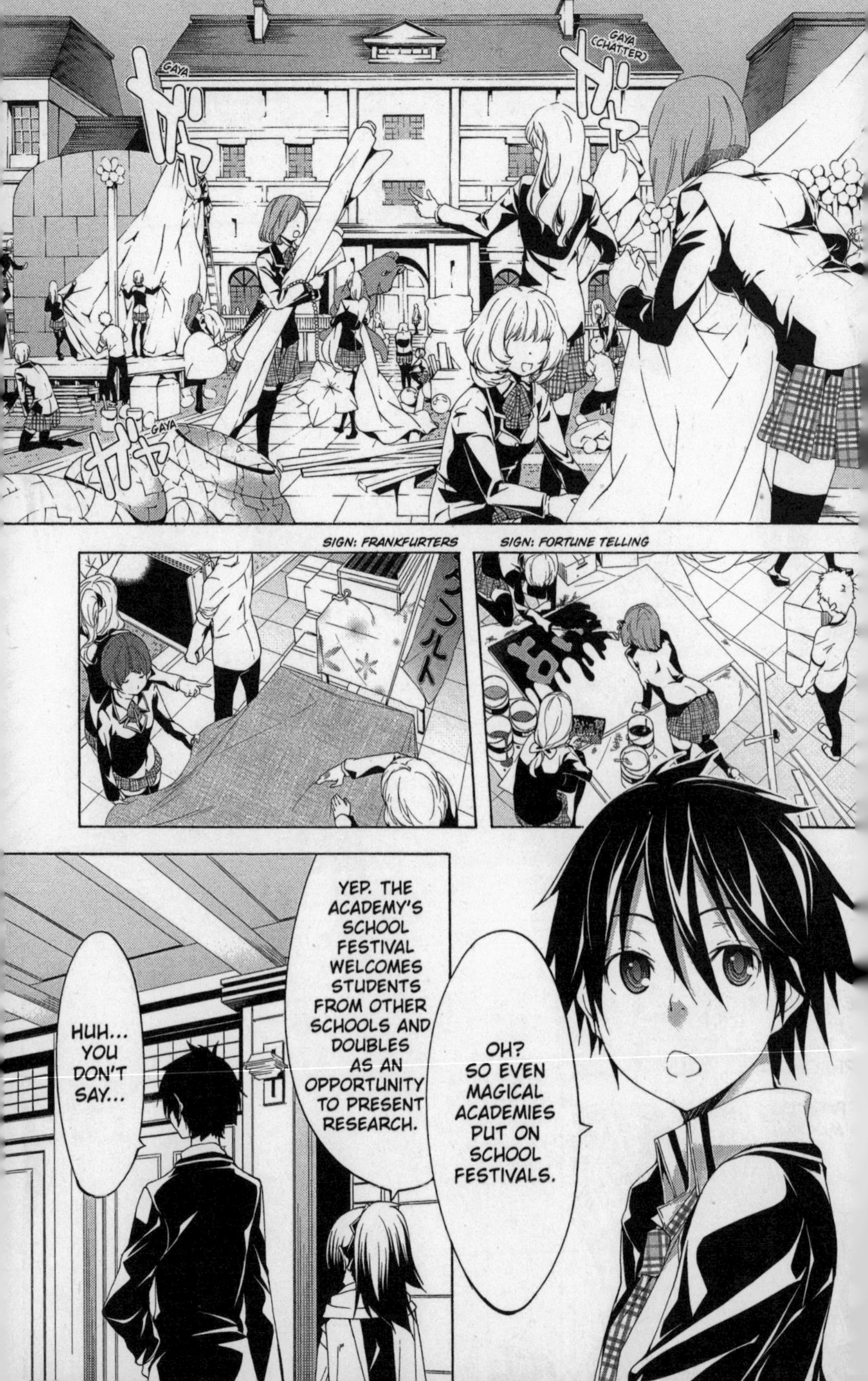
GAYA (CHATTER)
GAYA
GAYA
SIGN: FORTUNE TELLING
SIGN: FRANKFURTERS
OH? SO EVEN MAGICAL ACADEMIES PUT ON SCHOOL FESTIVALS.
YEP. THE ACADEMY'S SCHOOL FESTIVAL WELCOMES STUDENTS FROM OTHER SCHOOLS AND DOUBLES AS AN OPPORTUNITY TO PRESENT RESEARCH.
HUH... YOU DON'T SAY...

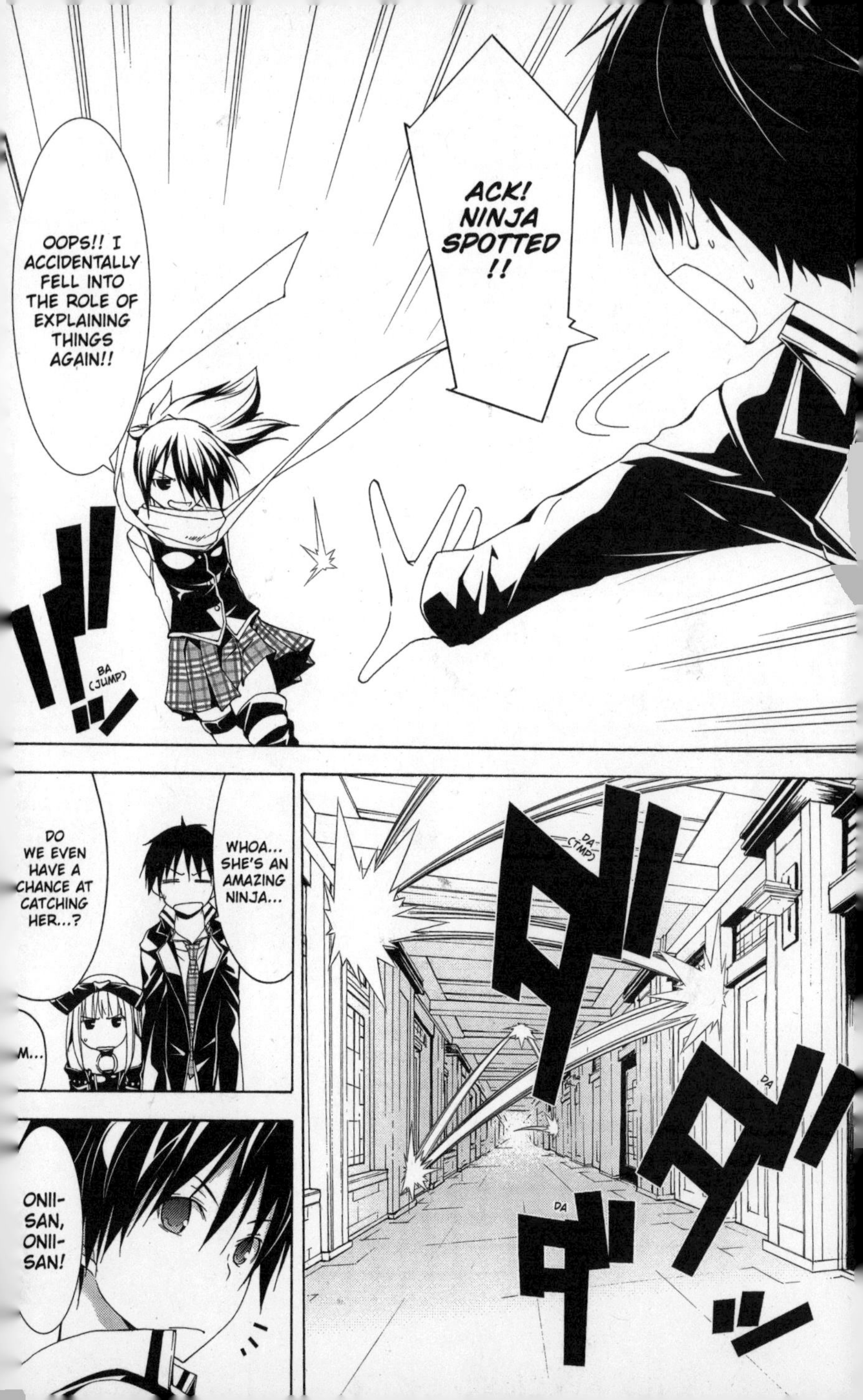
ACK! NINJA SPOTTED!!
OOPS!! I ACCIDENTALLY FELL INTO THE ROLE OF EXPLAINING THINGS AGAIN!!
BA (JUMP)
DA (TMP)
DA
DA
WHOA... SHE'S AN AMAZING NINJA...
DO WE EVEN HAVE A CHANCE AT CATCHING HER...?
M...
ONII-SAN, ONII-SAN!

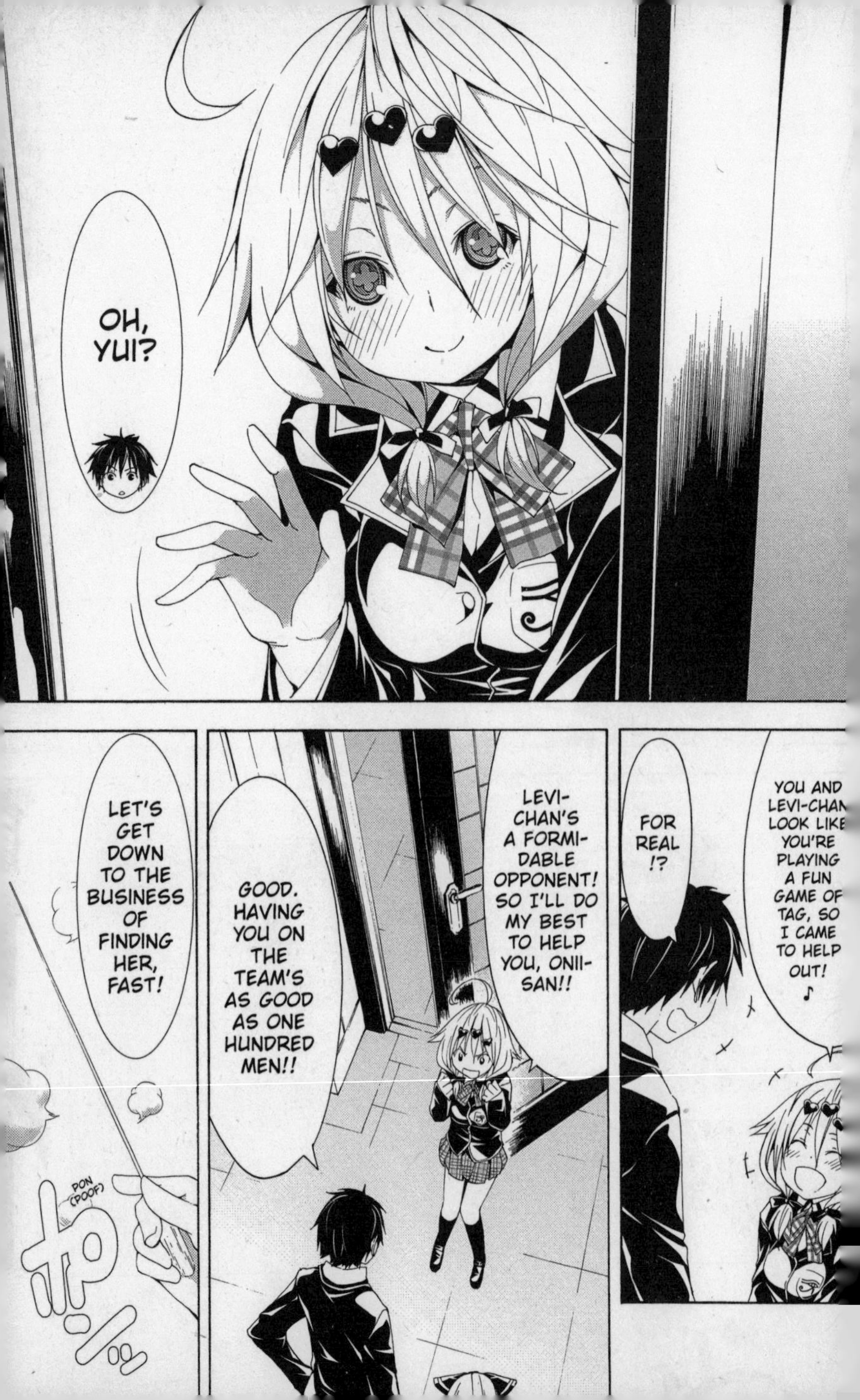
OH, YUI?
YOU AND LEVI-CHAN LOOK LIKE YOU'RE PLAYING A FUN GAME OF TAG, SO I CAME TO HELP OUT! ♪
FOR REAL!?
LEVI-CHAN'S A FORMIDABLE OPPONENT! SO I'LL DO MY BEST TO HELP YOU, ONII-SAN!!
GOOD. HAVING YOU ON THE TEAM'S AS GOOD AS ONE HUNDRED MEN!!
LET'S GET DOWN TO THE BUSINESS OF FINDING HER, FAST!
PON (POOF)

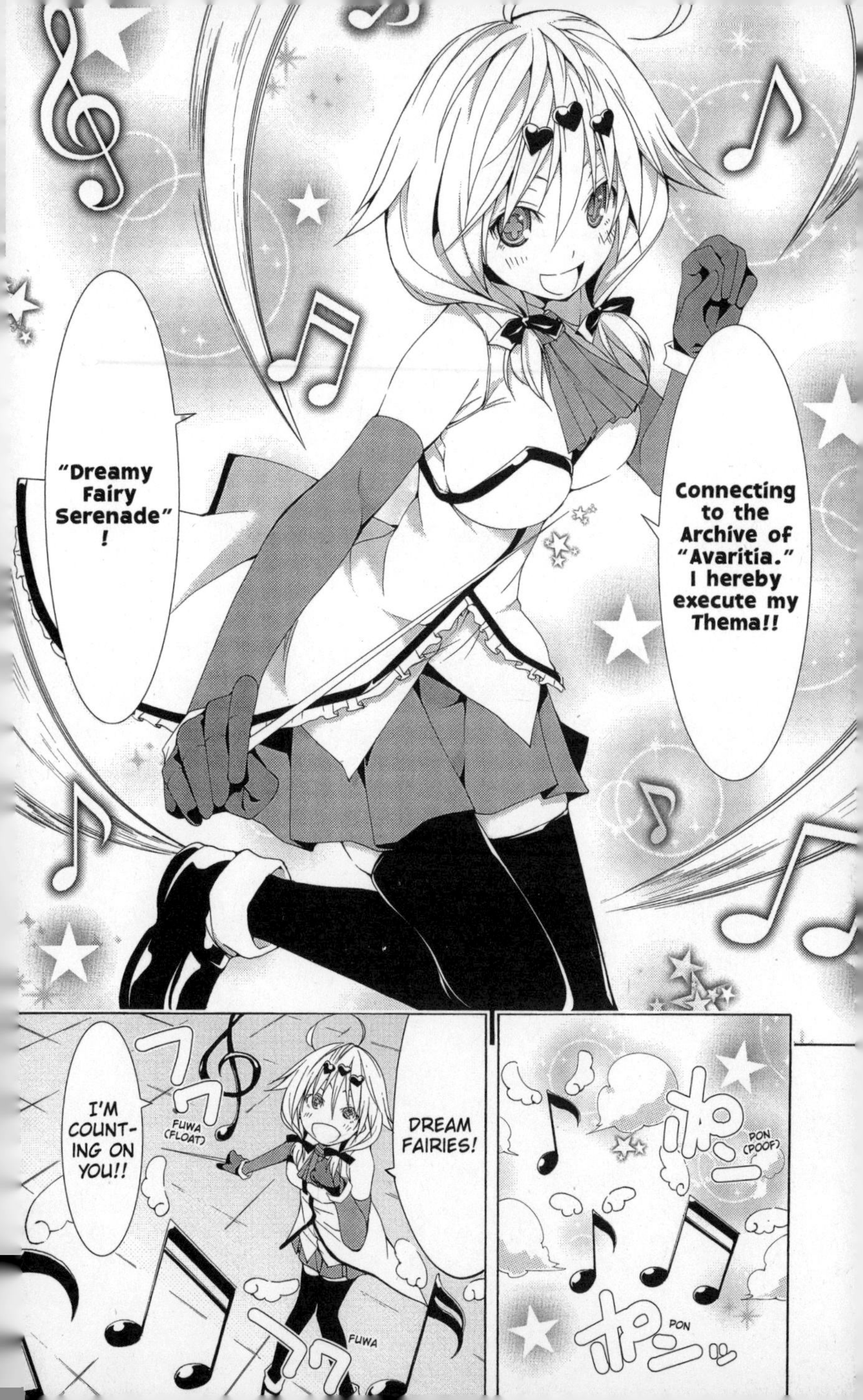
Connecting to the Archive of "Avaritia." I hereby execute my Thema!!
"Dreamy Fairy Serenade" !
PON (POOF)
PON
DREAM FAIRIES!
FUWA (FLOAT)
I'M COUNTING ON YOU!!
FUWA

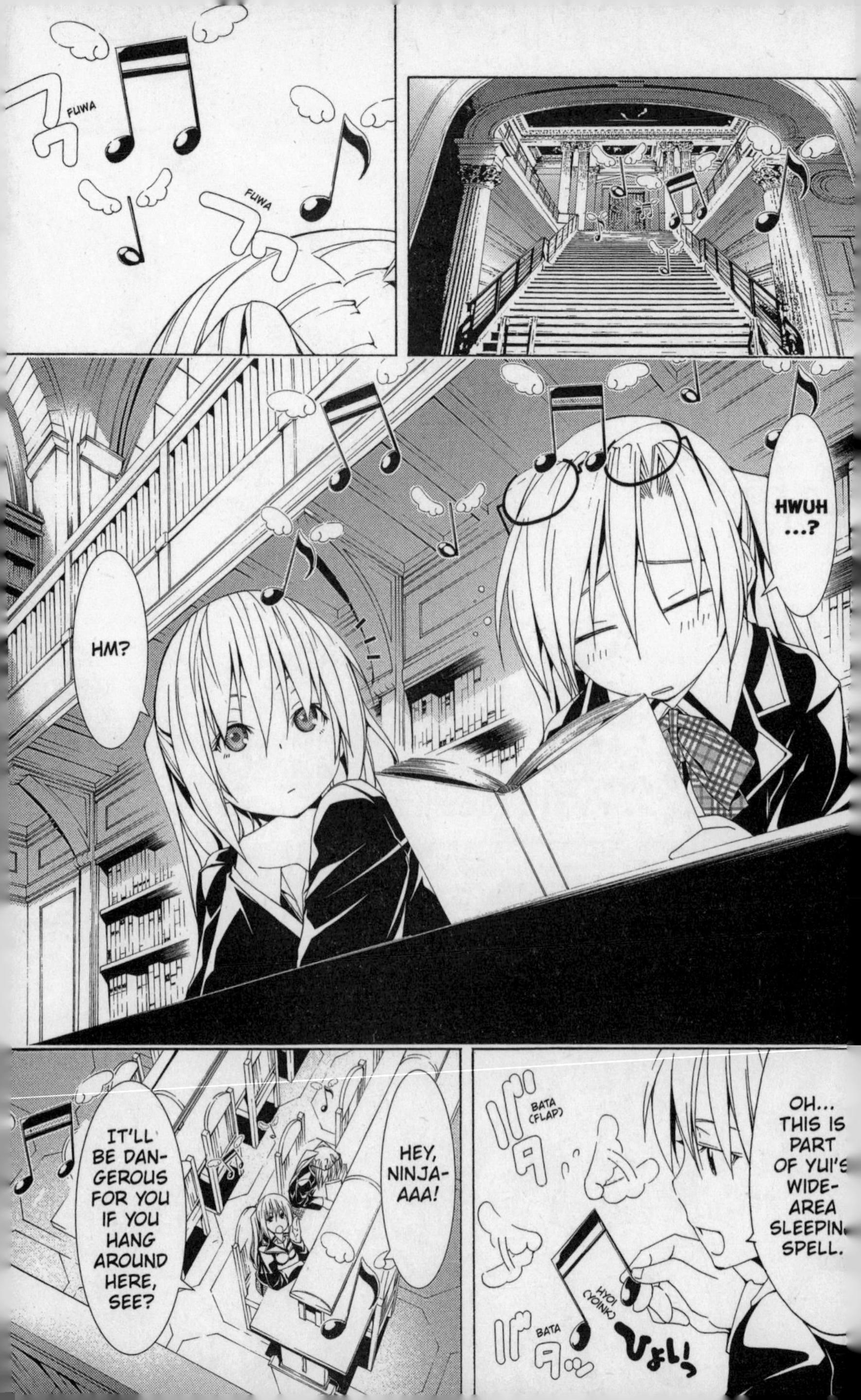
FUWA
FUWA
HWUH ...?
HM?
OH... THIS IS PART OF YUI'
WIDE-AREA SLEEPIN
SPELL.
BATA (FLAP)
HYOI (YOINK)
BATA
HEY, NINJA-AAA!
IT'LL BE DAN-GEROUS FOR YOU IF YOU HANG AROUND HERE, SEE?

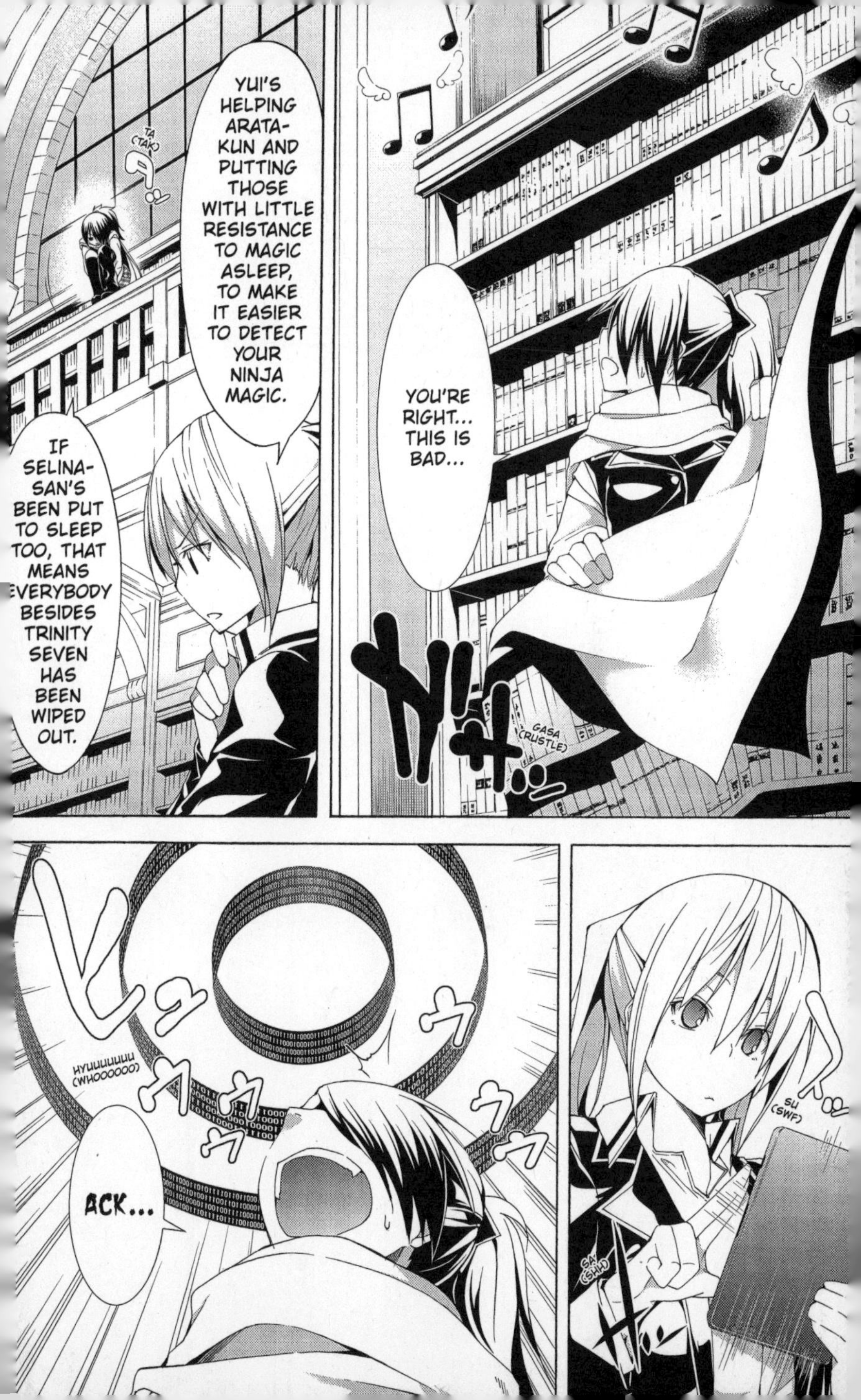
YOU'RE RIGHT... THIS IS BAD...
GASA (RUSTLE)
YUI'S HELPING ARATA-KUN AND PUTTING THOSE WITH LITTLE RESISTANCE TO MAGIC ASLEEP, TO MAKE IT EASIER TO DETECT YOUR NINJA MAGIC.
TA (TAK)
IF SELINA-SAN'S BEEN PUT TO SLEEP TOO, THAT MEANS EVERYBODY BESIDES TRINITY SEVEN HAS BEEN WIPED OUT.
SU (SWF)
SA (SHH)
HYUUUUUUU (WHOOOOOO)
ACK...

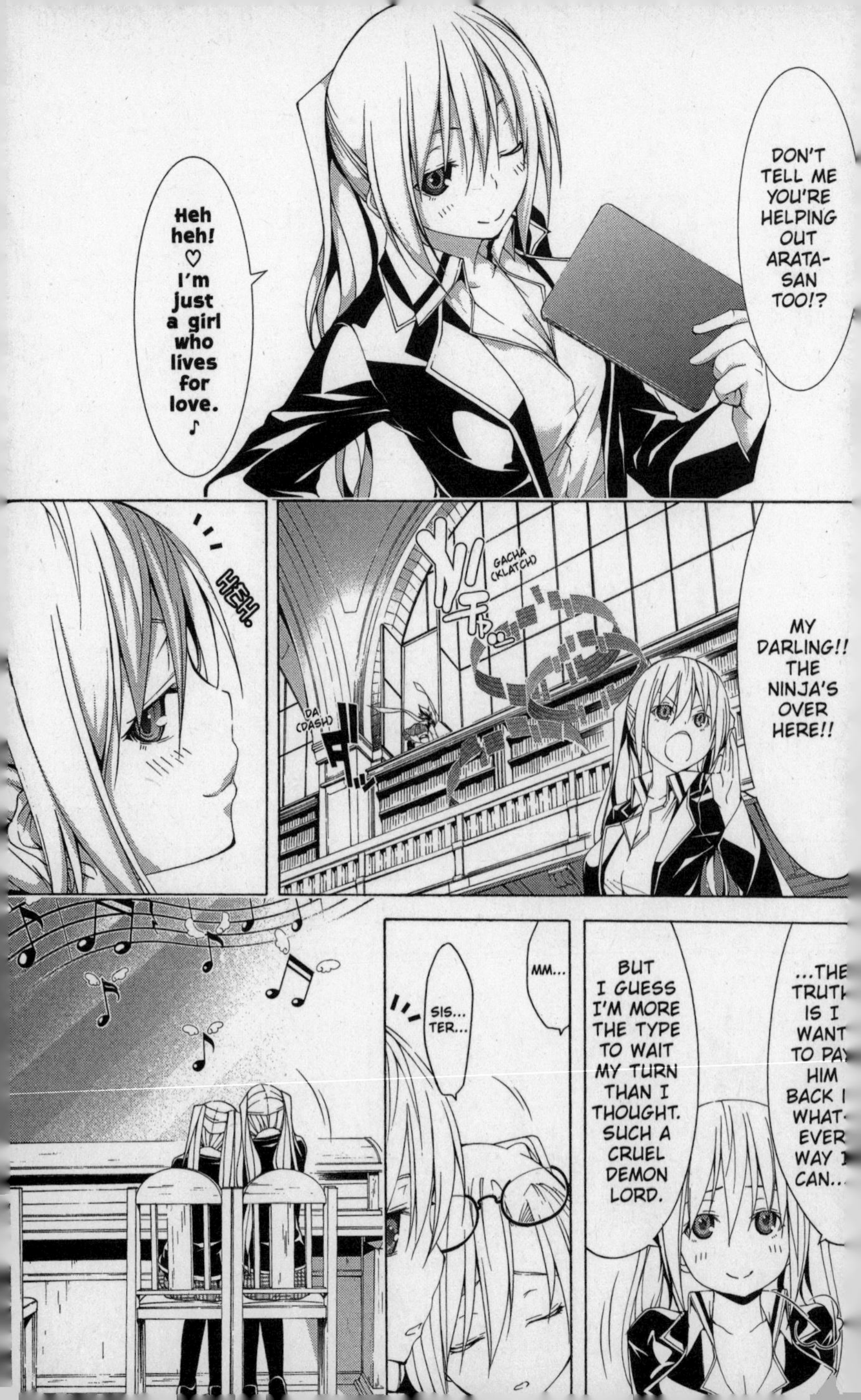
DON'T TELL ME YOU'RE HELPING OUT ARATA-SAN TOO!?
Heh heh! ♡ I'm just a girl who lives for love. ♪
MY DARLING!! THE NINJA'S OVER HERE!!
GACHA (KLATCH)
DA (DASH)
HEH.
...THE TRUTH IS I WANT TO PAY HIM BACK IN WHATEVER WAY I CAN...
BUT I GUESS I'M MORE THE TYPE TO WAIT MY TURN THAN I THOUGHT. SUCH A CRUEL DEMON LORD.
MM...
SIS... TER...

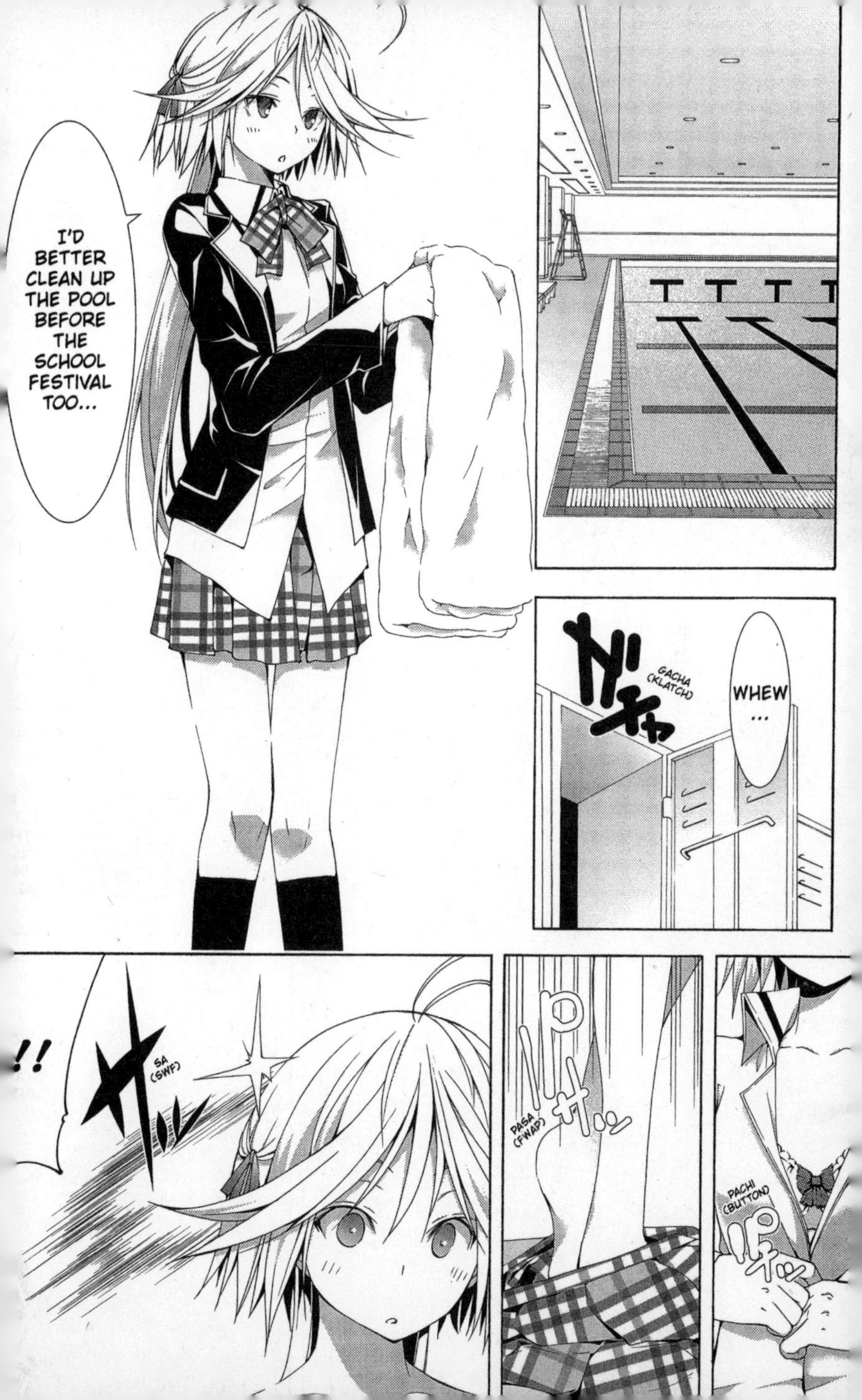
WHEW ...
GACHA (KLATCH)
I'D BETTER CLEAN UP THE POOL BEFORE THE SCHOOL FESTIVAL TOO...
PACHI (BUTTON)
PASA (FWAP)
!!
SA (SWF)

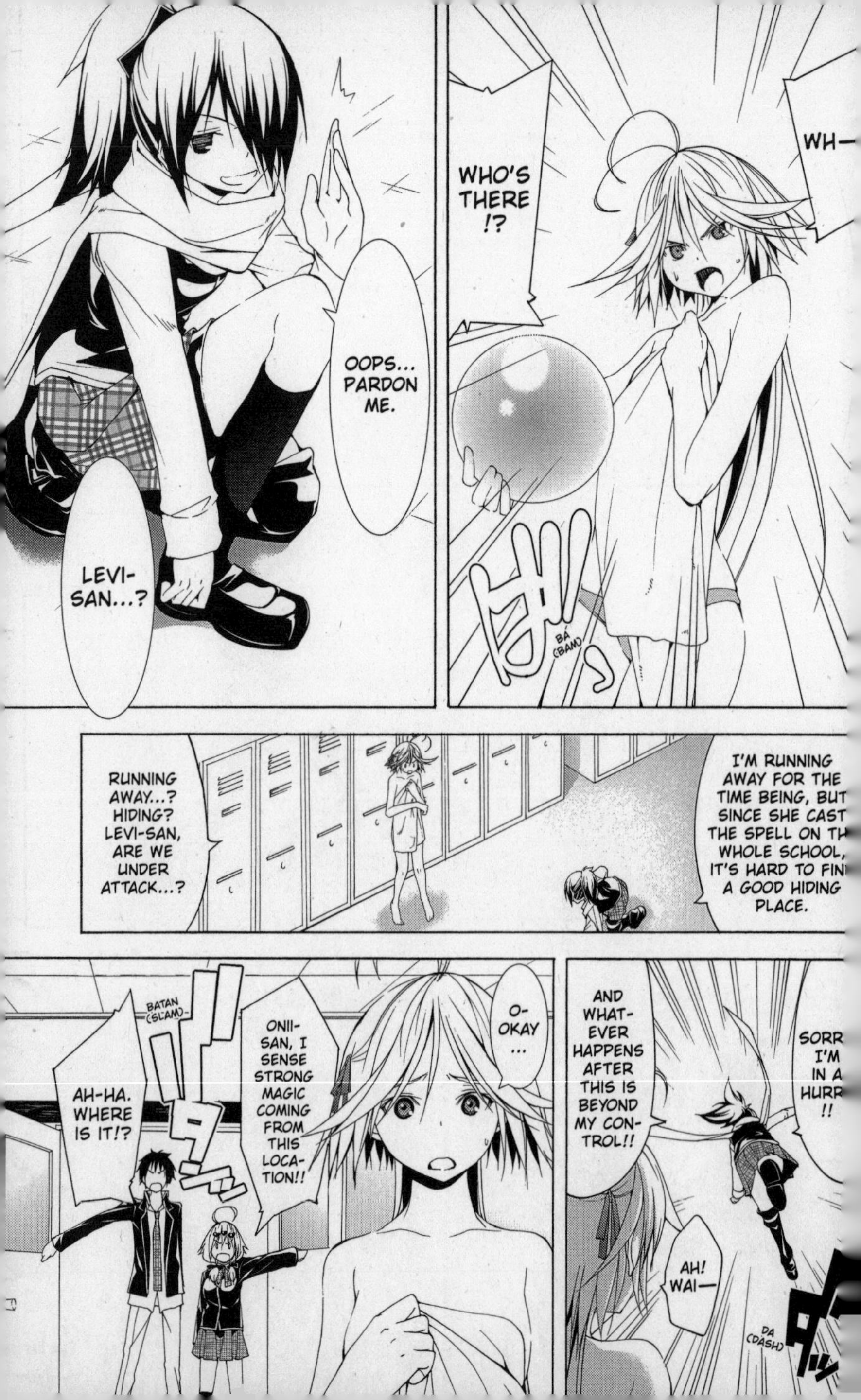
WH—
WHO'S THERE !?
BA (BAM)
OOPS... PARDON ME.
LEVI-SAN...?
I'M RUNNING AWAY FOR THE TIME BEING, BUT SINCE SHE CAST THE SPELL ON TH WHOLE SCHOOL, IT'S HARD TO FIN A GOOD HIDING PLACE.
RUNNING AWAY...? HIDING? LEVI-SAN, ARE WE UNDER ATTACK...?
SORR I'M IN A HURR !!
AND WHAT-EVER HAPPENS AFTER THIS IS BEYOND MY CON-TROL!!
AH! WAI—
DA (DASH)
O-OKAY ...
ONII-SAN, I SENSE STRONG MAGIC COMING FROM THIS LOCA-TION!!
BATAN (SLAM)
AH-HA. WHERE IS IT!?

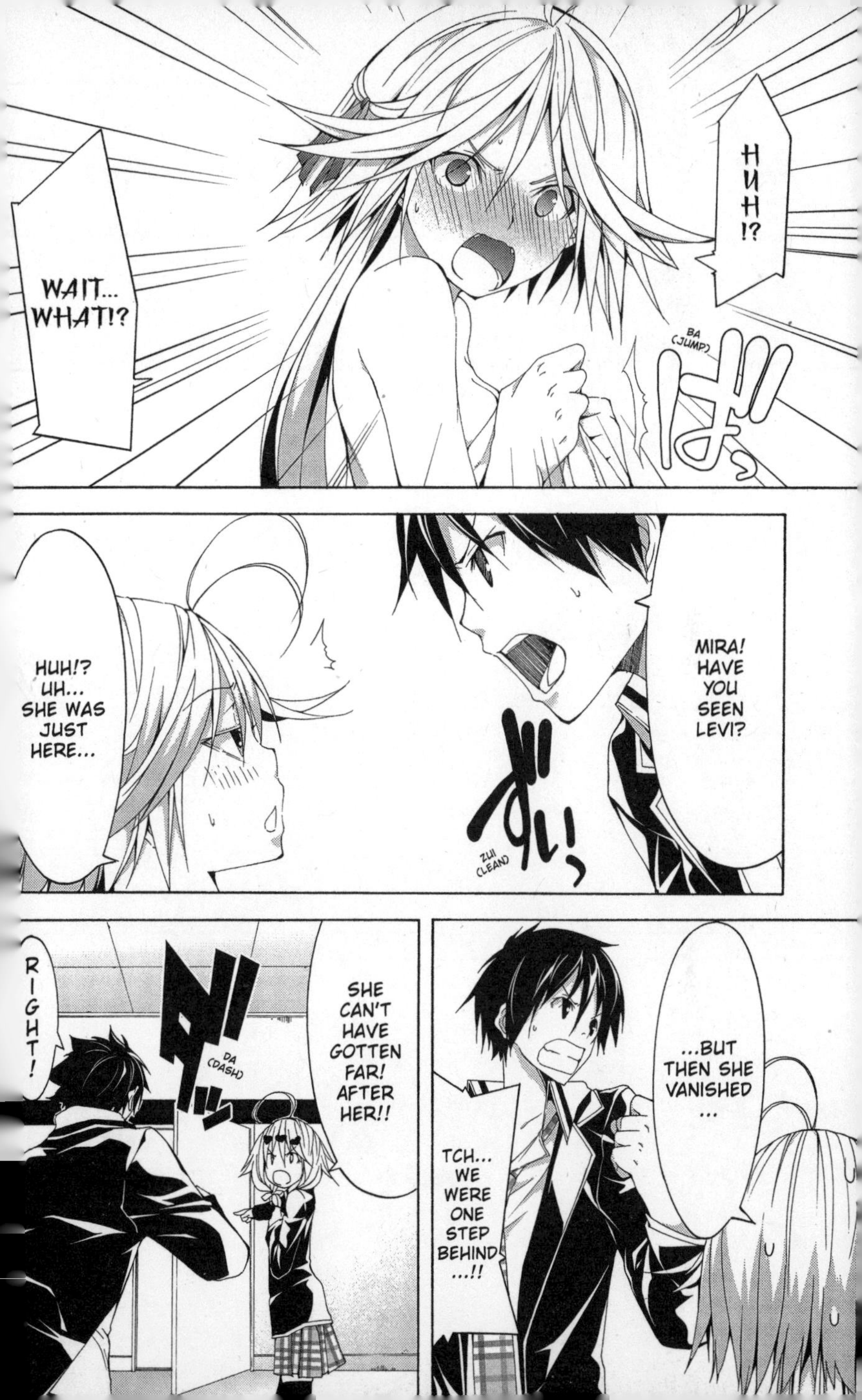
HUH!?
ばっ
BA (JUMP)
WAIT... WHAT!?
MIRA! HAVE YOU SEEN LEVI?
ずいっ
ZUI (LEAN)
HUH!? UH... SHE WAS JUST HERE...
...BUT THEN SHE VANISHED ...
TCH... WE WERE ONE STEP BEHIND ...!!
SHE CAN'T HAVE GOTTEN FAR! AFTER HER!!
ダッ
DA (DASH)
RIGHT!

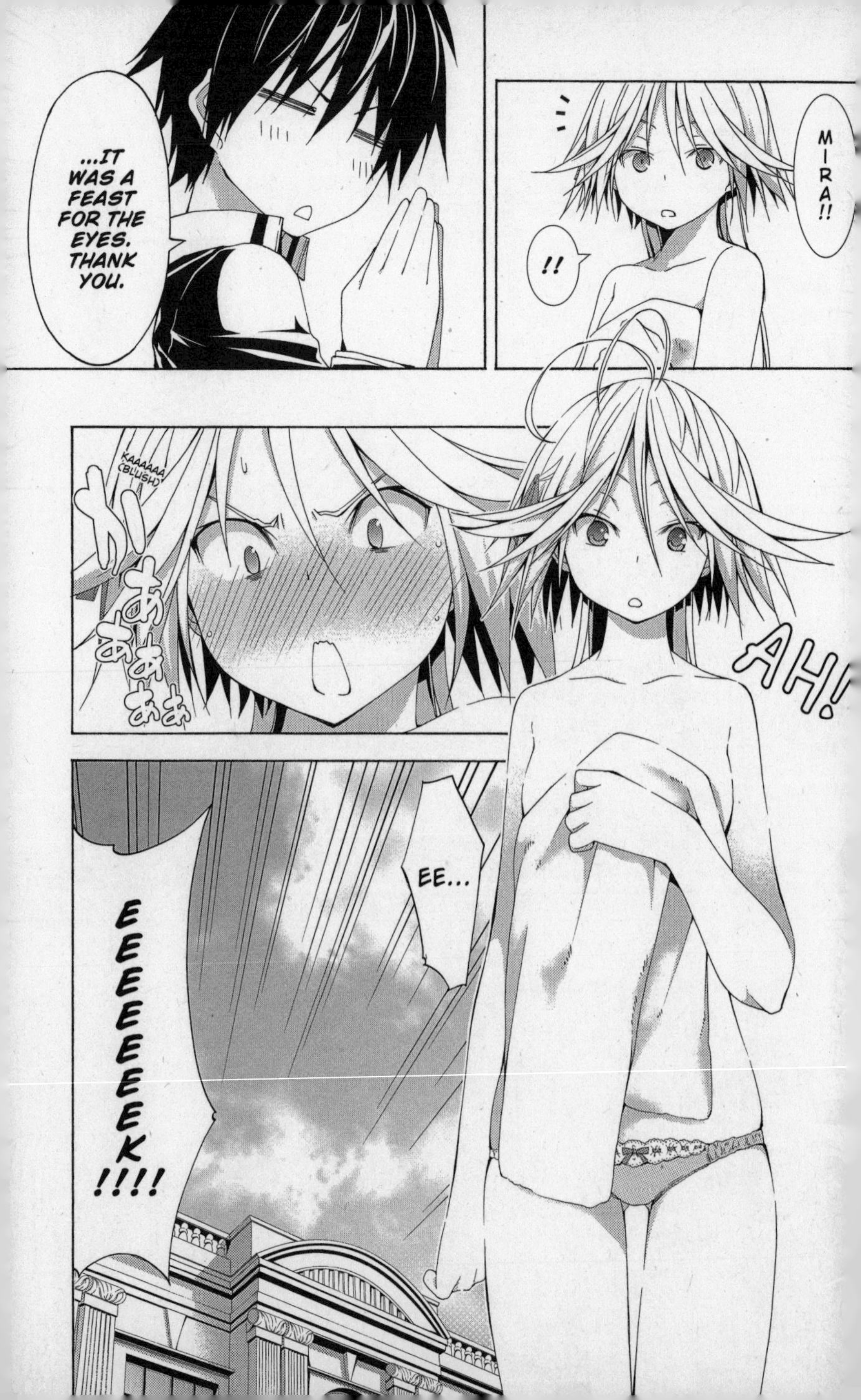
MIRA!!
!!
...IT WAS A FEAST FOR THE EYES. THANK YOU.
AH!
KAAAAAA (BLUSH)
EE...
EEEEEEEEK!!!!

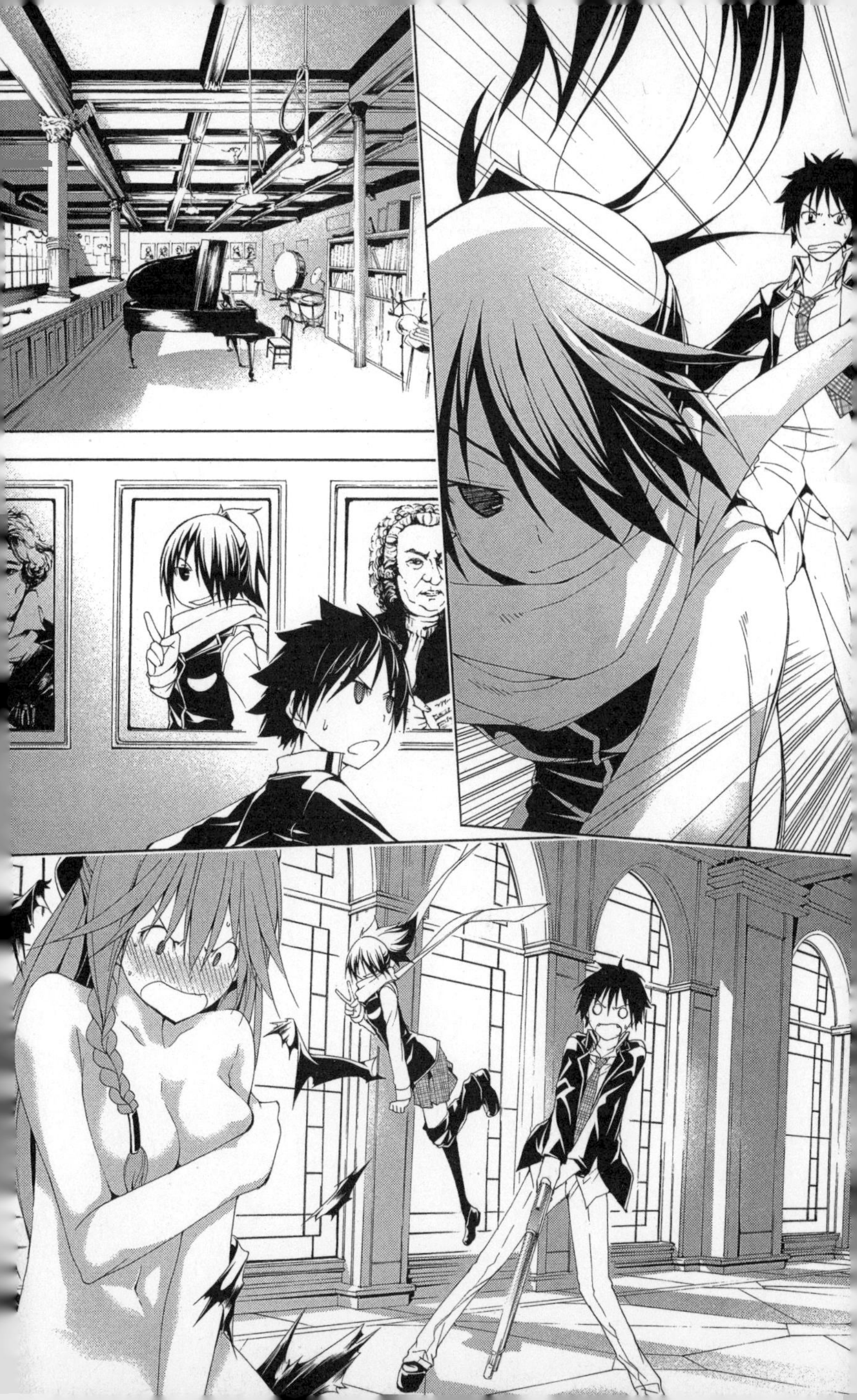

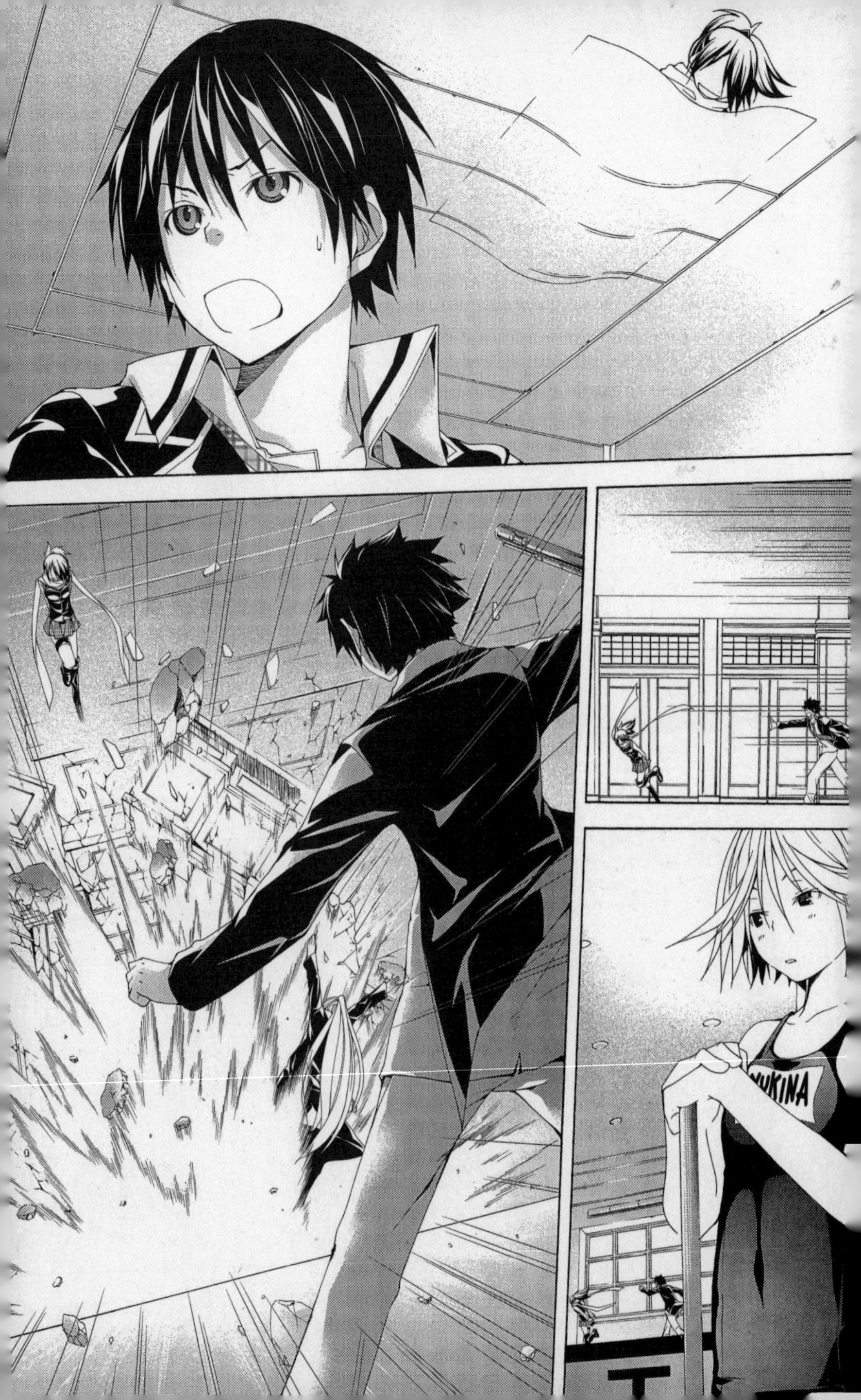

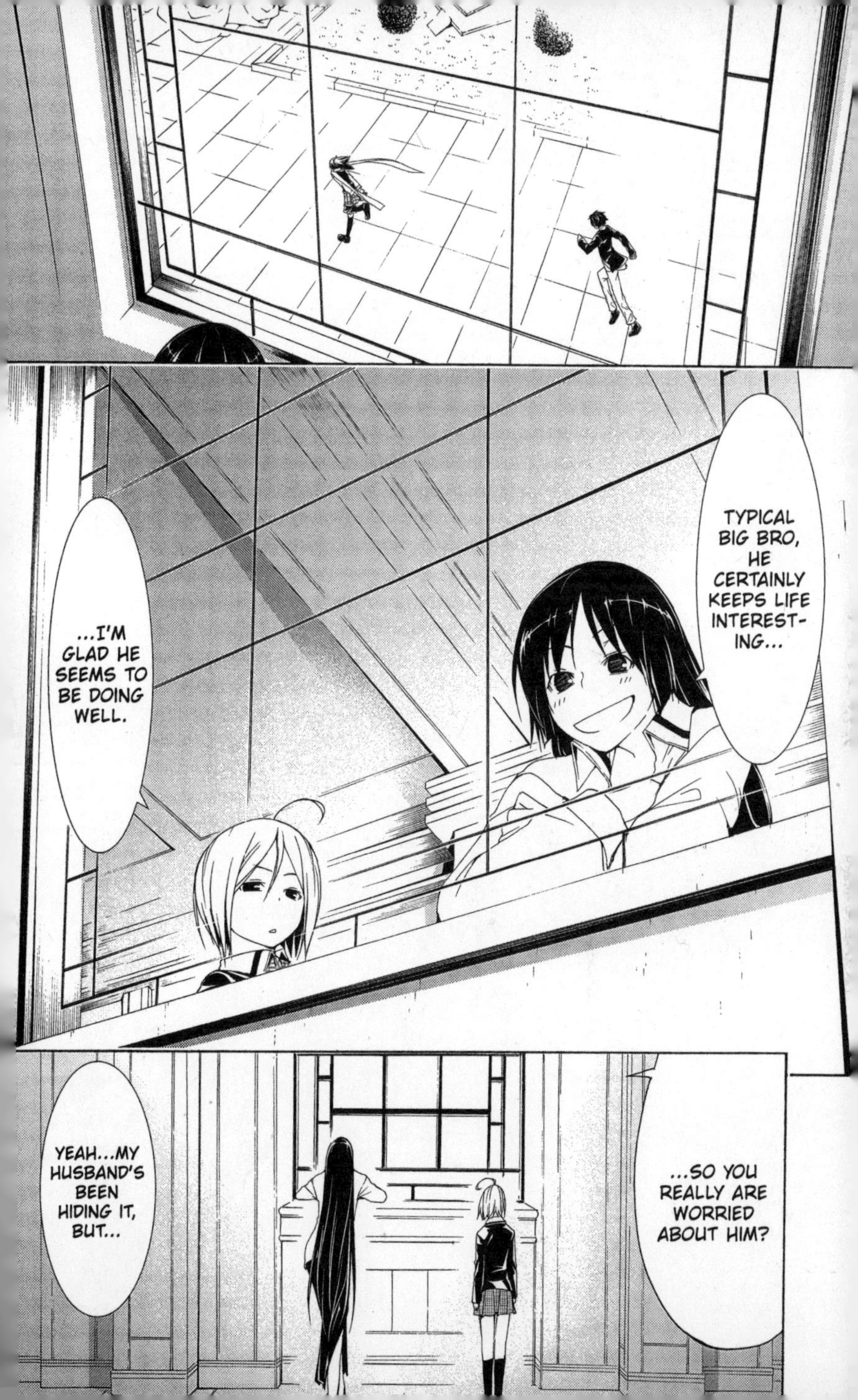
TYPICAL BIG BRO, HE CERTAINLY KEEPS LIFE INTEREST-ING...
...I'M GLAD HE SEEMS TO BE DOING WELL.
...SO YOU REALLY ARE WORRIED ABOUT HIM?
YEAH...MY HUSBAND'S BEEN HIDING IT, BUT...

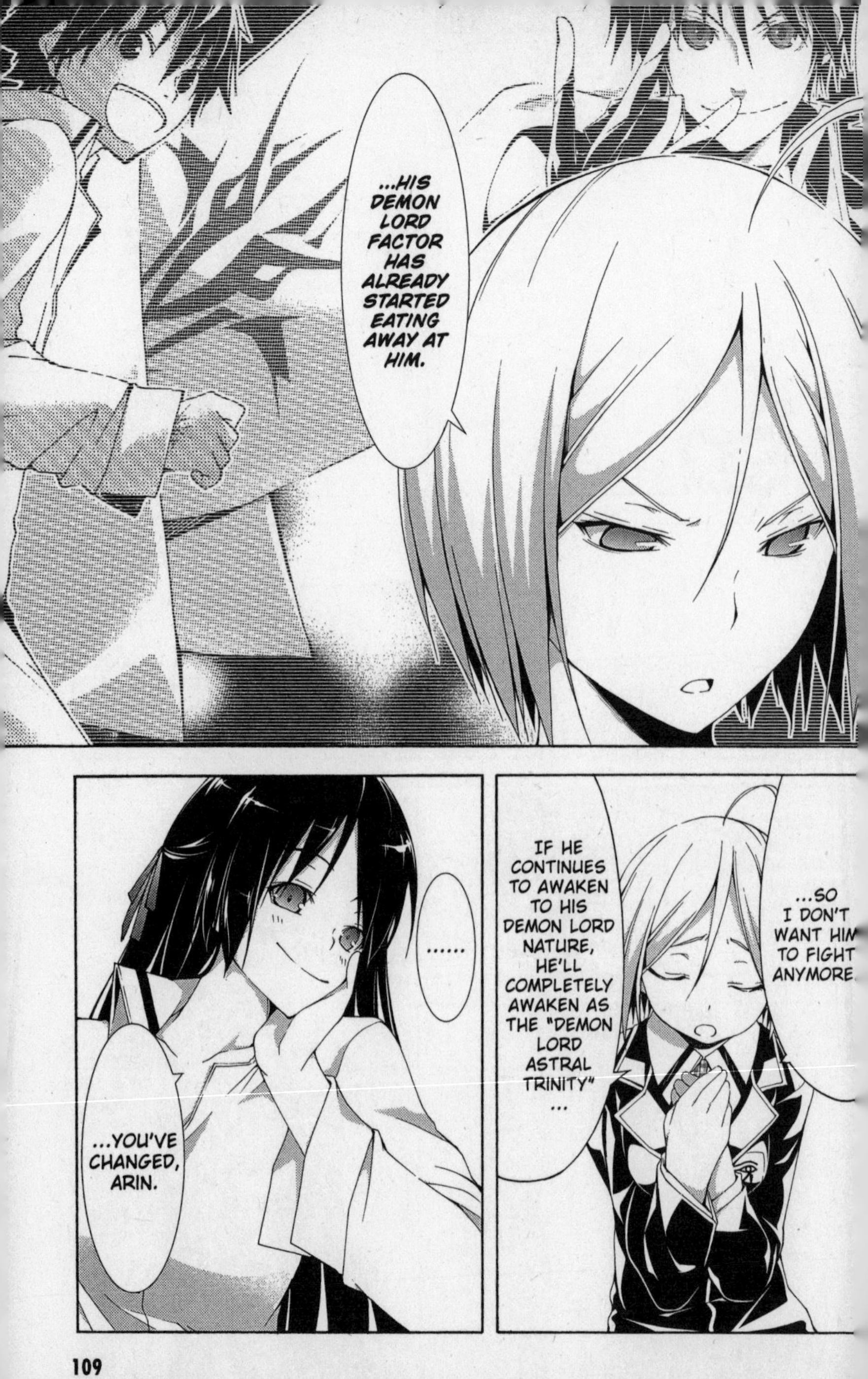
...HIS DEMON LORD FACTOR HAS ALREADY STARTED EATING AWAY AT HIM.
IF HE CONTINUES TO AWAKEN TO HIS DEMON LORD NATURE, HE'LL COMPLETELY AWAKEN AS THE "DEMON LORD ASTRAL TRINITY"...
...SO I DON'T WANT HIM TO FIGHT ANYMORE.
......
...YOU'VE CHANGED, ARIN.

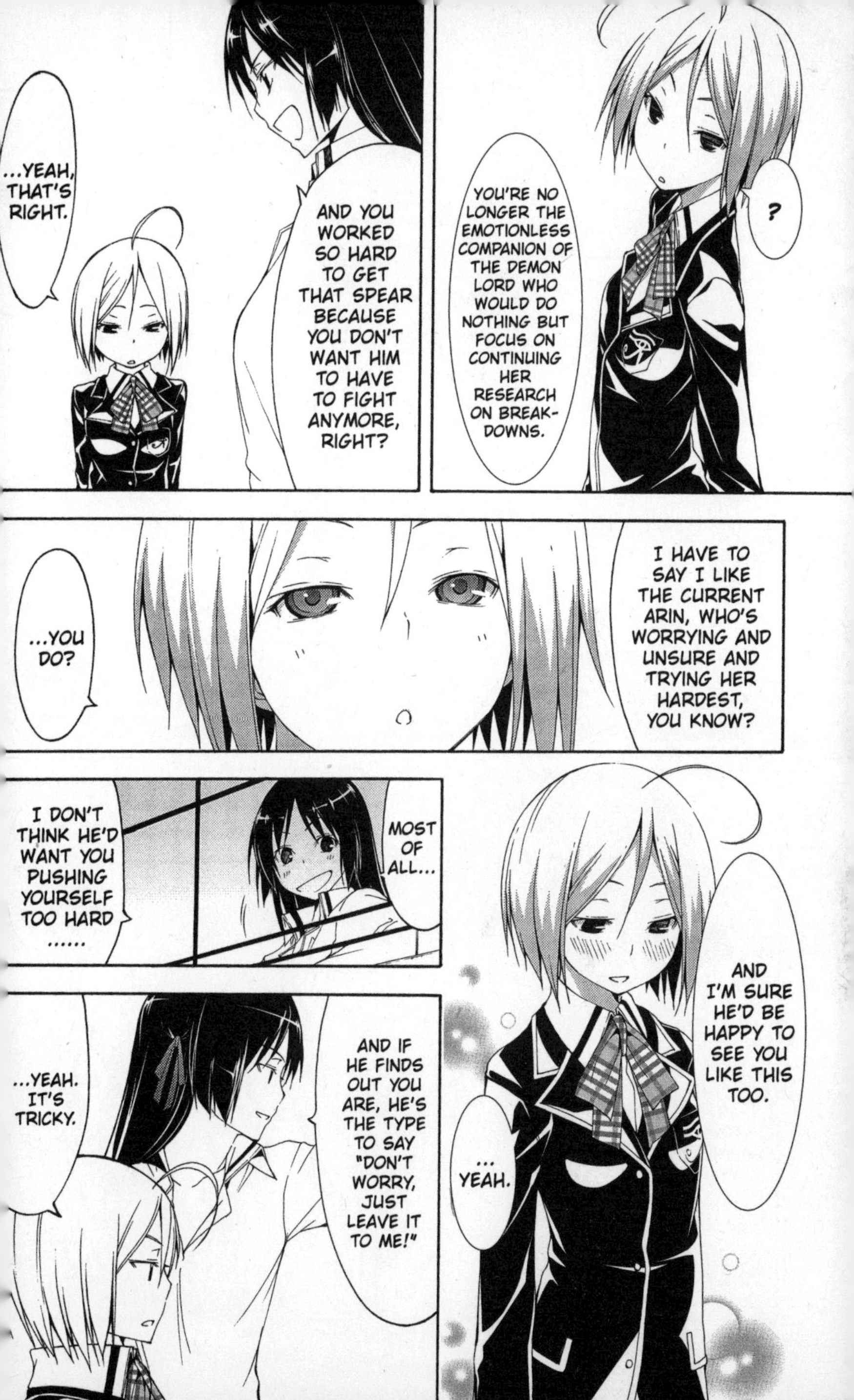
?
YOU'RE NO LONGER THE EMOTIONLESS COMPANION OF THE DEMON LORD WHO WOULD DO NOTHING BUT FOCUS ON CONTINUING HER RESEARCH ON BREAK-DOWNS.
AND YOU WORKED SO HARD TO GET THAT SPEAR BECAUSE YOU DON'T WANT HIM TO HAVE TO FIGHT ANYMORE, RIGHT?
...YEAH, THAT'S RIGHT.
I HAVE TO SAY I LIKE THE CURRENT ARIN, WHO'S WORRYING AND UNSURE AND TRYING HER HARDEST, YOU KNOW?
...YOU DO?
AND I'M SURE HE'D BE HAPPY TO SEE YOU LIKE THIS TOO.
...YEAH.
MOST OF ALL...
I DON'T THINK HE'D WANT YOU PUSHING YOURSELF TOO HARD ......
AND IF HE FINDS OUT YOU ARE, HE'S THE TYPE TO SAY "DON'T WORRY, JUST LEAVE IT TO ME!"
...YEAH. IT'S TRICKY.

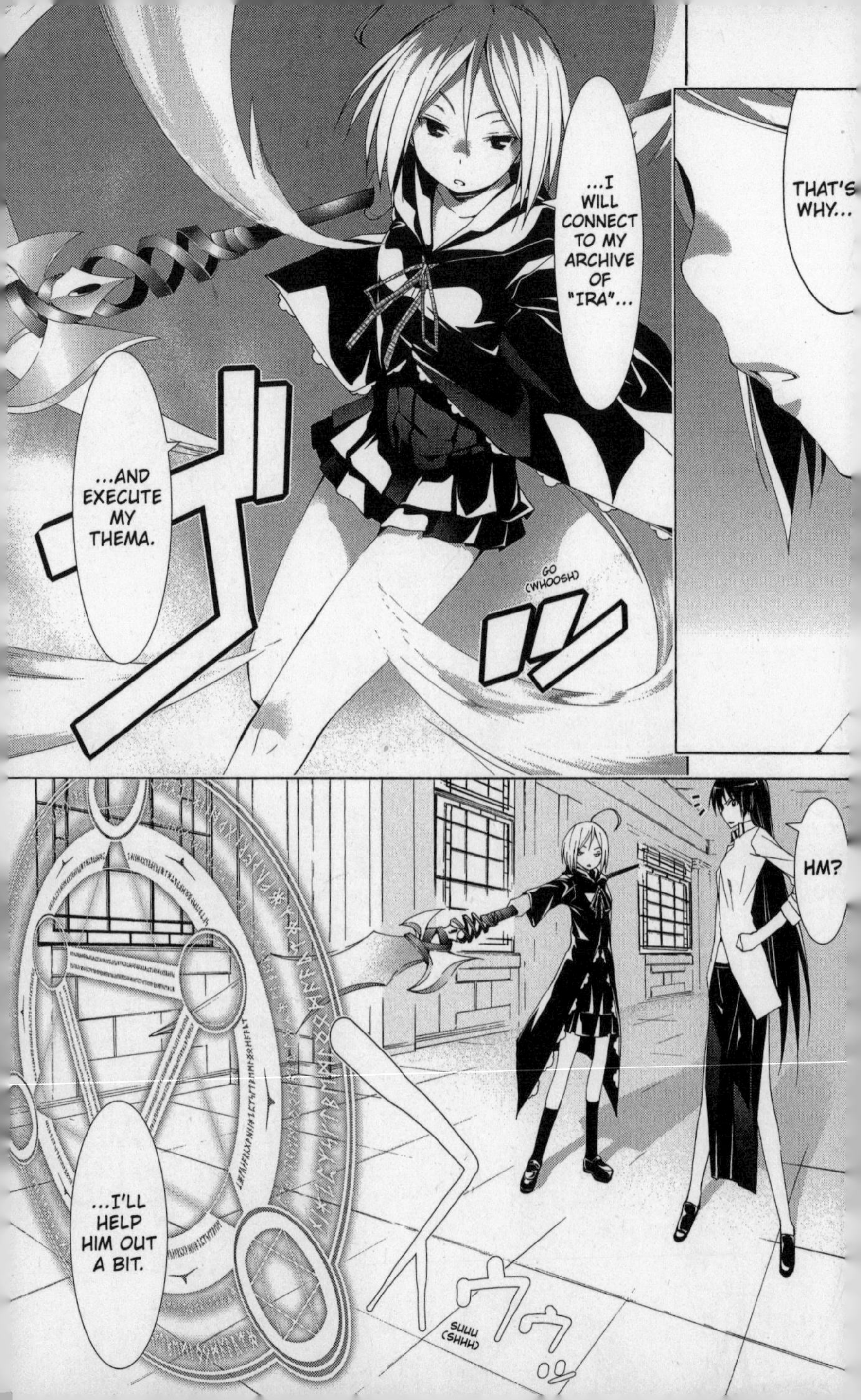
THAT'S WHY...
...I WILL CONNECT TO MY ARCHIVE OF "IRA"...
...AND EXECUTE MY THEMA.
GO (WHOOSH)
HM?
...I'LL HELP HIM OUT A BIT.
SUUU (SHHH)

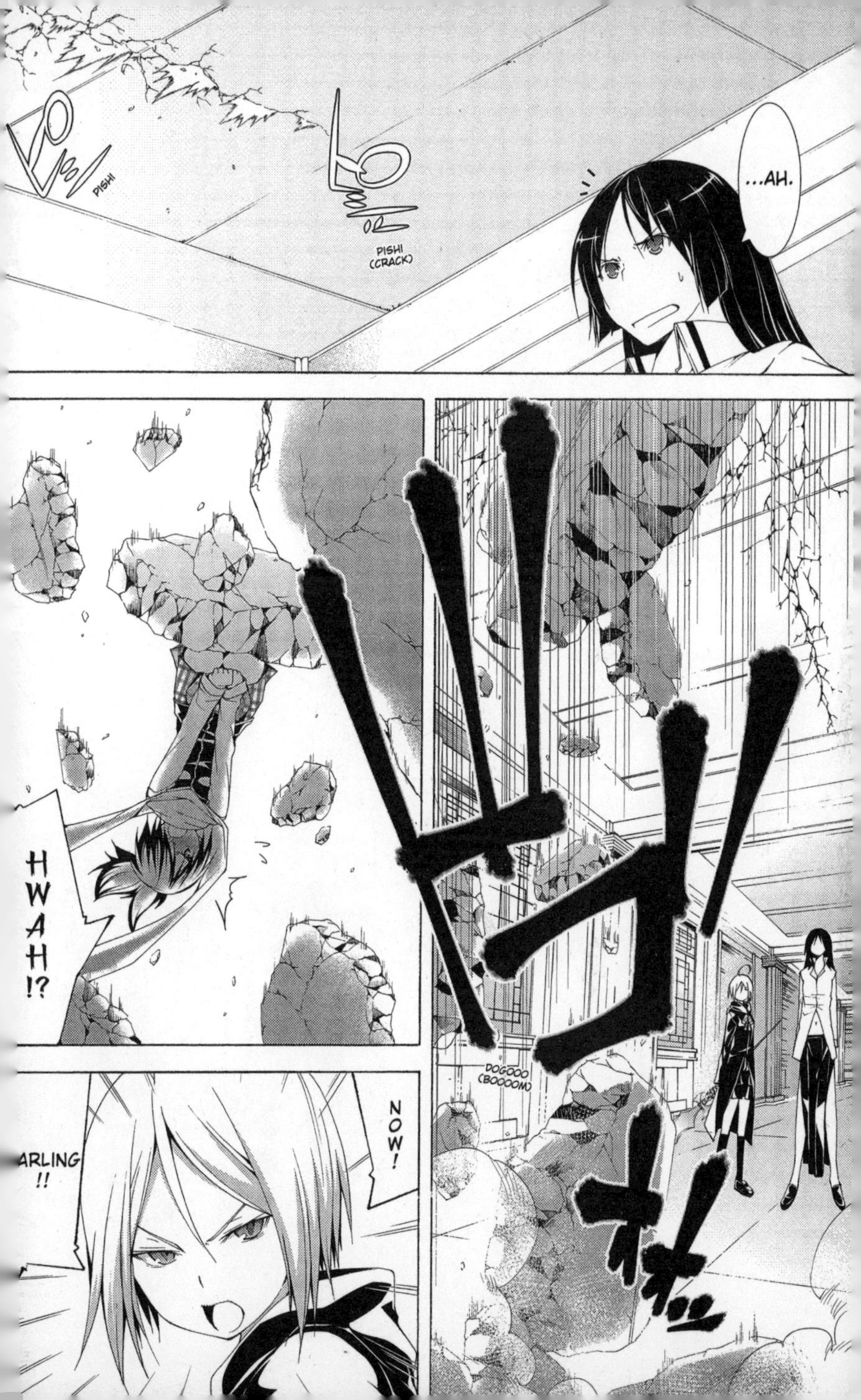
...AH.
PISHI (CRACK)
PISHI
DOGOOO (BOOOOM)
HWAH!?
NOW!
ARLING !!

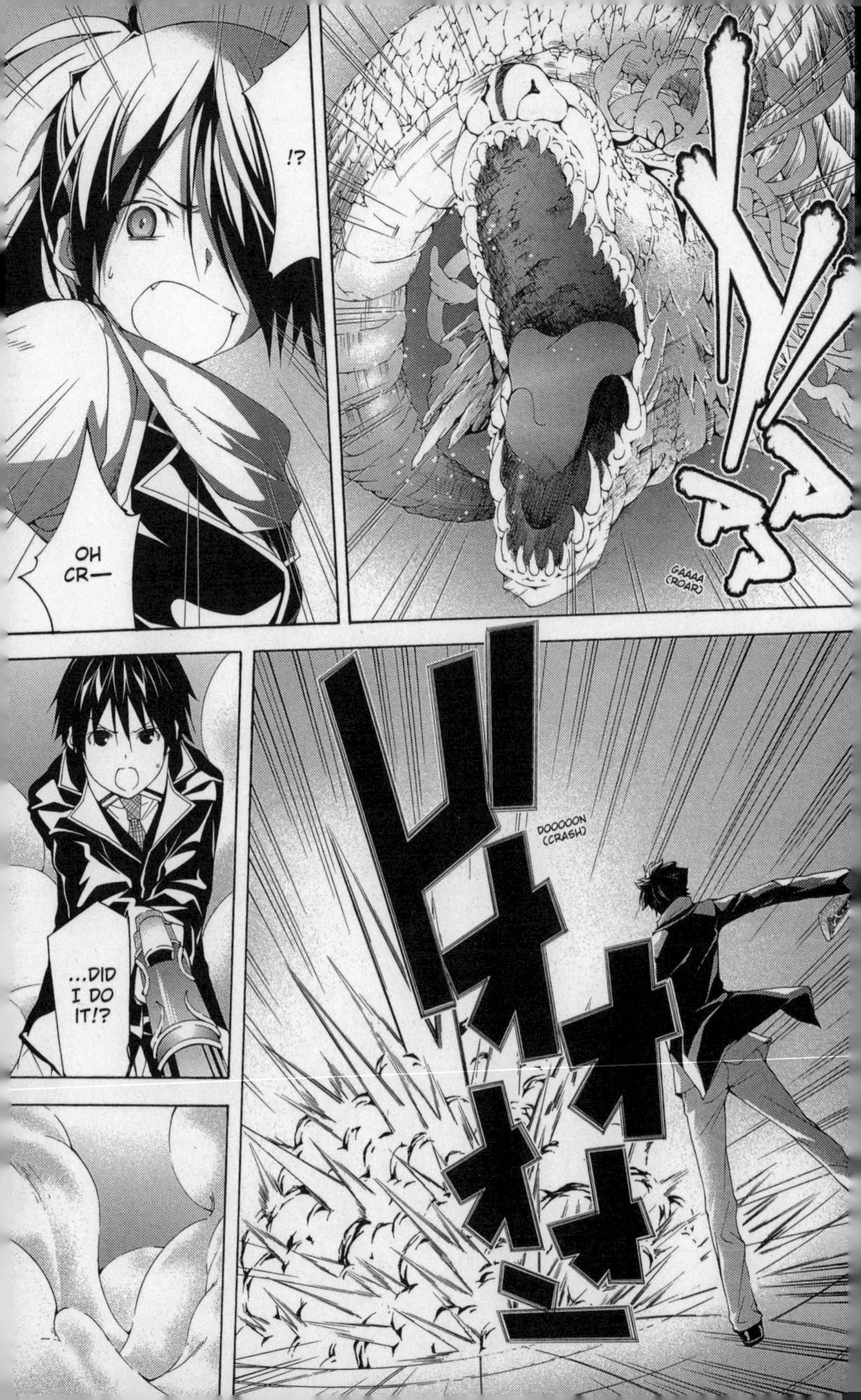
GAAAA (ROAR)
!?
OH CR—
DOOOOON (CRASH)
...DID I DO IT!?

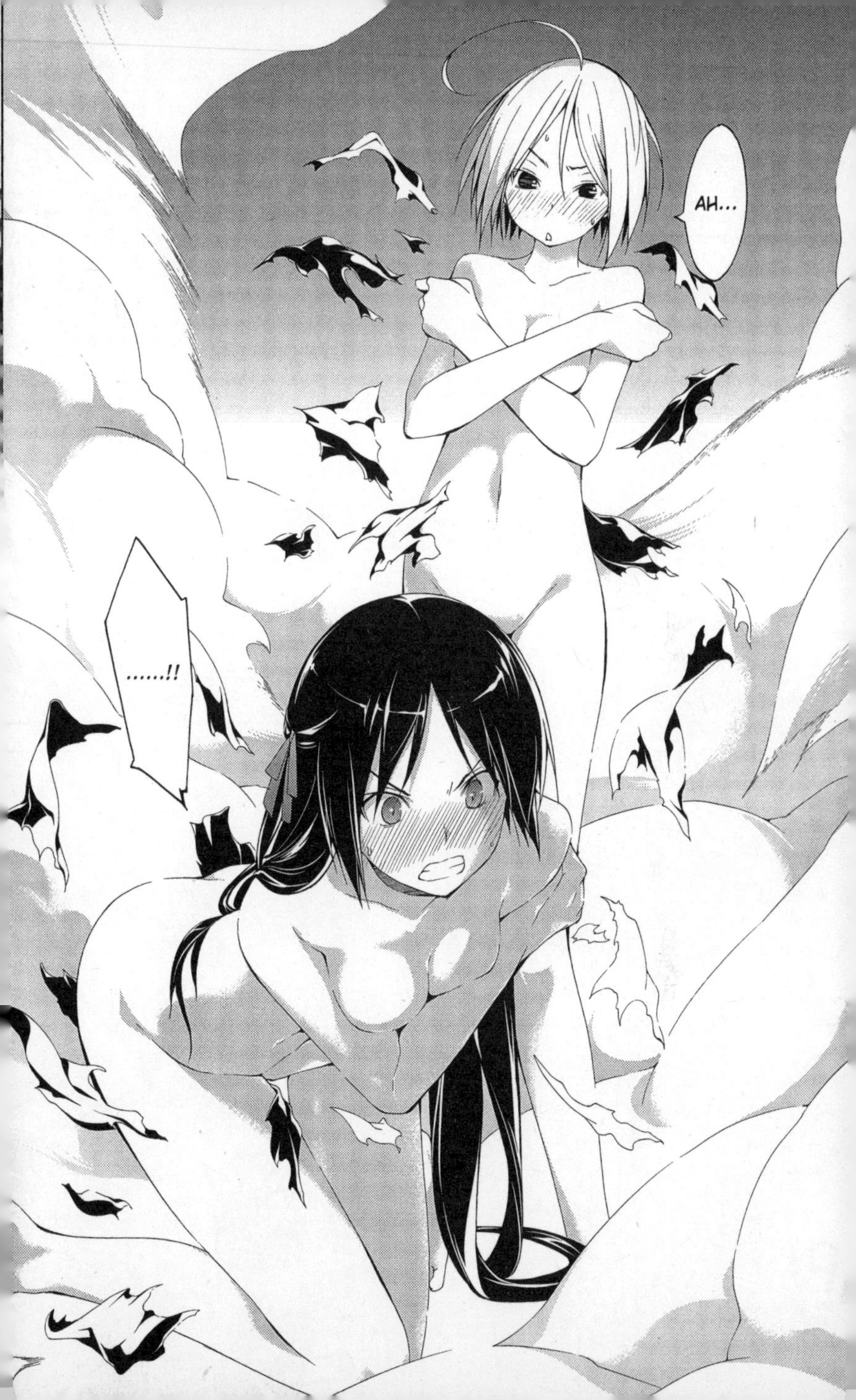
AH...
......!!

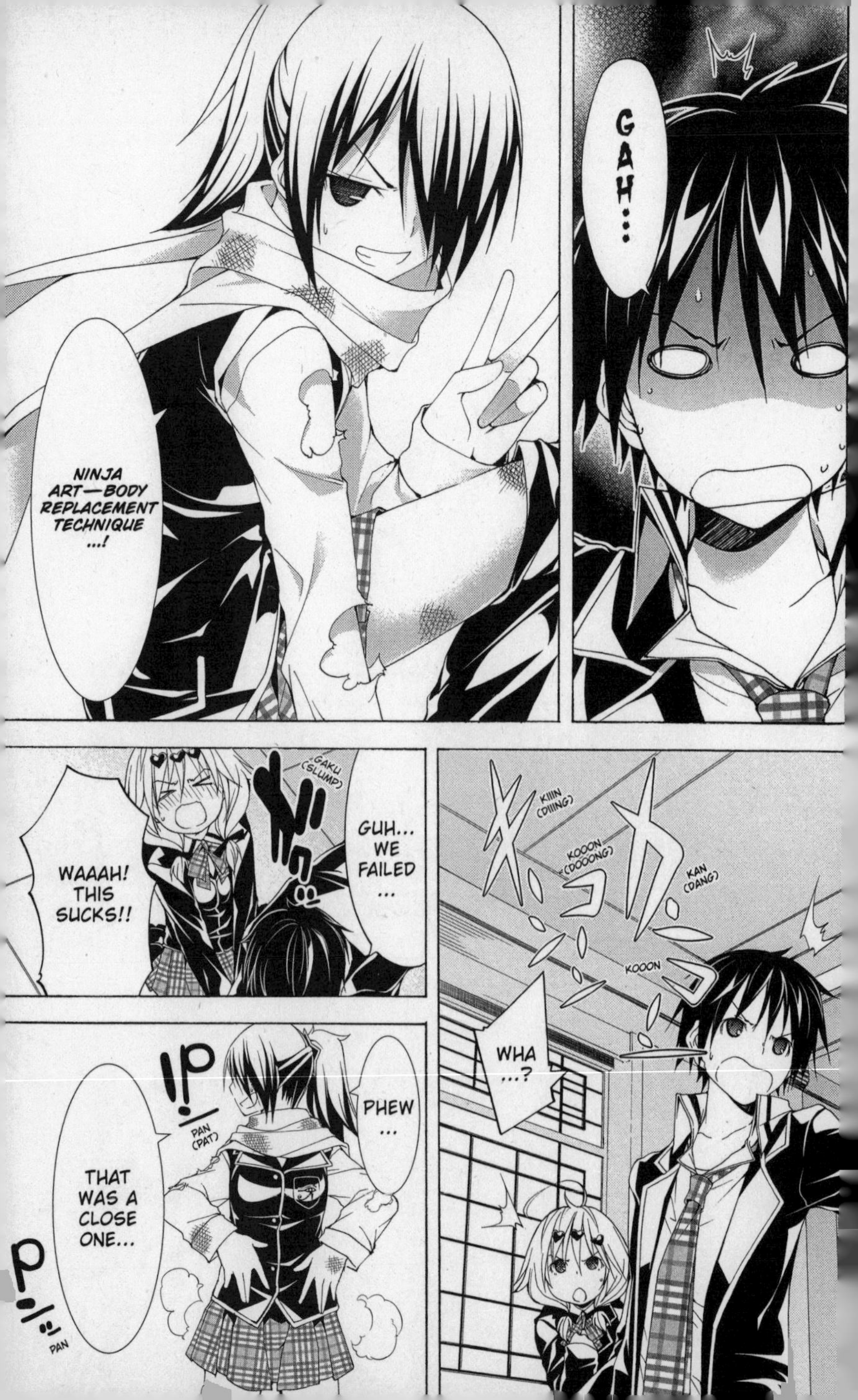
GAH...
NINJA ART—BODY REPLACEMENT TECHNIQUE ...!
KIIIN (DIIING)
KOOON (DOOONG)
KAN (DANG)
KOOON
WHA ...?
GAKU (SLUMP)
GUH... WE FAILED ...
WAAAH! THIS SUCKS!!
PHEW ...
PAN (PAT)
THAT WAS A CLOSE ONE...
PAN

NO USING YOUR DEMON LORD POWERS UNTIL YOU'VE REALLY CAPTURED ME, ARATA-SAN.

AND WITH THAT —

...SO YOU'RE BASICALLY TELLING ME TO BECOME A GOOD ENOUGH MAGUS...

...THAT I COULD CAPTURE YOU JUST THE WAY I AM, RIGHT...?

UH......

YEP...

GU (GRAB)

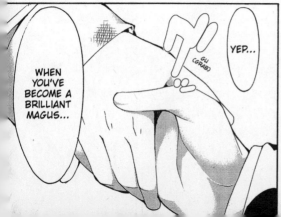

WHEN YOU'VE BECOME A BRILLIANT MAGUS...

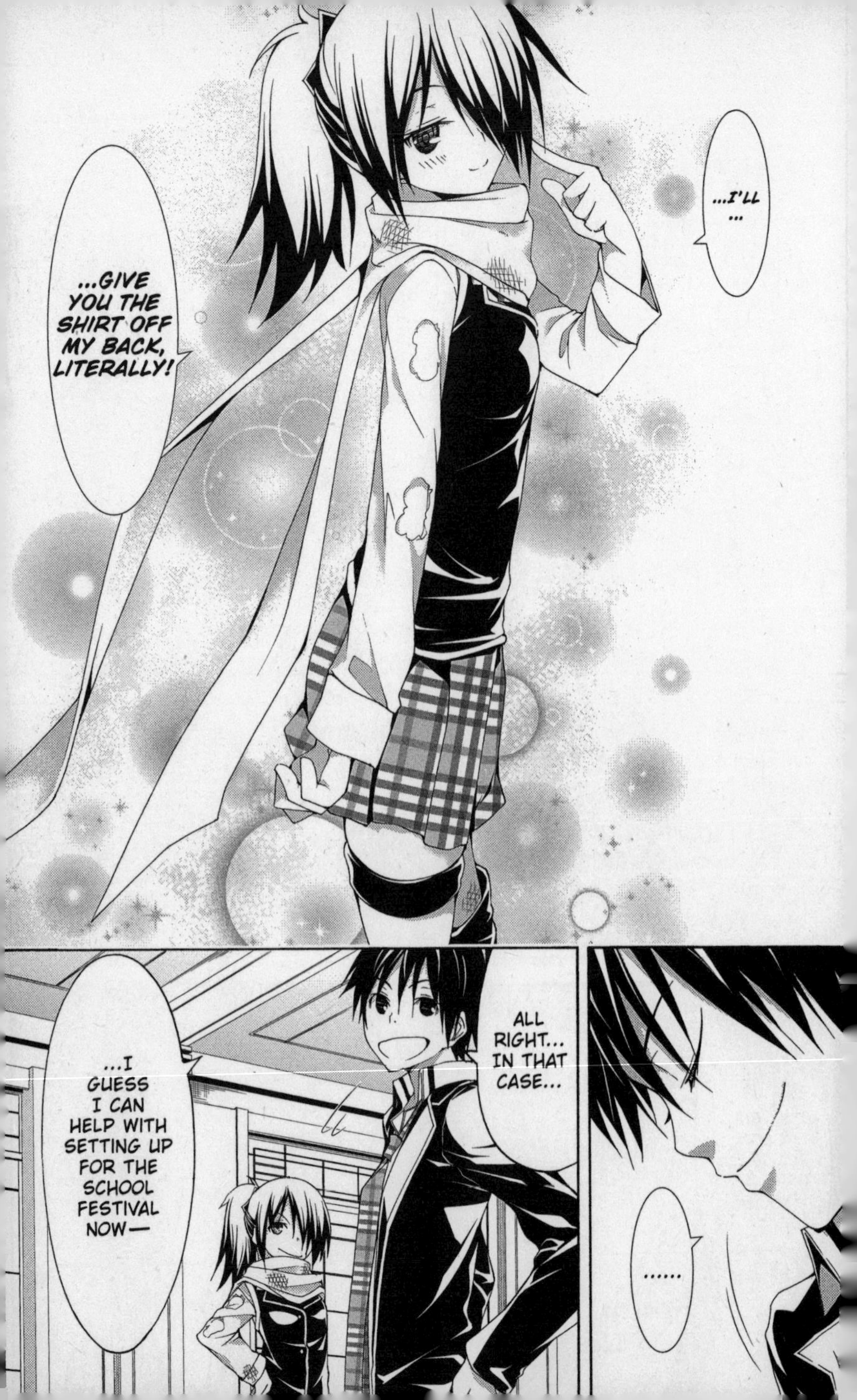
...I'LL ...
...GIVE YOU THE SHIRT OFF MY BACK, LITERALLY!
......
ALL RIGHT... IN THAT CASE...
...I GUESS I CAN HELP WITH SETTING UP FOR THE SCHOOL FESTIVAL NOW—

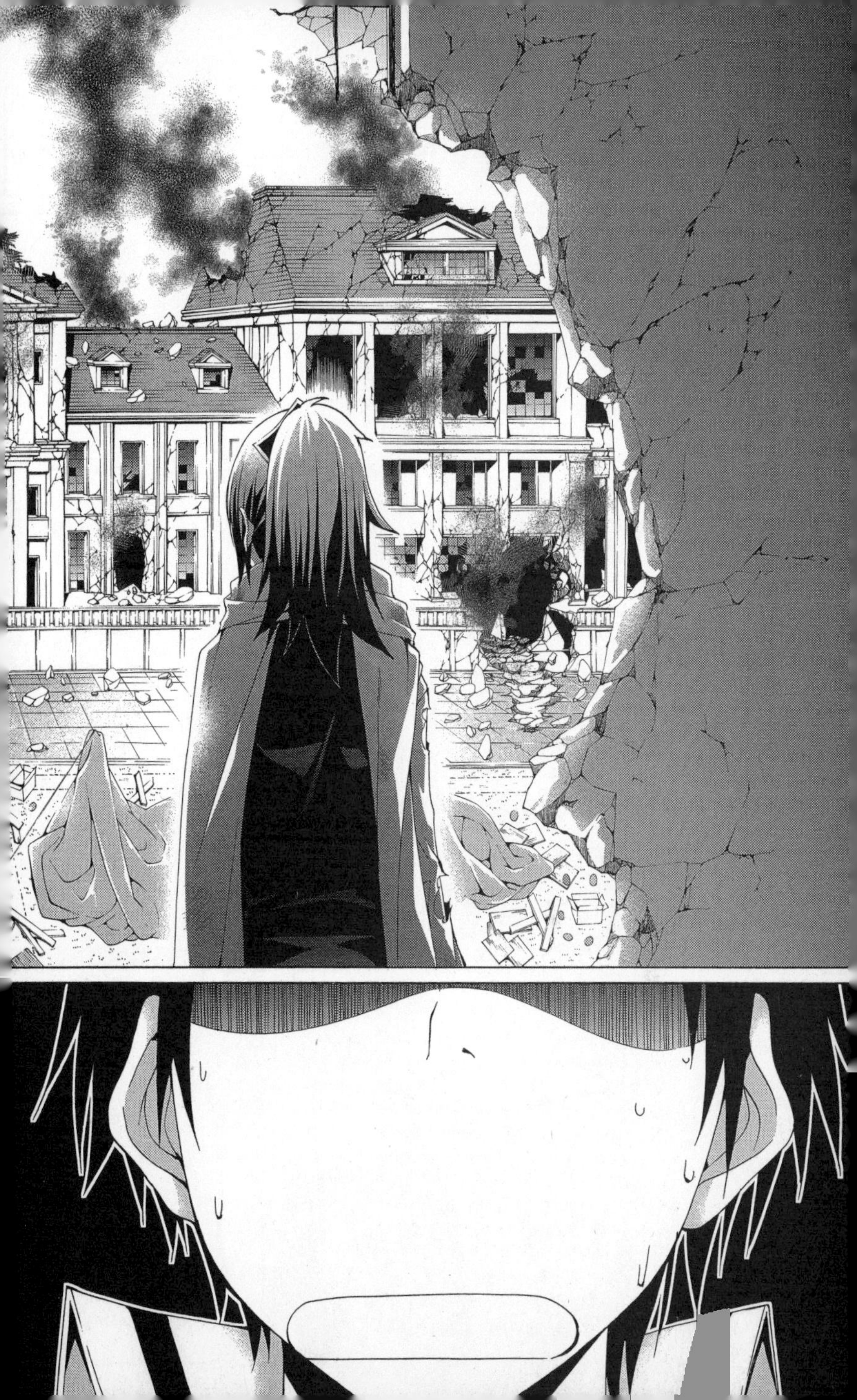

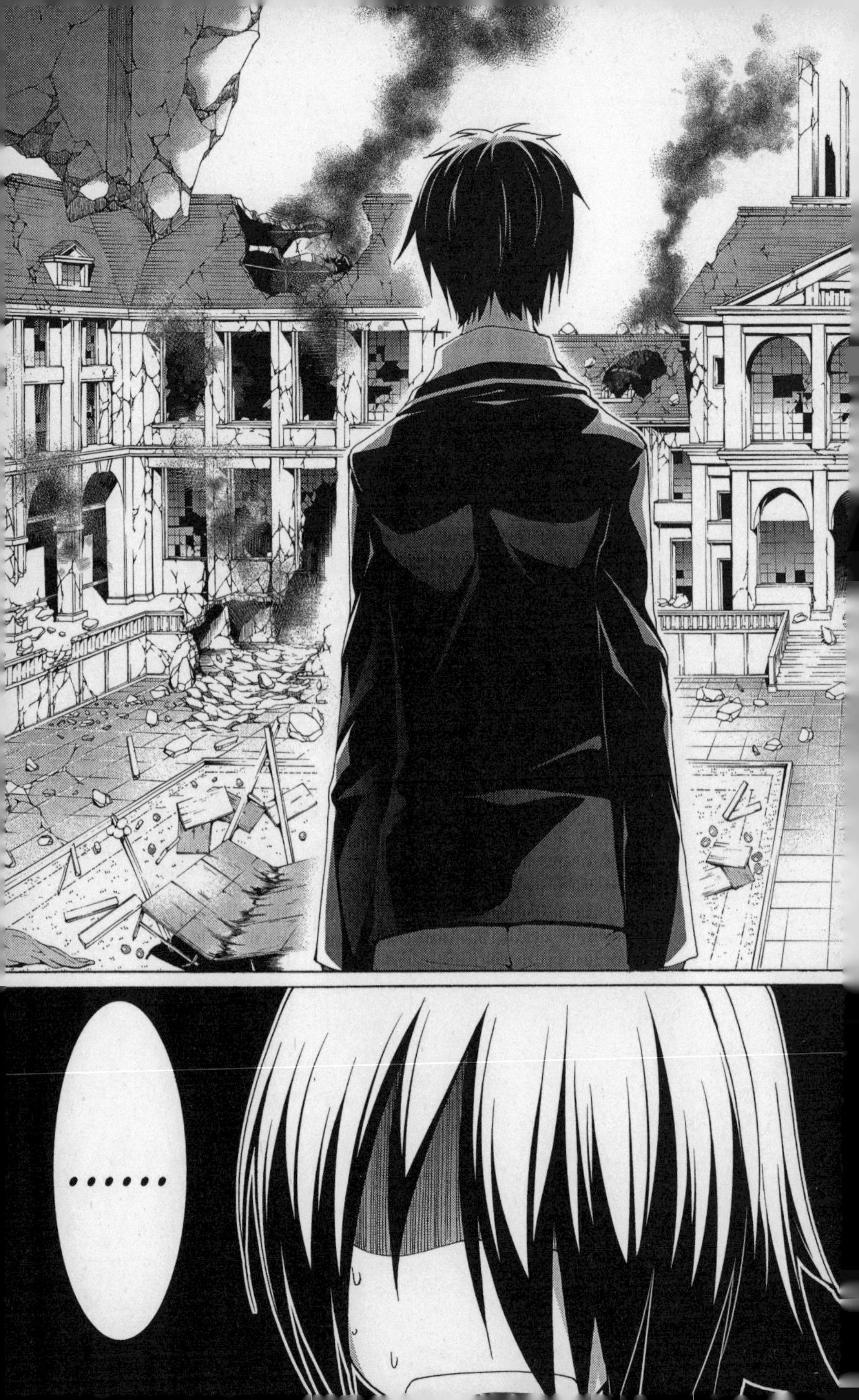
......

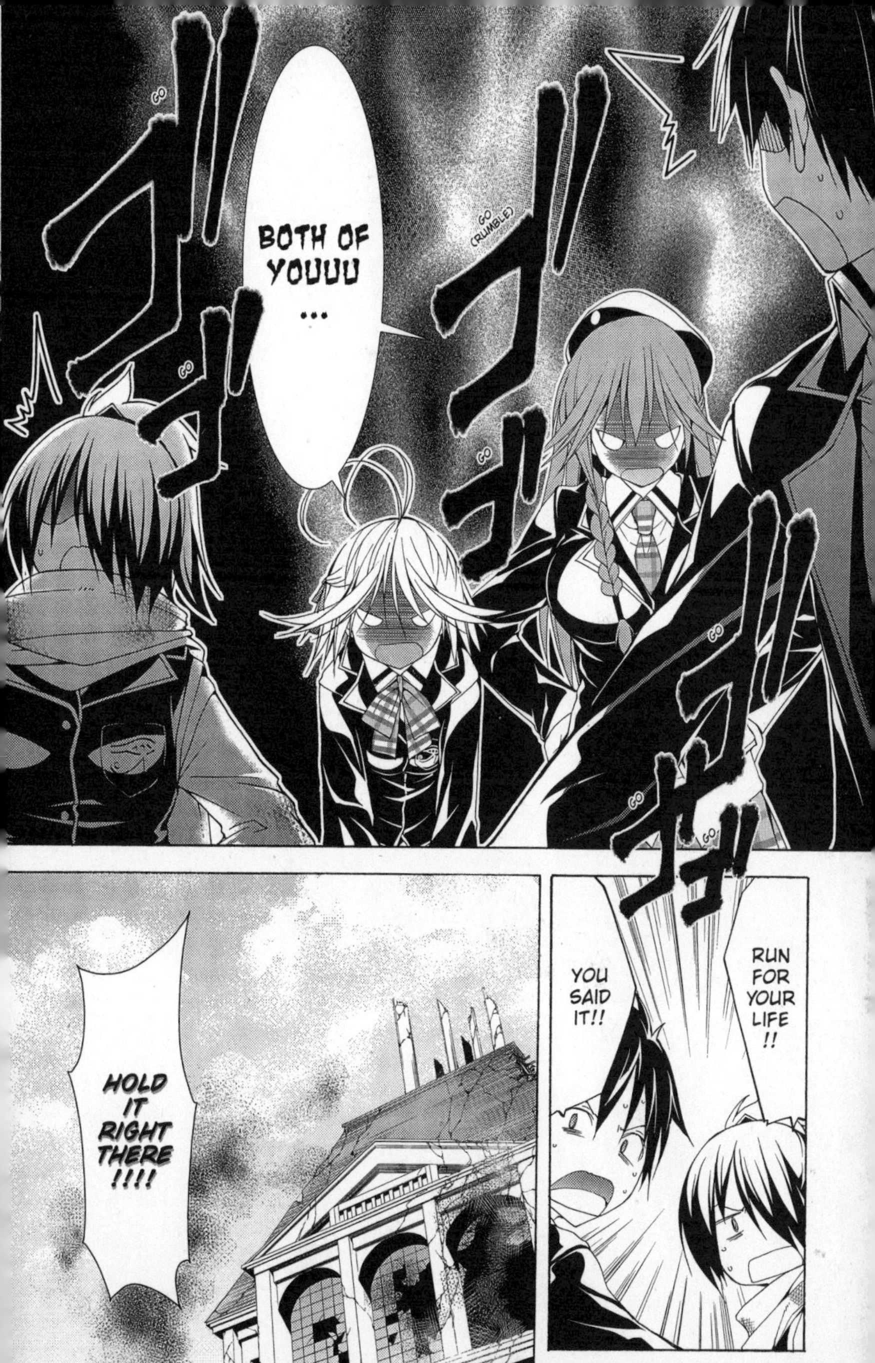
GO
(RUMBLE)
BOTH OF YOUUU ...
GO
GO
GO
GO
GO
GO
RUN FOR YOUR LIFE !!
YOU SAID IT!!
HOLD IT RIGHT THERE !!!!

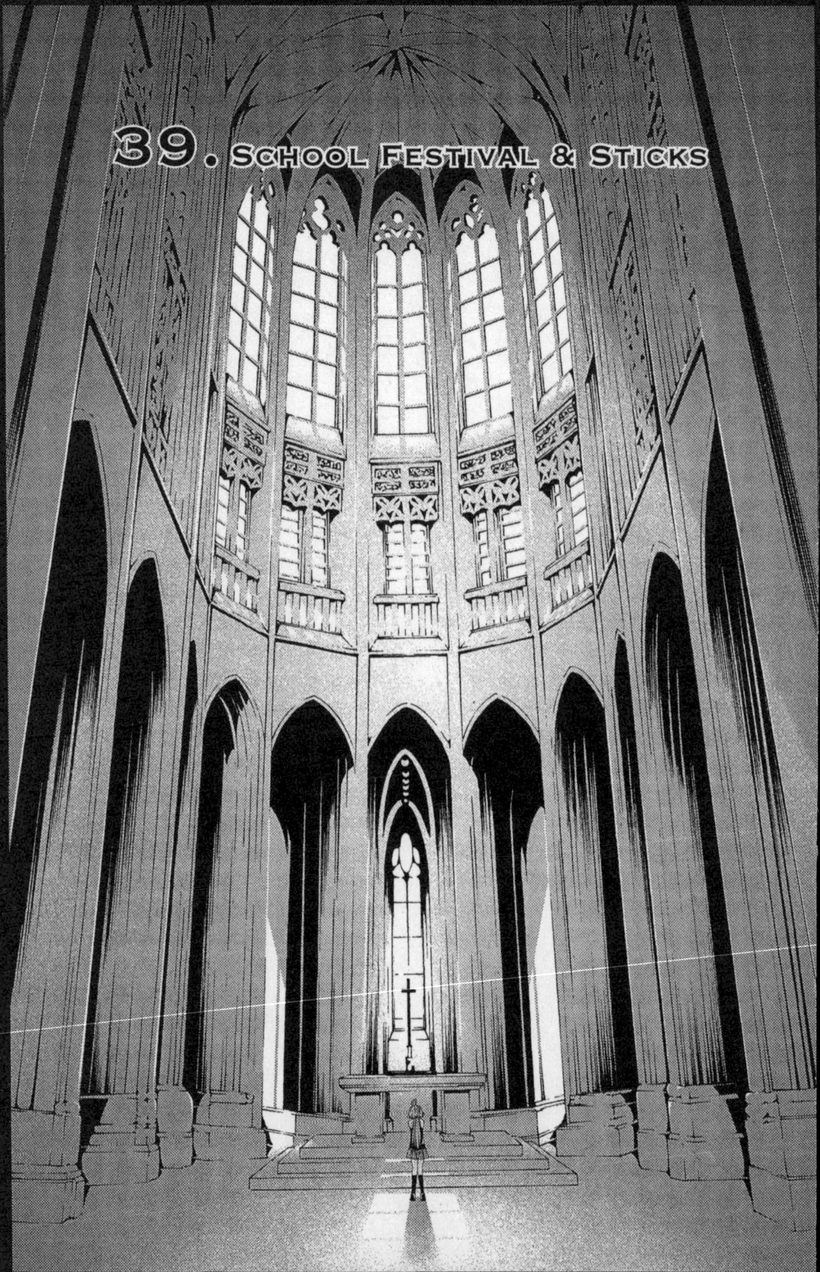
39. School Festival & Sticks

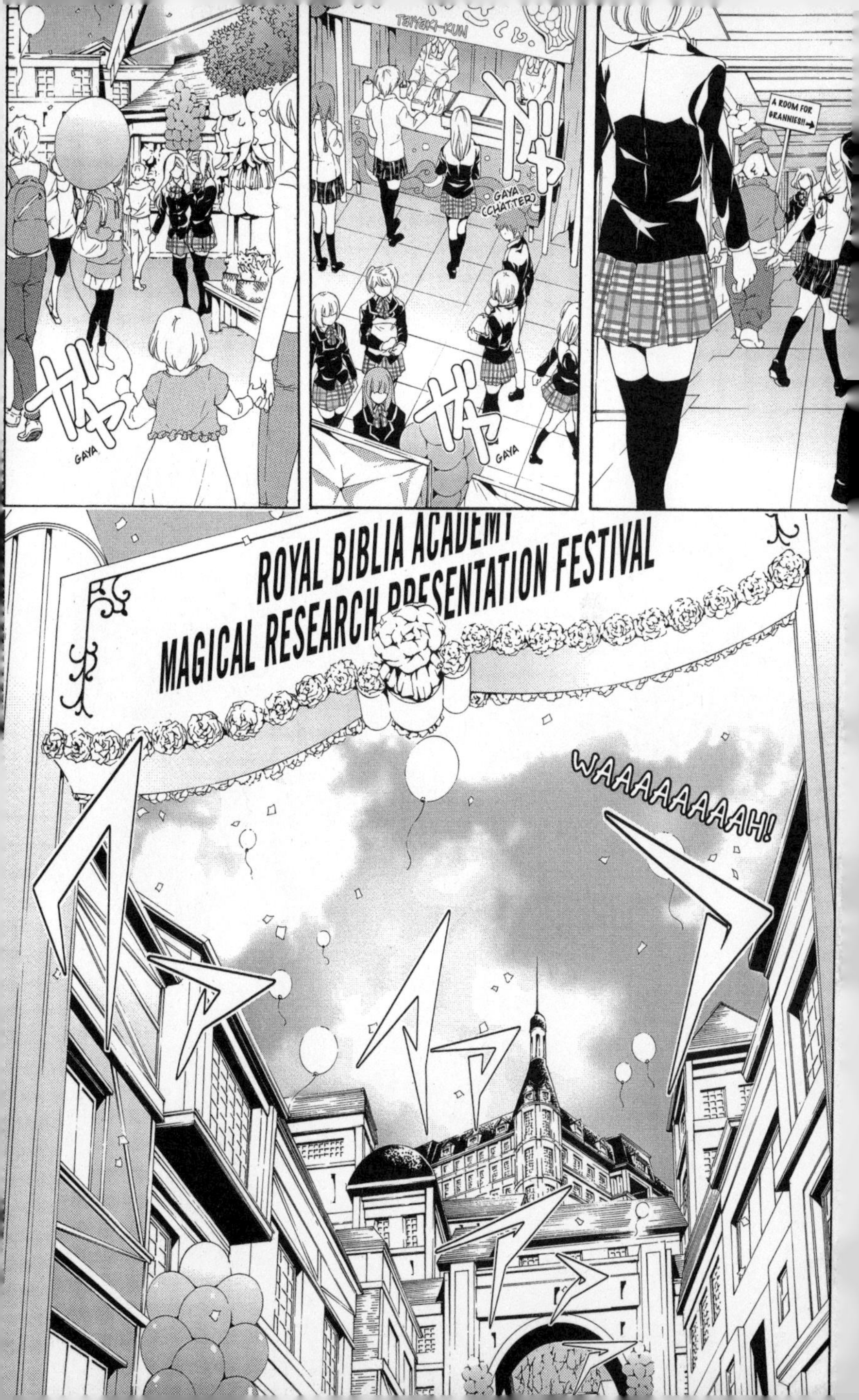

A ROOM FOR GRANNIES!!
TAIYAKI-KUN
GAYA (CHATTER)
GAYA
GAYA
ROYAL BIBLIA ACADEMY
MAGICAL RESEARCH PRESENTATION FESTIVAL
WAAAAAAAAAH!

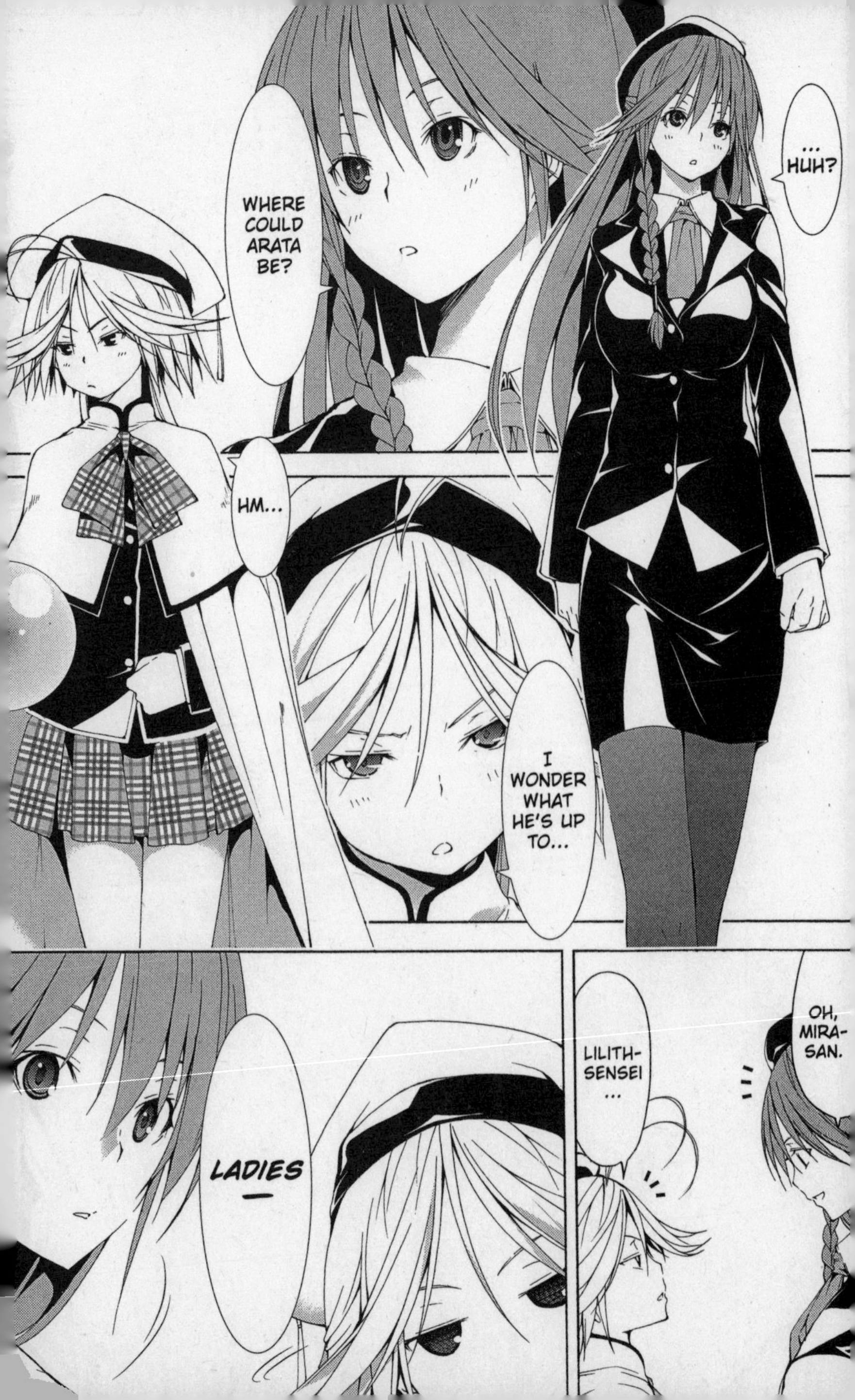
...HUH?
WHERE COULD ARATA BE?
HM...
I WONDER WHAT HE'S UP TO...
OH, MIRA-SAN.
LILITH-SENSEI...
LADIES —

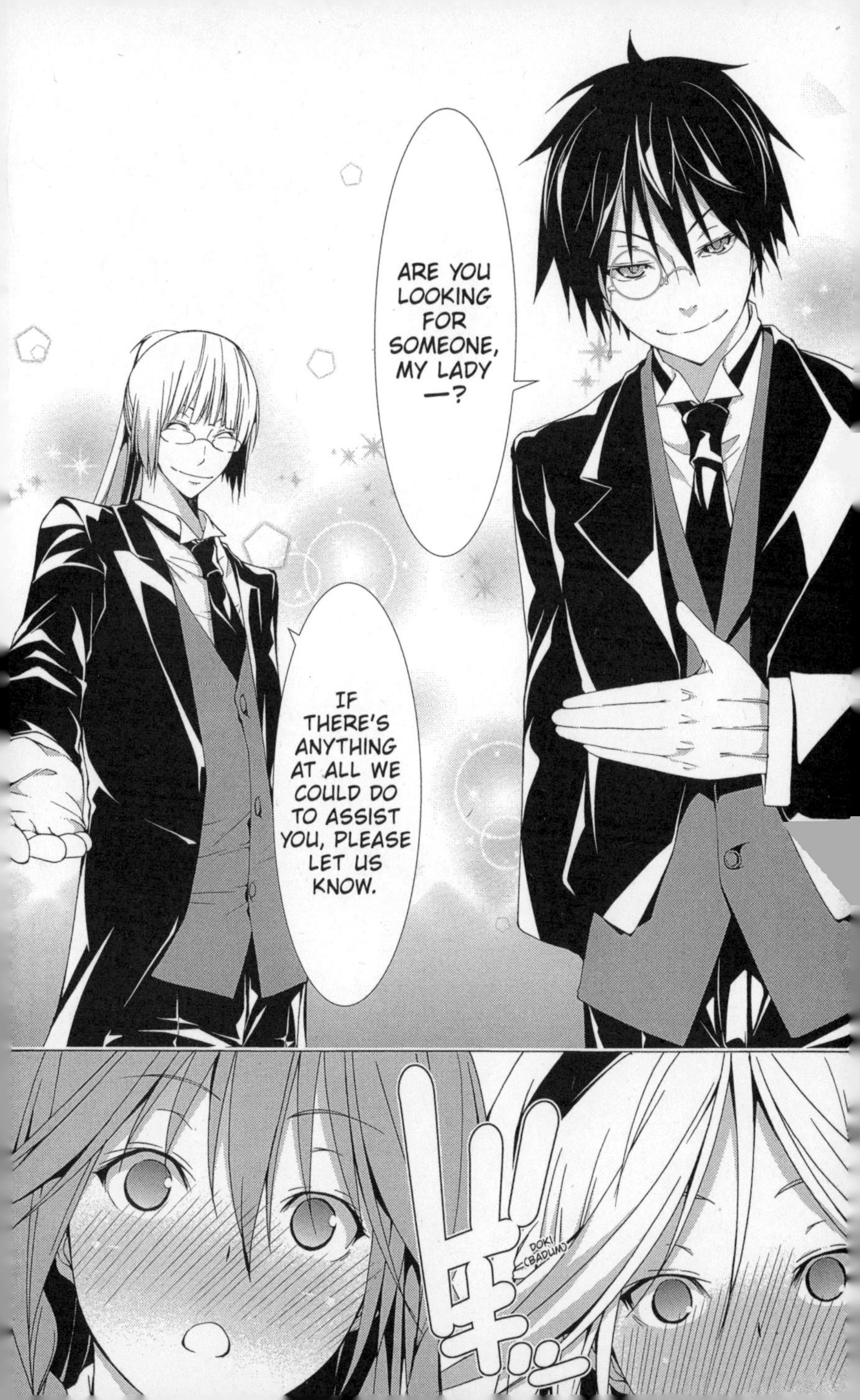
ARE YOU LOOKING FOR SOMEONE, MY LADY —?
IF THERE'S ANYTHING AT ALL WE COULD DO TO ASSIST YOU, PLEASE LET US KNOW.
DOKI (BADUM)

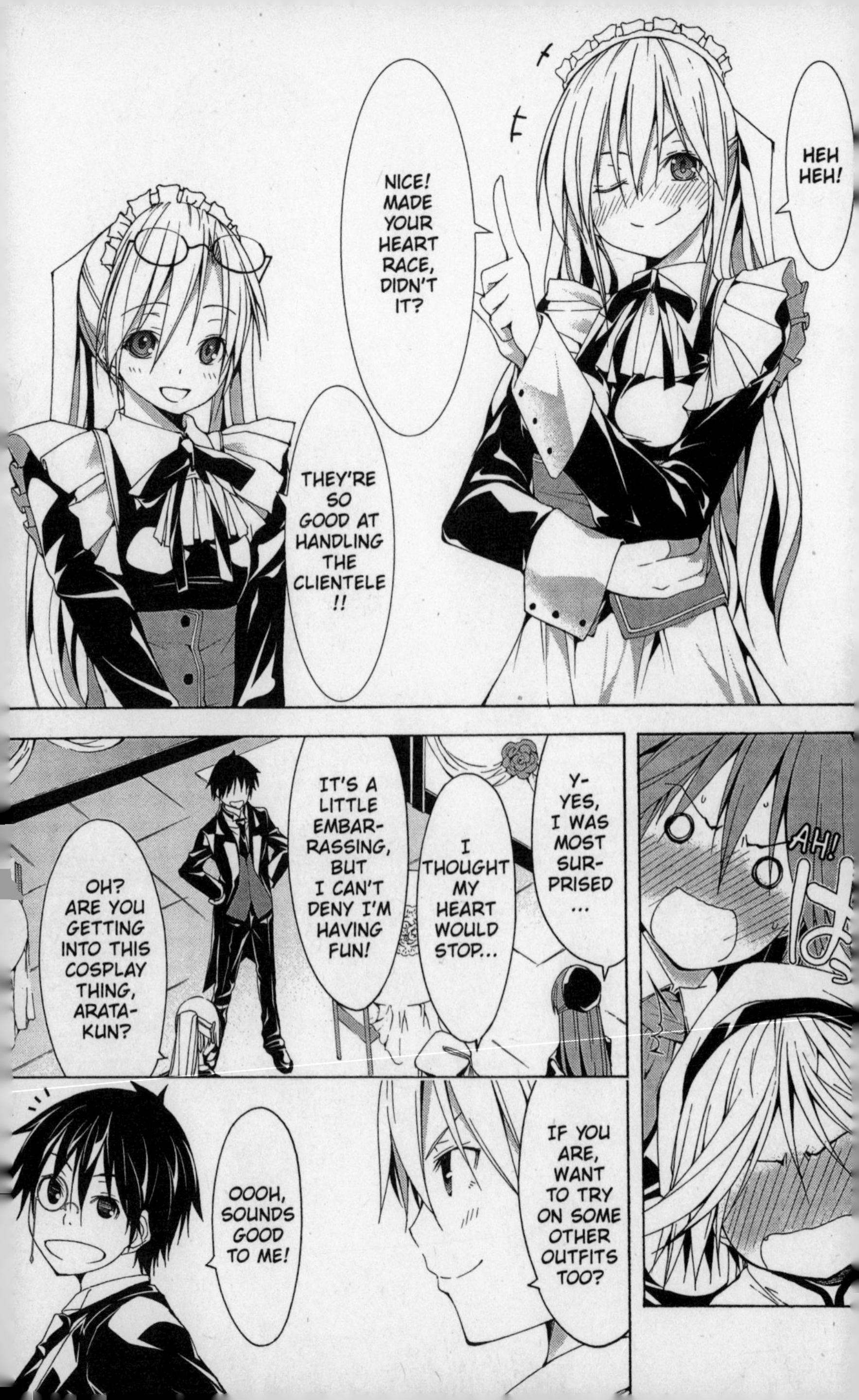
HEH HEH!
NICE! MADE YOUR HEART RACE, DIDN'T IT?
THEY'RE SO GOOD AT HANDLING THE CLIENTELE!!
AH!
Y-YES, I WAS MOST SURPRISED...
I THOUGHT MY HEART WOULD STOP...
IT'S A LITTLE EMBARRASSING, BUT I CAN'T DENY I'M HAVING FUN!
OH? ARE YOU GETTING INTO THIS COSPLAY THING, ARATA-KUN?
IF YOU ARE, WANT TO TRY ON SOME OTHER OUTFITS TOO?
OOOH, SOUNDS GOOD TO ME!

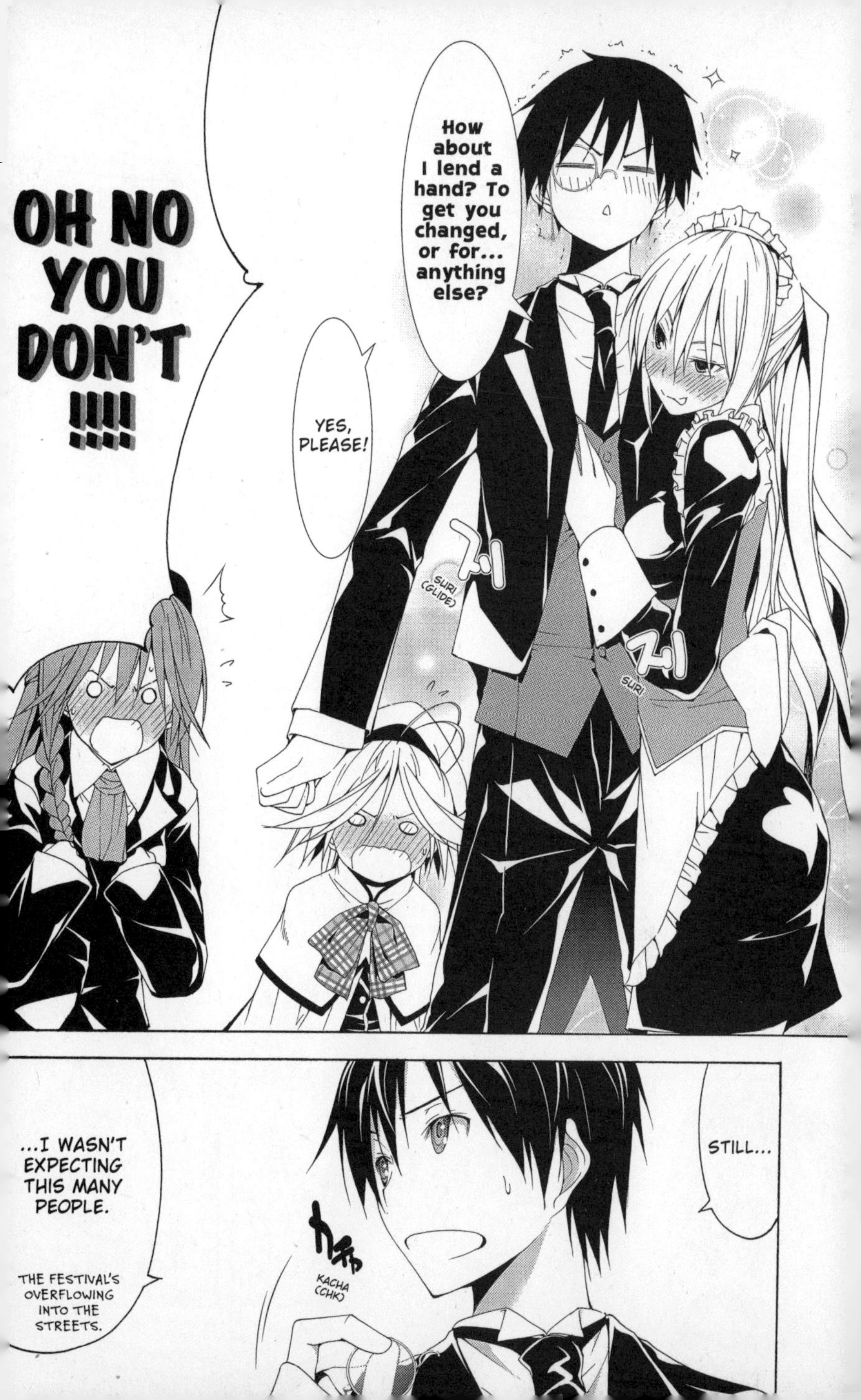
How about I lend a hand? To get you changed, or for... anything else?
YES, PLEASE!
SURI (GLIDE)
SURI
OH NO YOU DON'T!!!!
STILL...
...I WASN'T EXPECTING THIS MANY PEOPLE.
KACHA (CHK)
THE FESTIVAL'S OVERFLOWING INTO THE STREETS.

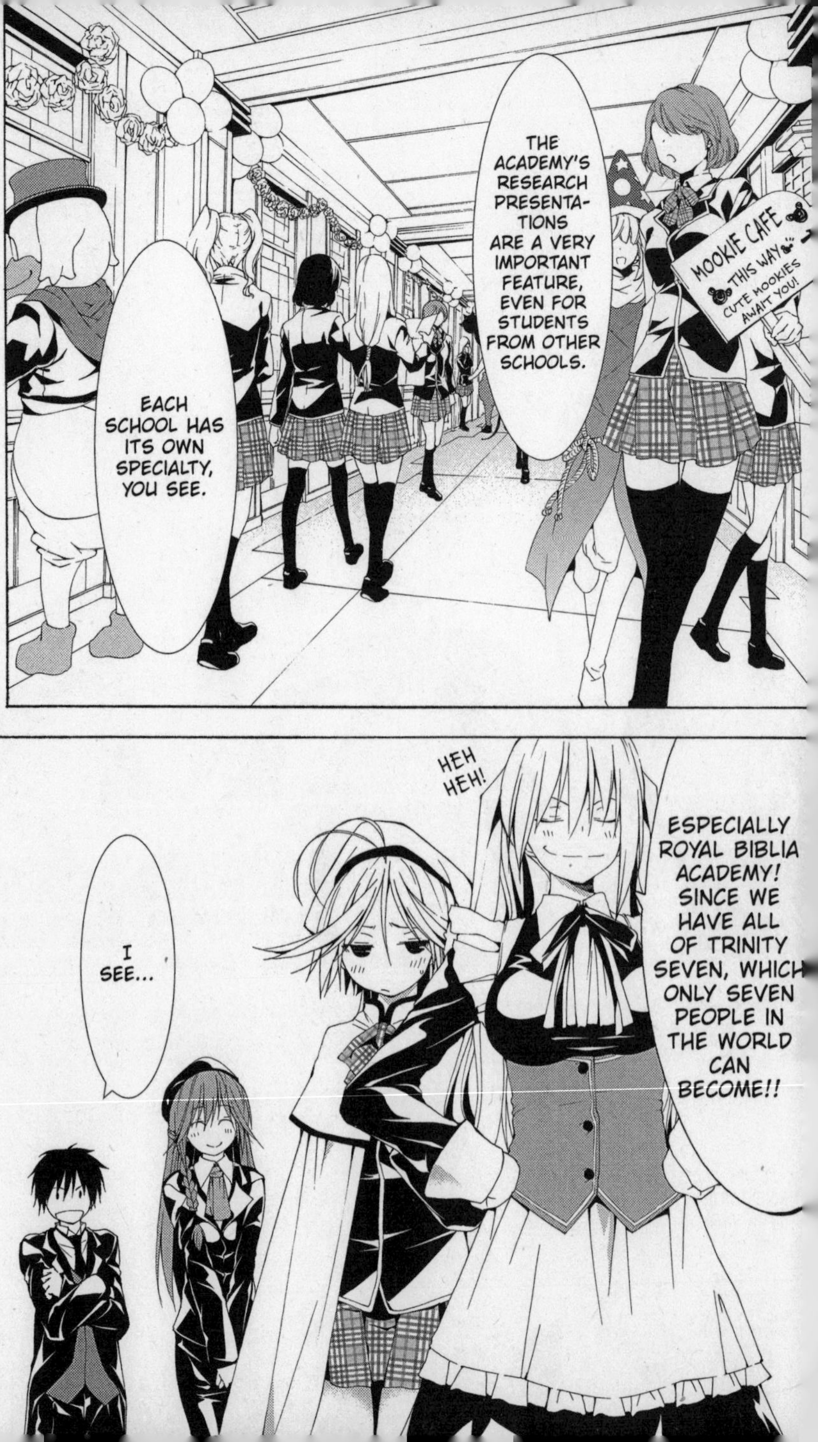
MOOKIE CAFE THIS WAY CUTE MOOKIES AWAIT YOU!
THE ACADEMY'S RESEARCH PRESENTATIONS ARE A VERY IMPORTANT FEATURE, EVEN FOR STUDENTS FROM OTHER SCHOOLS.
EACH SCHOOL HAS ITS OWN SPECIALTY, YOU SEE.
HEH HEH!
ESPECIALLY ROYAL BIBLIA ACADEMY! SINCE WE HAVE ALL OF TRINITY SEVEN, WHICH ONLY SEVEN PEOPLE IN THE WORLD CAN BECOME!!
I SEE...

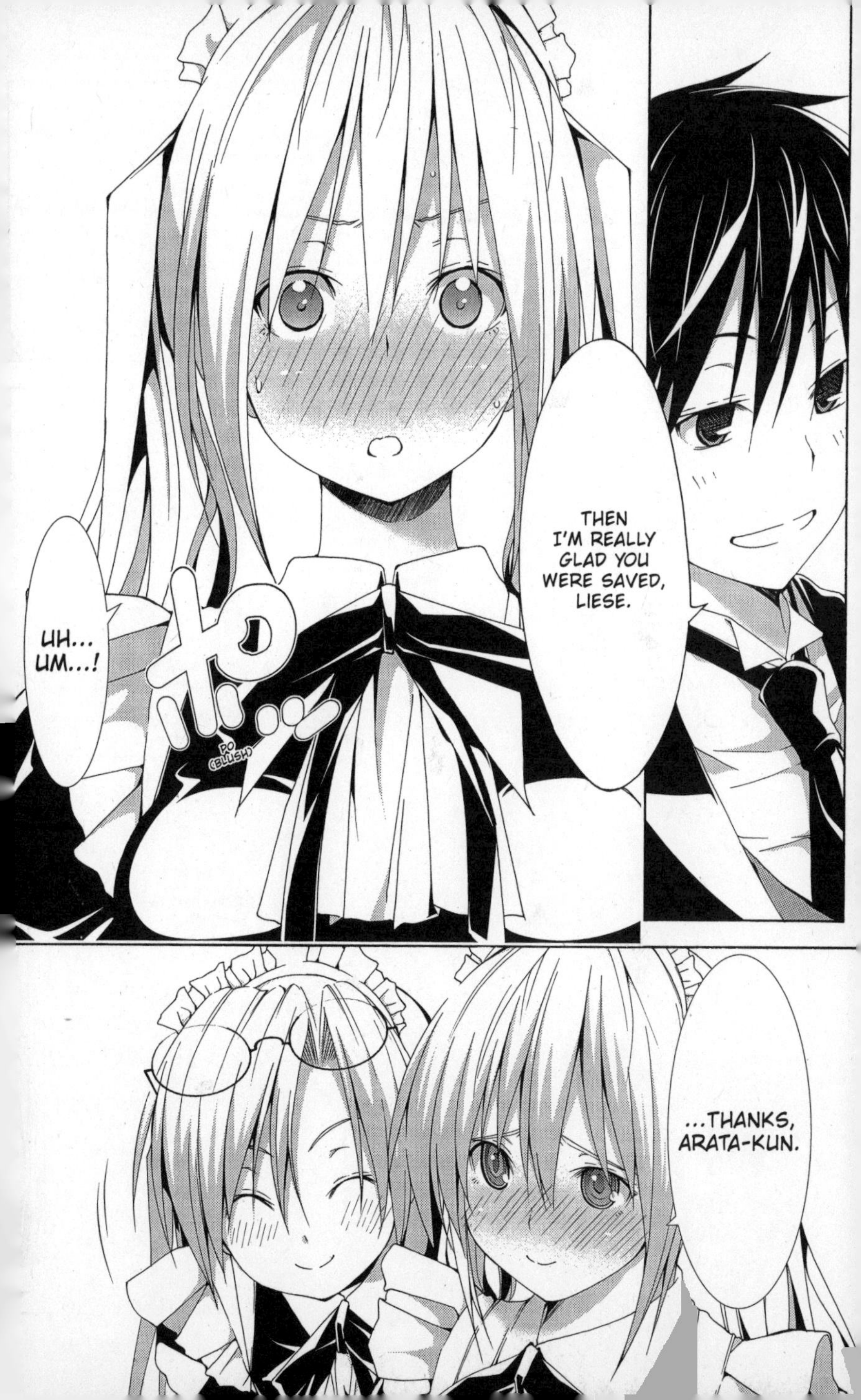
THEN I'M REALLY GLAD YOU WERE SAVED, LIESE.
UH... UM...!
PO (BLUSH)
...THANKS, ARATA-KUN.

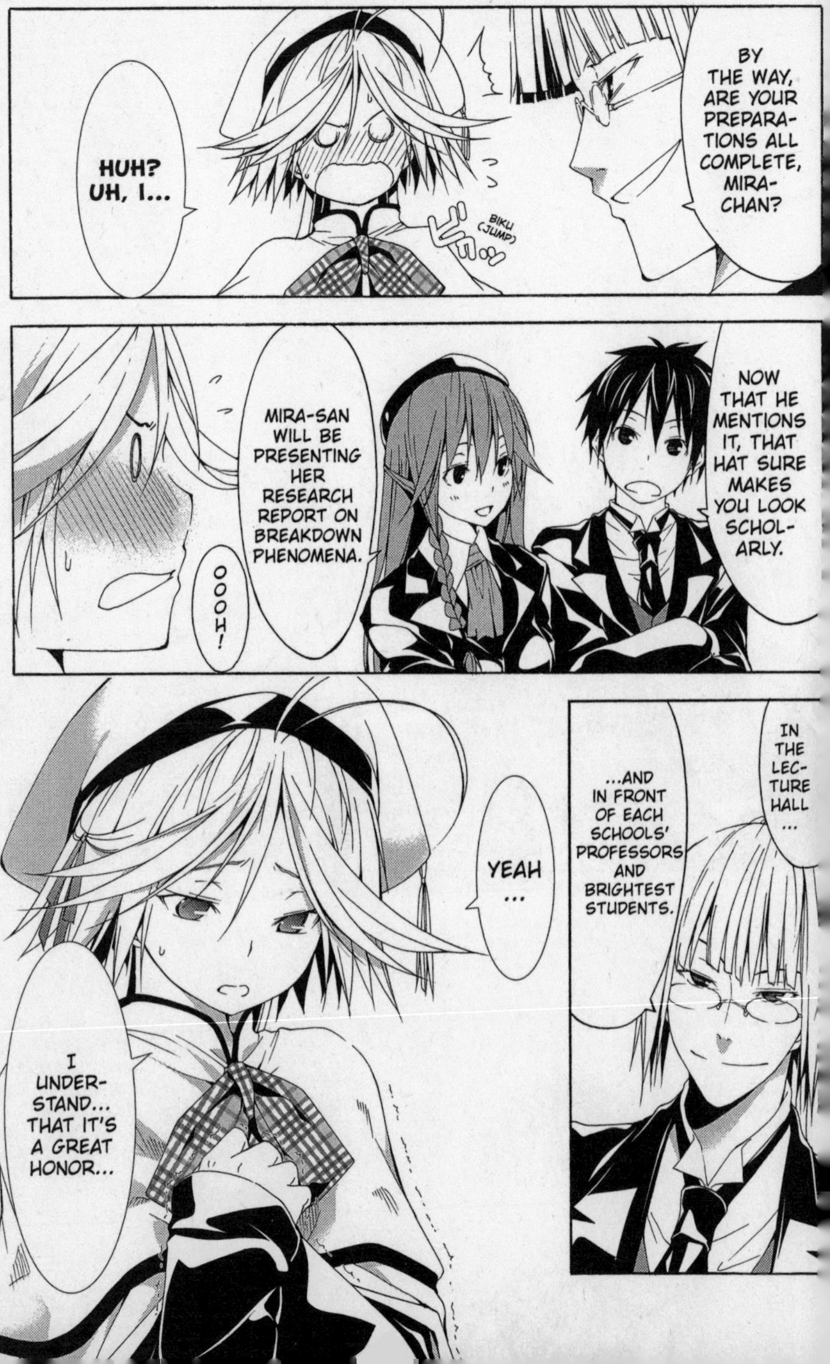
BY THE WAY, ARE YOUR PREPARATIONS ALL COMPLETE, MIRA-CHAN?
BIKU (JUMP)
HUH? UH, I...
NOW THAT HE MENTIONS IT, THAT HAT SURE MAKES YOU LOOK SCHOLARLY.
MIRA-SAN WILL BE PRESENTING HER RESEARCH REPORT ON BREAKDOWN PHENOMENA.
OOOH!
IN THE LECTURE HALL...
...AND IN FRONT OF EACH SCHOOLS' PROFESSORS AND BRIGHTEST STUDENTS.
YEAH...
I UNDERSTAND... THAT IT'S A GREAT HONOR...

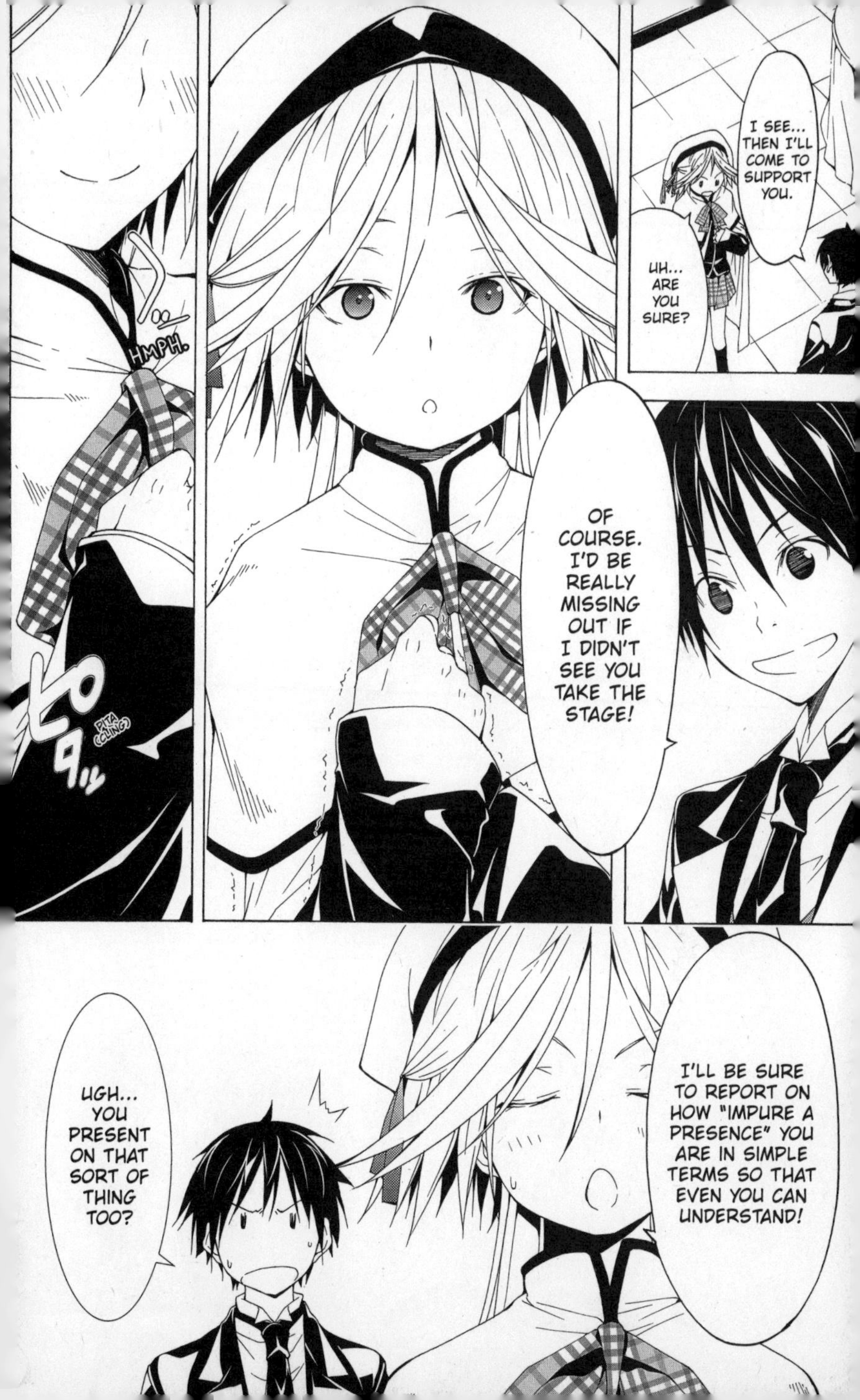
I SEE... THEN I'LL COME TO SUPPORT YOU.
UH... ARE YOU SURE?
OF COURSE. I'D BE REALLY MISSING OUT IF I DIDN'T SEE YOU TAKE THE STAGE!
HMPH.
ピタッ
PITA (CLING)
I'LL BE SURE TO REPORT ON HOW "IMPURE A PRESENCE" YOU ARE IN SIMPLE TERMS SO THAT EVEN YOU CAN UNDERSTAND!
UGH... YOU PRESENT ON THAT SORT OF THING TOO?

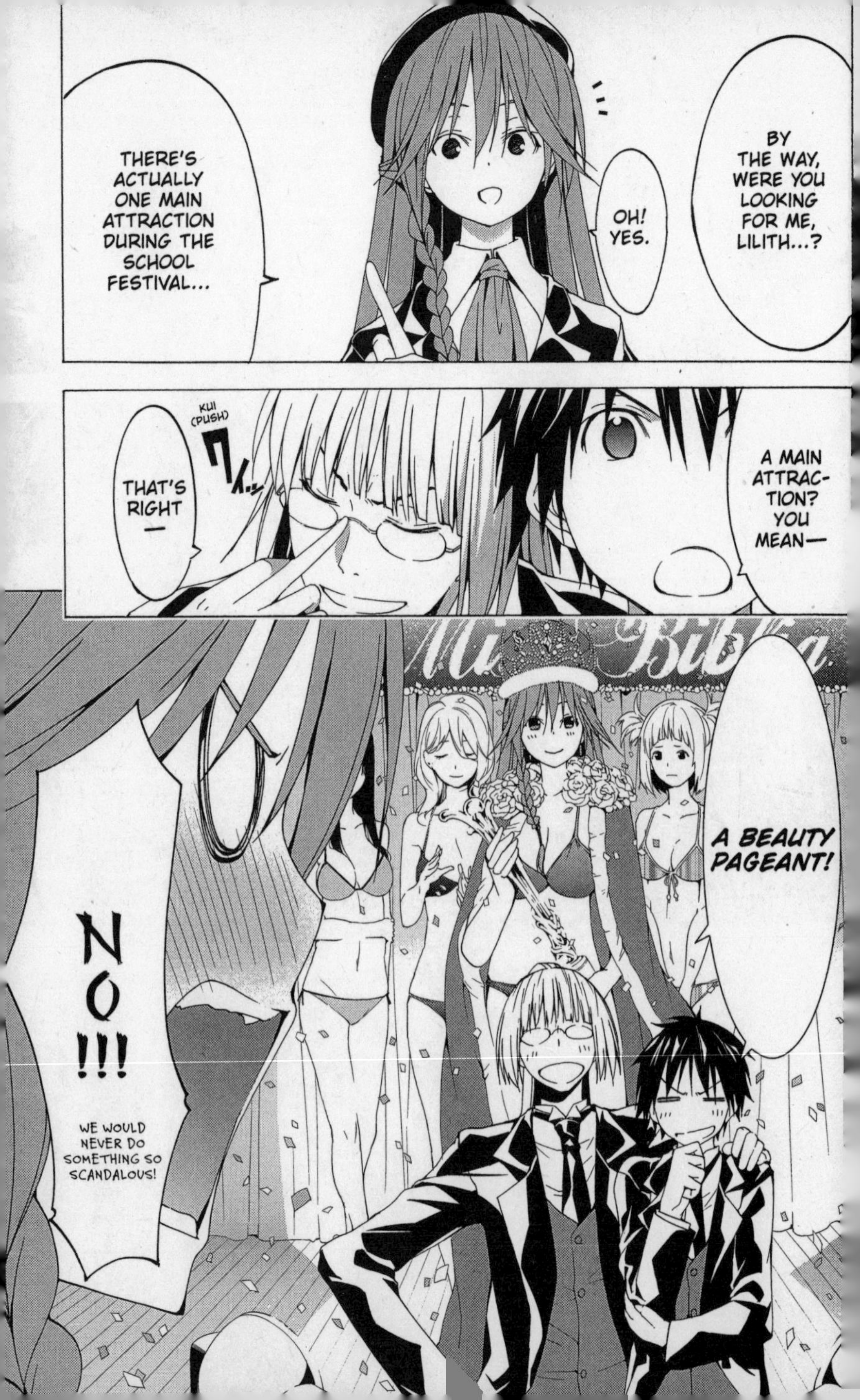
BY THE WAY, WERE YOU LOOKING FOR ME, LILITH...?
OH! YES.
THERE'S ACTUALLY ONE MAIN ATTRACTION DURING THE SCHOOL FESTIVAL...
A MAIN ATTRACTION? YOU MEAN—
KUI (PUSH)
THAT'S RIGHT —
A BEAUTY PAGEANT!
NO!!!
WE WOULD NEVER DO SOMETHING SO SCANDALOUS!

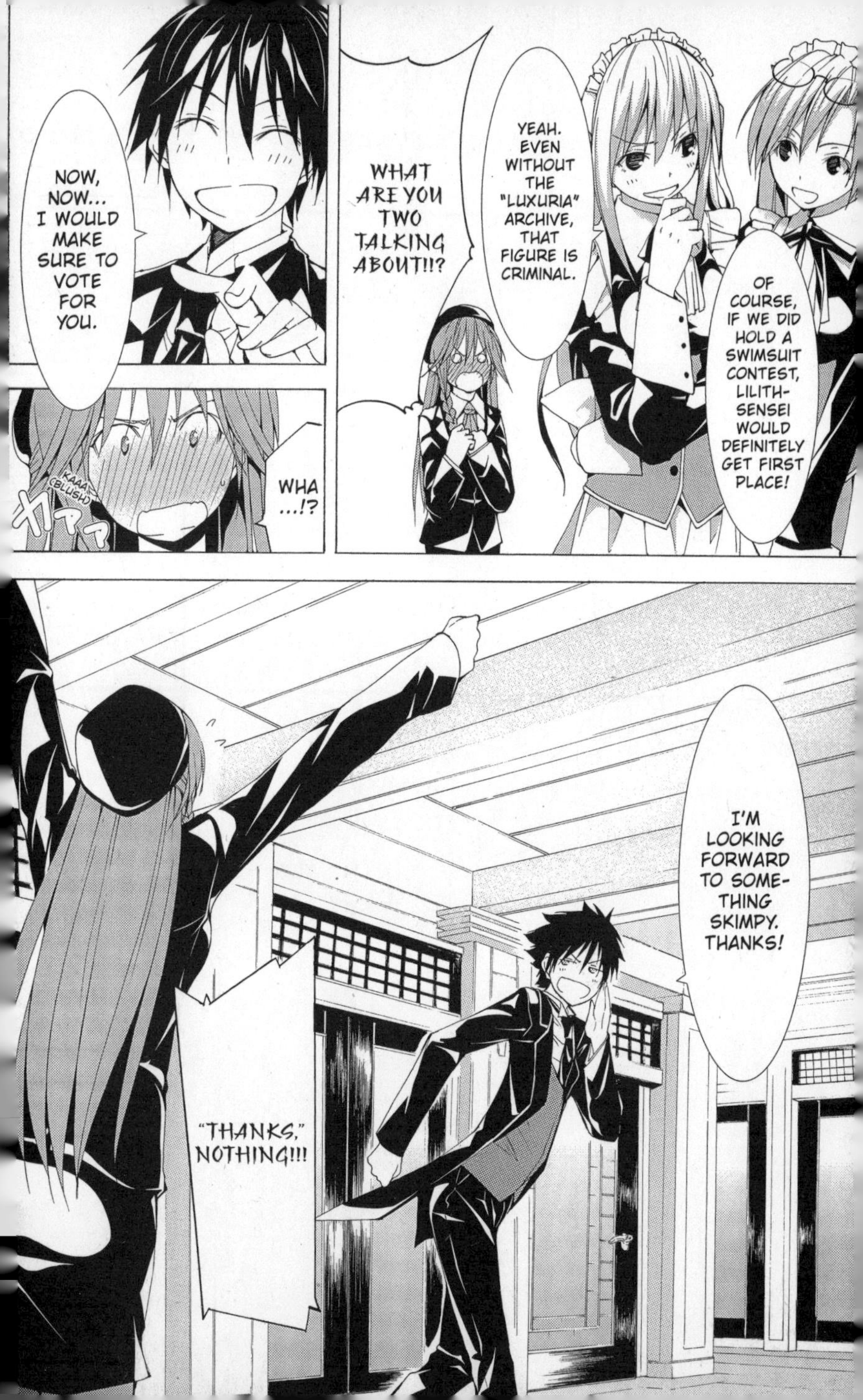
OF COURSE, IF WE DID HOLD A SWIMSUIT CONTEST, LILITH-SENSEI WOULD DEFINITELY GET FIRST PLACE!
YEAH. EVEN WITHOUT THE "LUXURIA" ARCHIVE, THAT FIGURE IS CRIMINAL.
WHAT ARE YOU TWO TALKING ABOUT!!?
NOW, NOW... I WOULD MAKE SURE TO VOTE FOR YOU.
WHA ...!?
KAAA (BLUSH)
I'M LOOKING FORWARD TO SOME-THING SKIMPY. THANKS!
"THANKS." NOTHING!!!

フ
FU
(FWIP)

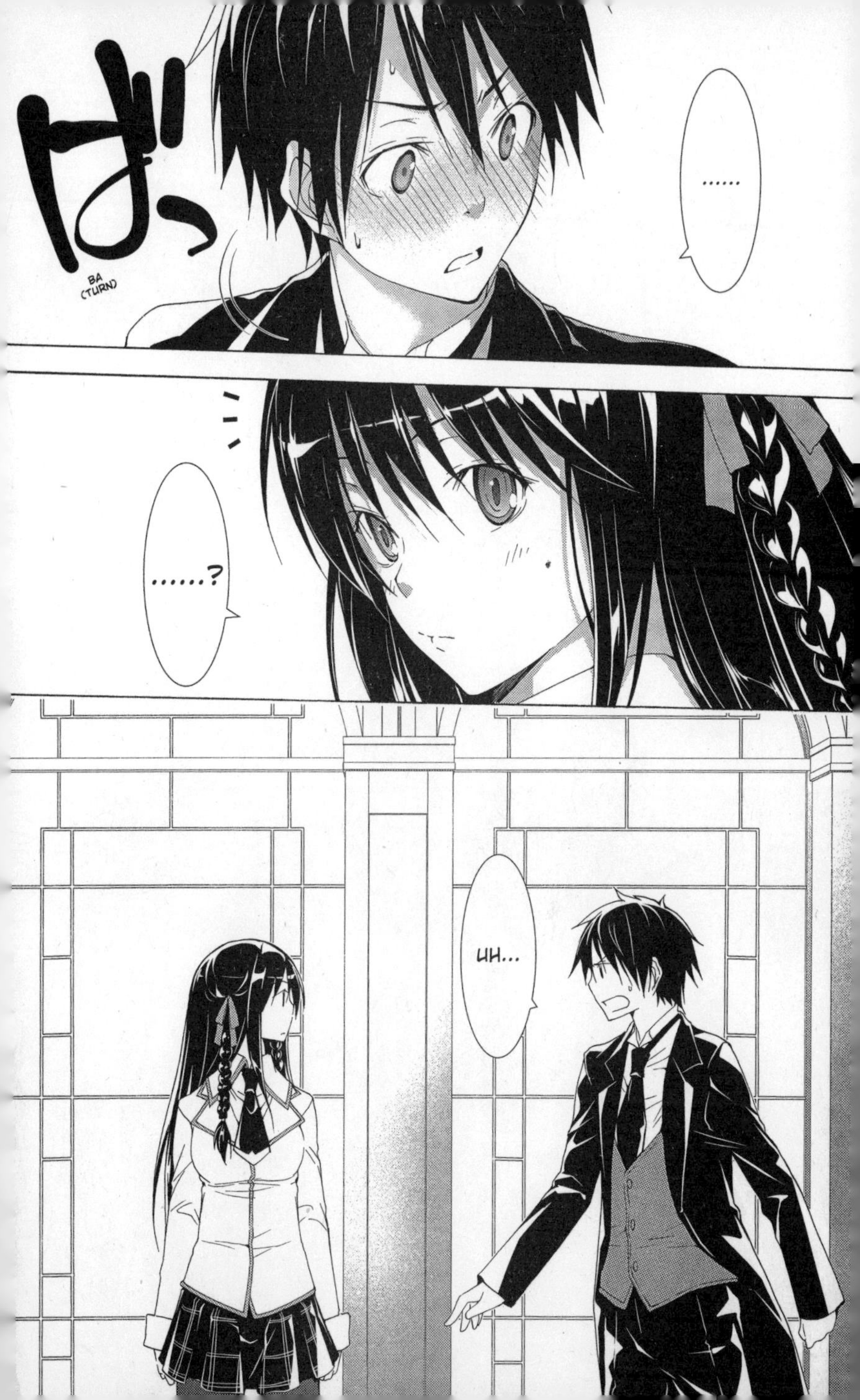
……
ぱっ
BA (TURN)
……?
UH…

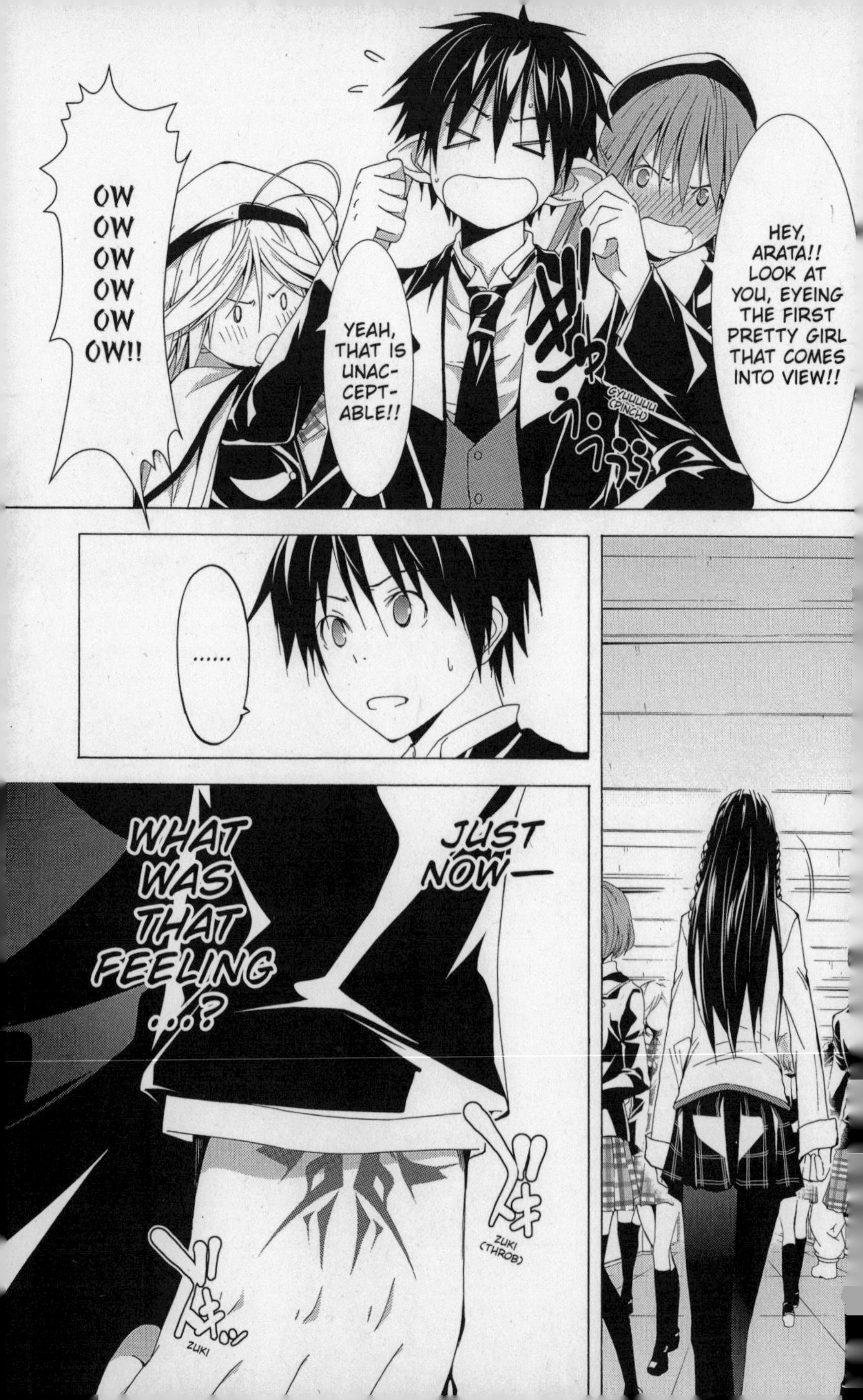
HEY, ARATA!! LOOK AT YOU, EYEING THE FIRST PRETTY GIRL THAT COMES INTO VIEW!!
GYUUUUU (PINCH)
YEAH, THAT IS UNACCEPTABLE!!
OW OW OW OW OW OW!!
......
JUST NOW—
WHAT WAS THAT FEELING ...?
ZUKI (THROB)
ZUKI

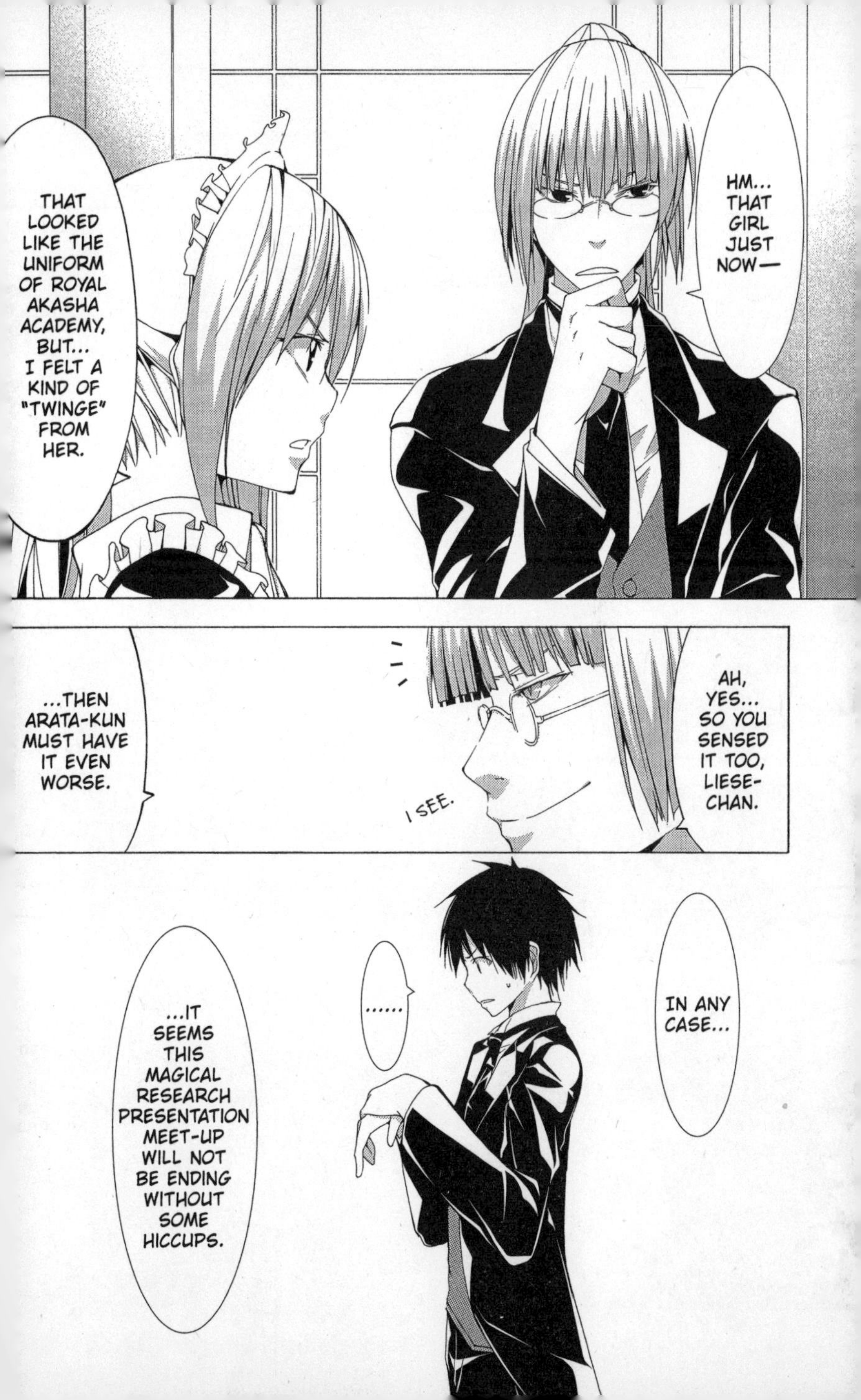
HM... THAT GIRL JUST NOW—
THAT LOOKED LIKE THE UNIFORM OF ROYAL AKASHA ACADEMY, BUT... I FELT A KIND OF "TWINGE" FROM HER.
AH, YES... SO YOU SENSED IT TOO, LIESE-CHAN.
I SEE.
...THEN ARATA-KUN MUST HAVE IT EVEN WORSE.
IN ANY CASE...
......
...IT SEEMS THIS MAGICAL RESEARCH PRESENTATION MEET-UP WILL NOT BE ENDING WITHOUT SOME HICCUPS.

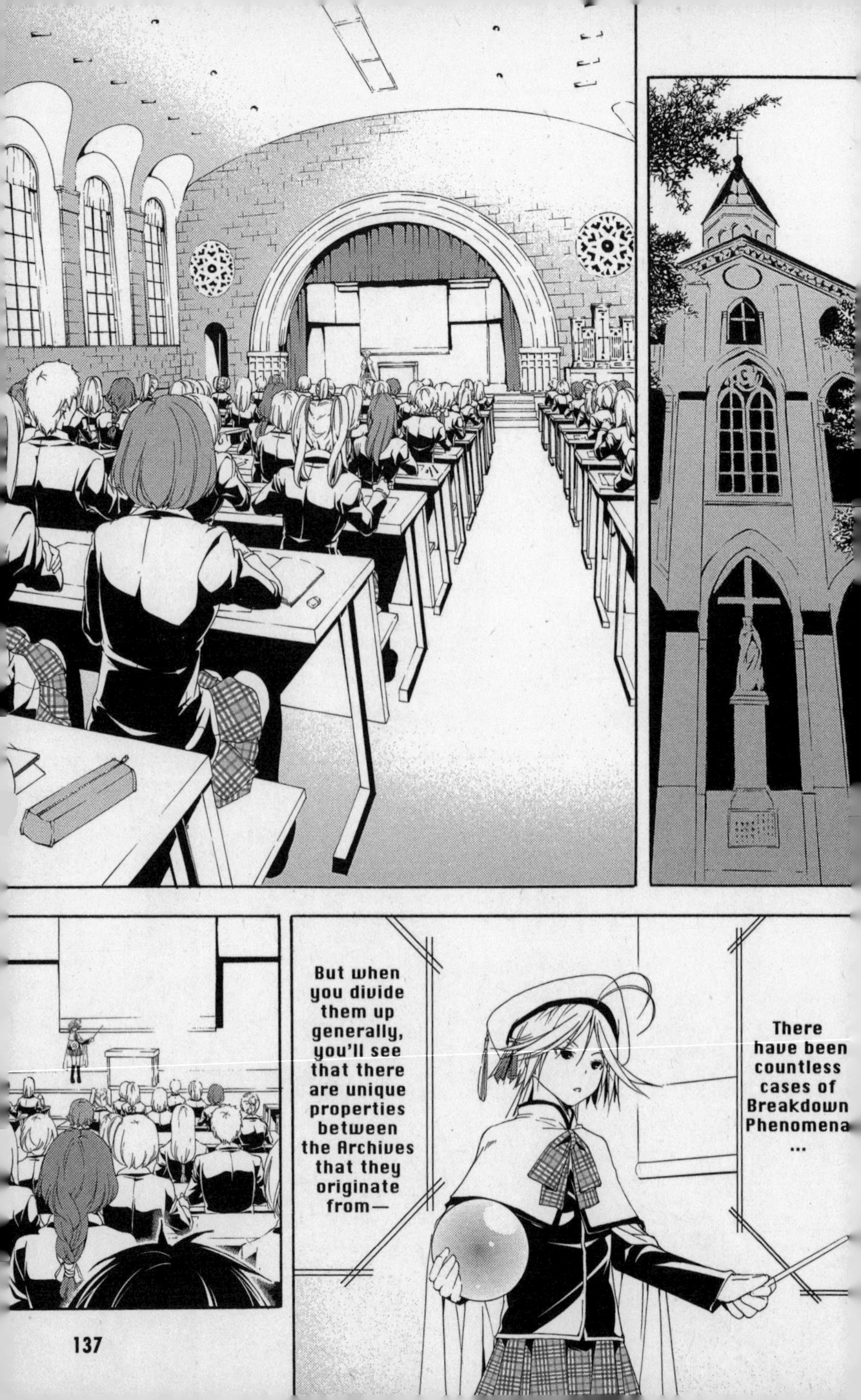
There have been countless cases of Breakdown Phenomena...
But when you divide them up generally, you'll see that there are unique properties between the Archives that they originate from—

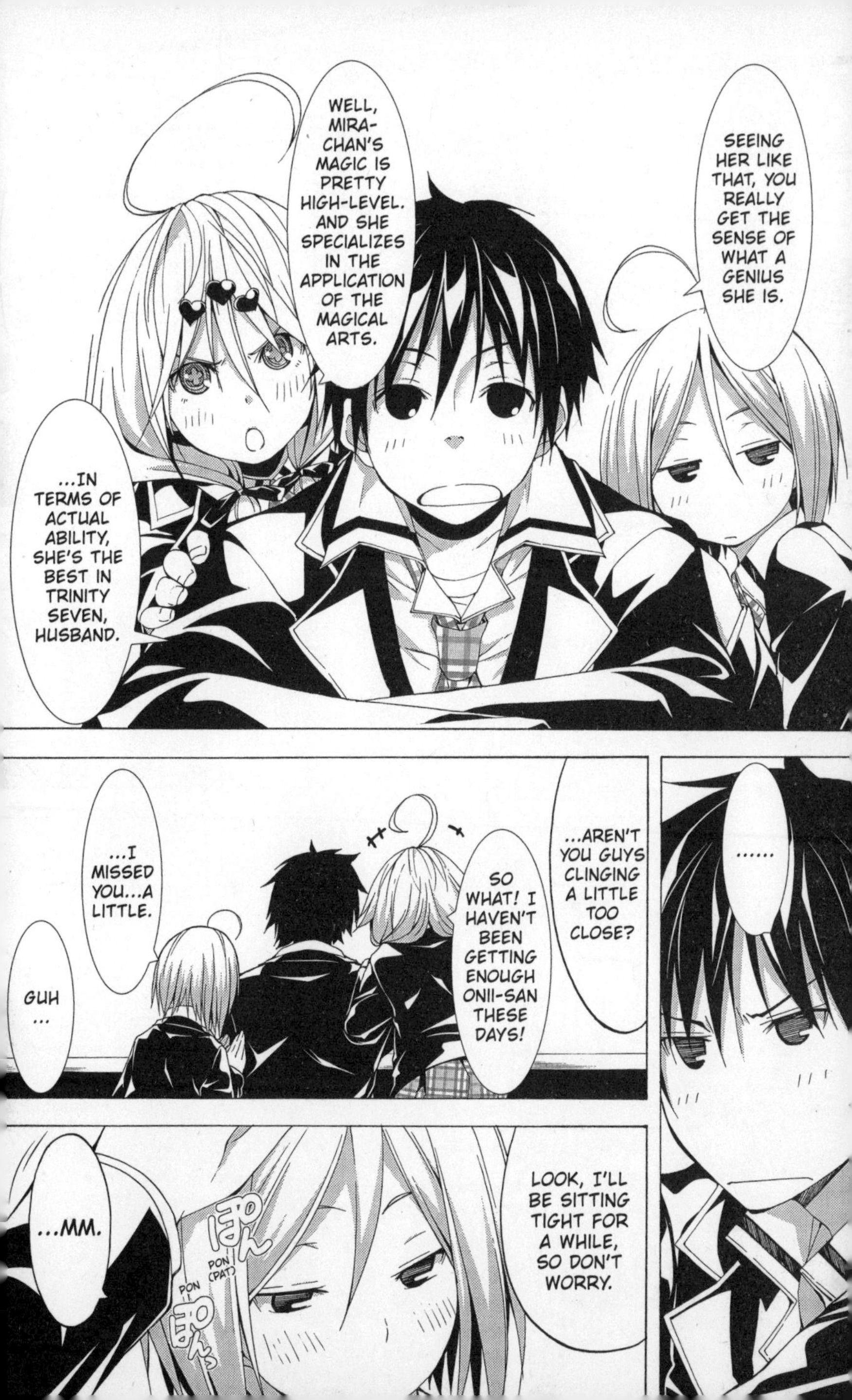
SEEING HER LIKE THAT, YOU REALLY GET THE SENSE OF WHAT A GENIUS SHE IS.
WELL, MIRA-CHAN'S MAGIC IS PRETTY HIGH-LEVEL. AND SHE SPECIALIZES IN THE APPLICATION OF THE MAGICAL ARTS.
...IN TERMS OF ACTUAL ABILITY, SHE'S THE BEST IN TRINITY SEVEN, HUSBAND.
......
...AREN'T YOU GUYS CLINGING A LITTLE TOO CLOSE?
SO WHAT! I HAVEN'T BEEN GETTING ENOUGH ONII-SAN THESE DAYS!
...I MISSED YOU...A LITTLE.
GUH ...
LOOK, I'LL BE SITTING TIGHT FOR A WHILE, SO DON'T WORRY.
ぽん
PON (PAT)
ぽん
PON
...MM.

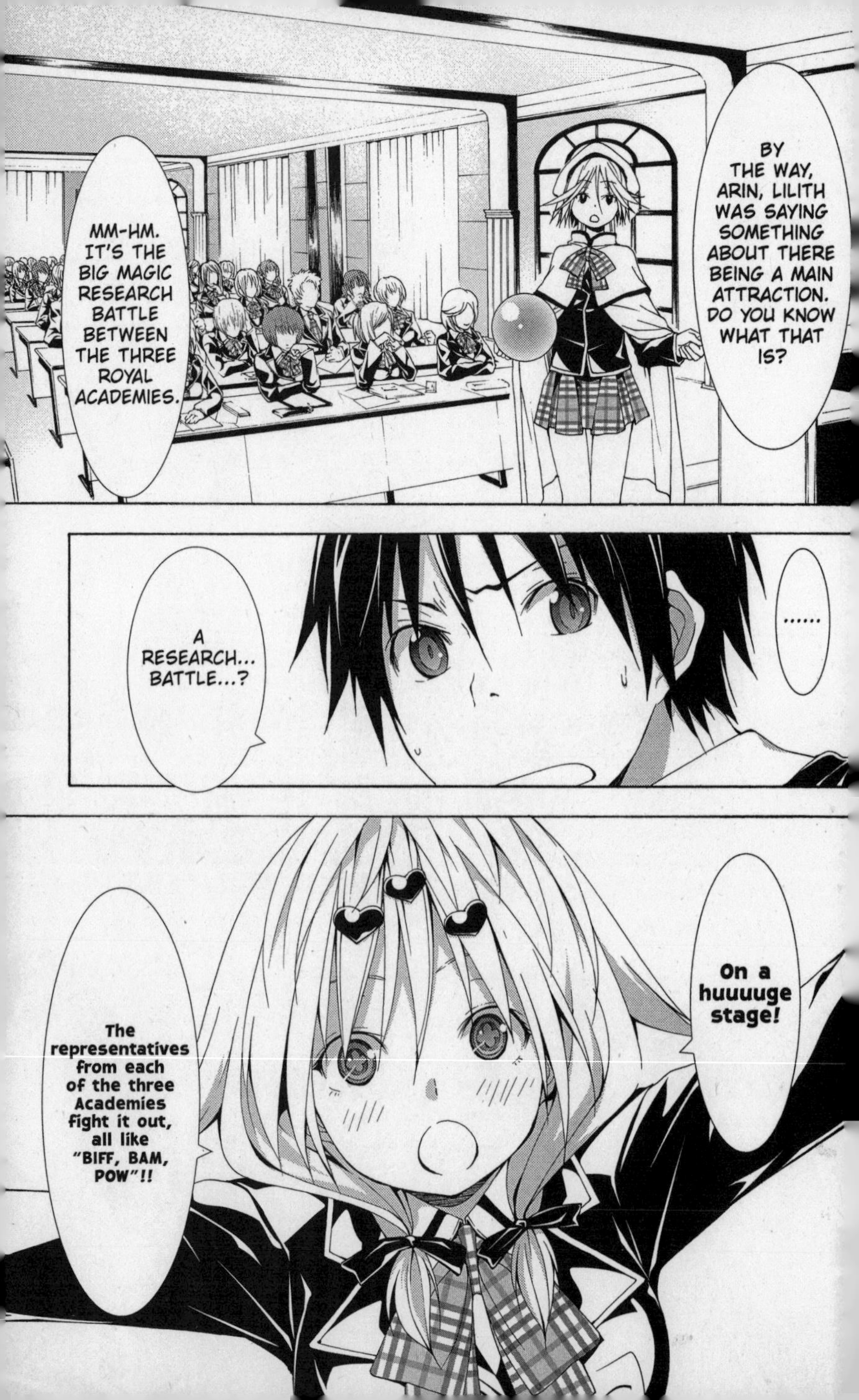
BY THE WAY, ARIN, LILITH WAS SAYING SOMETHING ABOUT THERE BEING A MAIN ATTRACTION. DO YOU KNOW WHAT THAT IS?
MM-HM. IT'S THE BIG MAGIC RESEARCH BATTLE BETWEEN THE THREE ROYAL ACADEMIES.
......
A RESEARCH... BATTLE...?
On a huuuuge stage!
The representatives from each of the three Academies fight it out, all like "BIFF, BAM, POW"!!

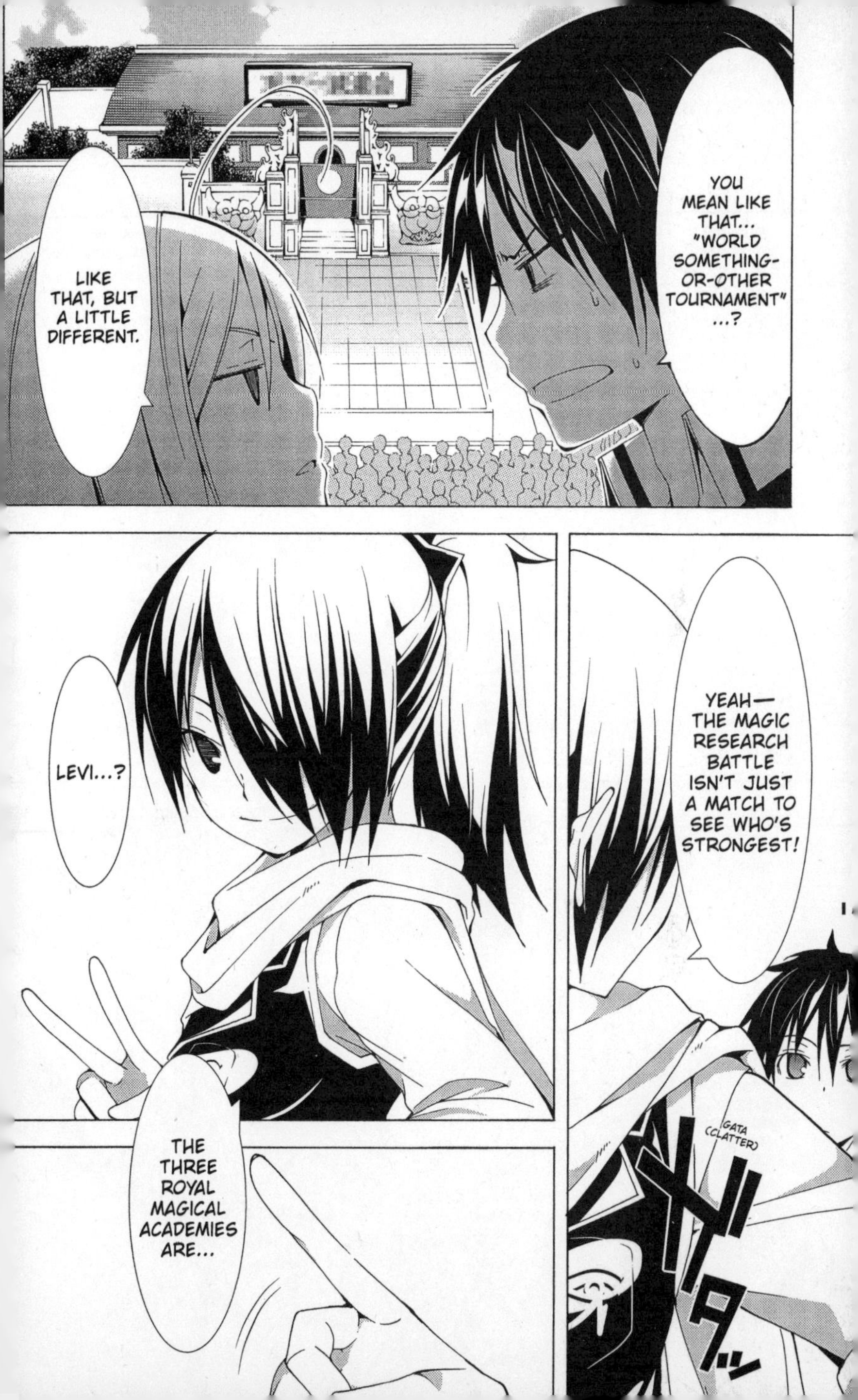
YOU MEAN LIKE THAT... "WORLD SOMETHING-OR-OTHER TOURNAMENT" ...?
LIKE THAT, BUT A LITTLE DIFFERENT.
YEAH— THE MAGIC RESEARCH BATTLE ISN'T JUST A MATCH TO SEE WHO'S STRONGEST!
GATA (CLATTER)
LEVI...?
THE THREE ROYAL MAGICAL ACADEMIES ARE...

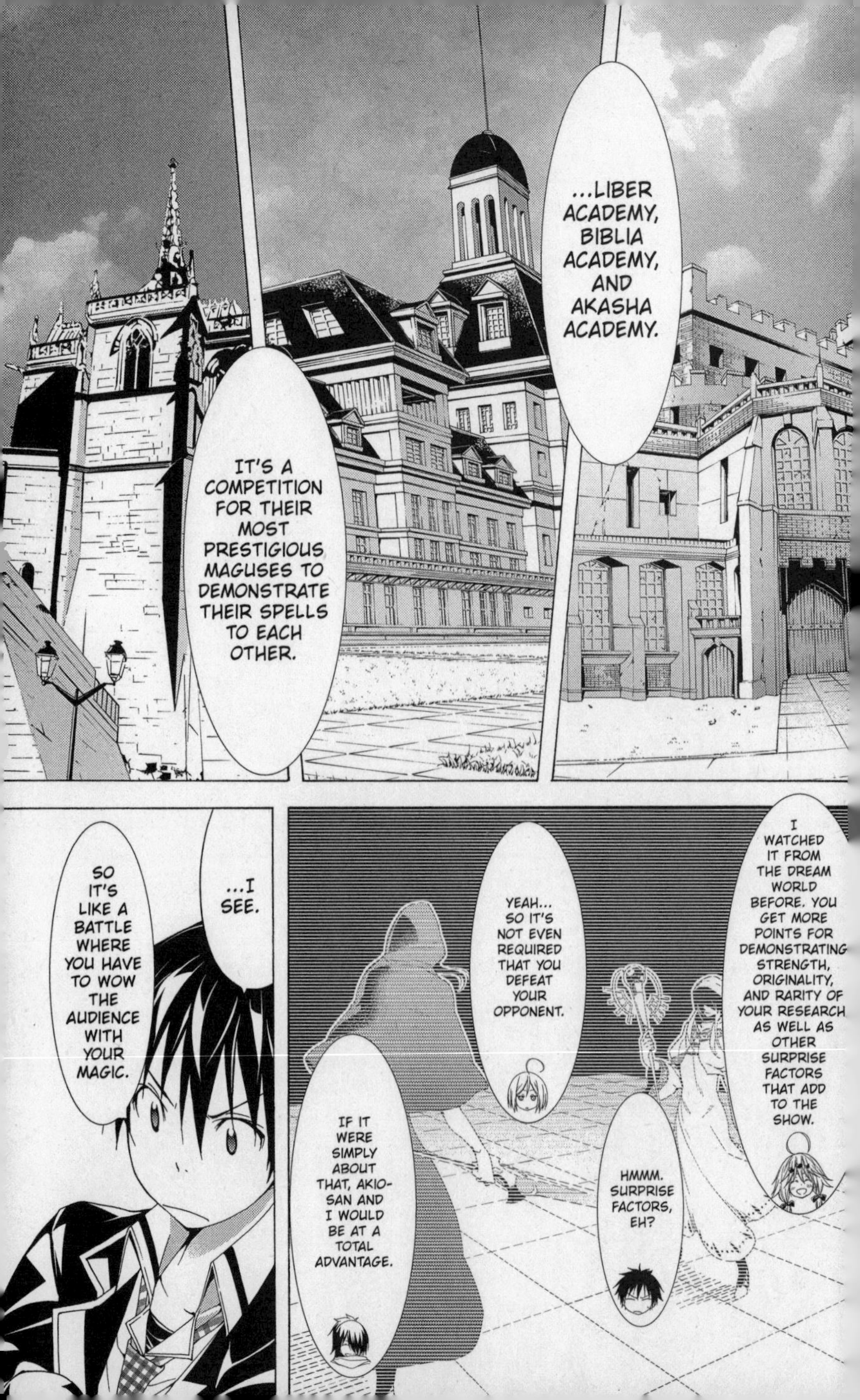
...LIBER ACADEMY, BIBLIA ACADEMY, AND AKASHA ACADEMY.
IT'S A COMPETITION FOR THEIR MOST PRESTIGIOUS MAGUSES TO DEMONSTRATE THEIR SPELLS TO EACH OTHER.
I WATCHED IT FROM THE DREAM WORLD BEFORE. YOU GET MORE POINTS FOR DEMONSTRATING STRENGTH, ORIGINALITY, AND RARITY OF YOUR RESEARCH AS WELL AS OTHER SURPRISE FACTORS THAT ADD TO THE SHOW.
YEAH... SO IT'S NOT EVEN REQUIRED THAT YOU DEFEAT YOUR OPPONENT.
HMMM. SURPRISE FACTORS, EH?
IF IT WERE SIMPLY ABOUT THAT, AKIO-SAN AND I WOULD BE AT A TOTAL ADVANTAGE.
...I SEE.
SO IT'S LIKE A BATTLE WHERE YOU HAVE TO WOW THE AUDIENCE WITH YOUR MAGIC.

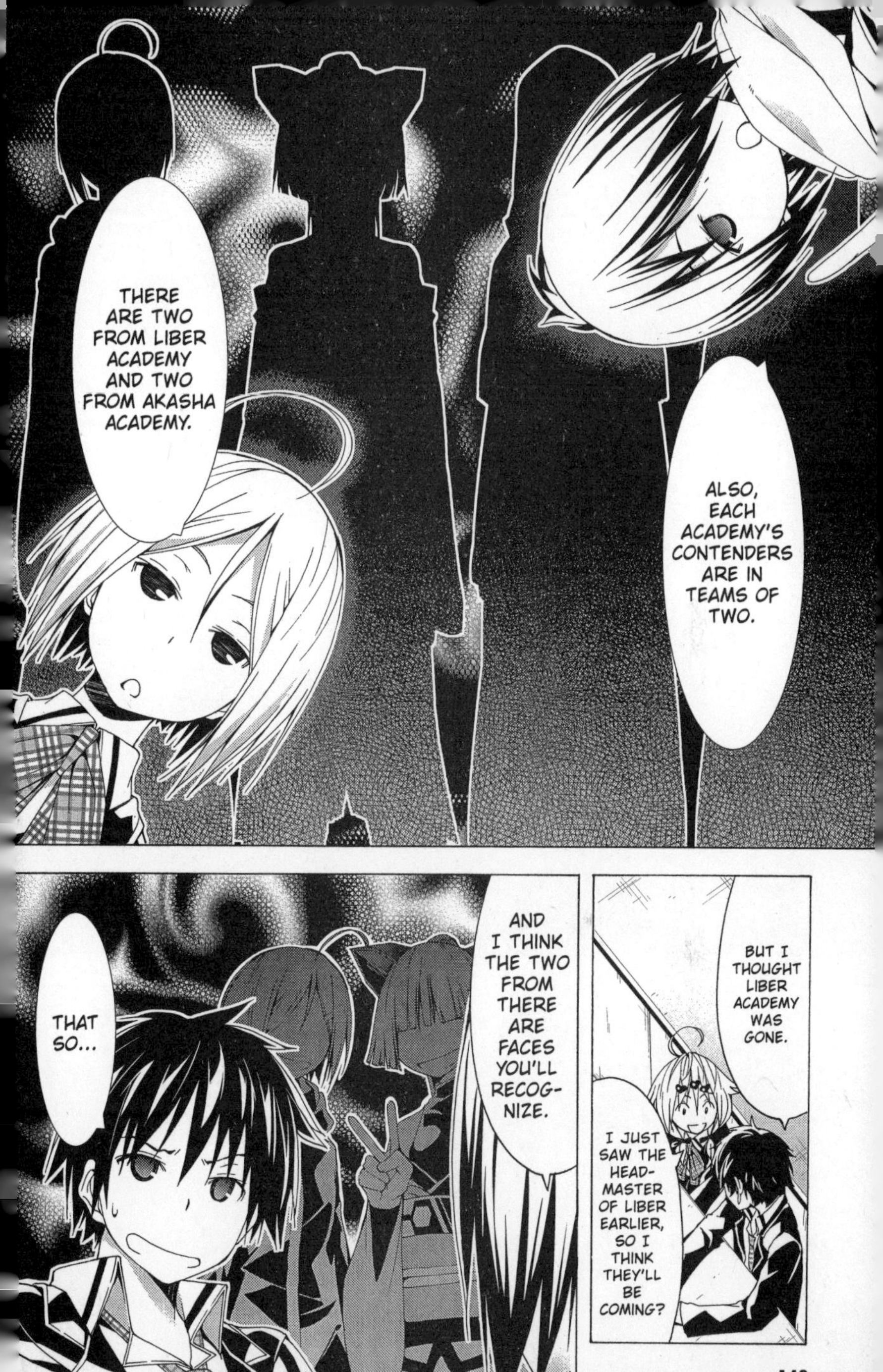
THERE ARE TWO FROM LIBER ACADEMY AND TWO FROM AKASHA ACADEMY.
ALSO, EACH ACADEMY'S CONTENDERS ARE IN TEAMS OF TWO.
BUT I THOUGHT LIBER ACADEMY WAS GONE.
I JUST SAW THE HEAD-MASTER OF LIBER EARLIER, SO I THINK THEY'LL BE COMING?
AND I THINK THE TWO FROM THERE ARE FACES YOU'LL RECOG-NIZE.
THAT SO...

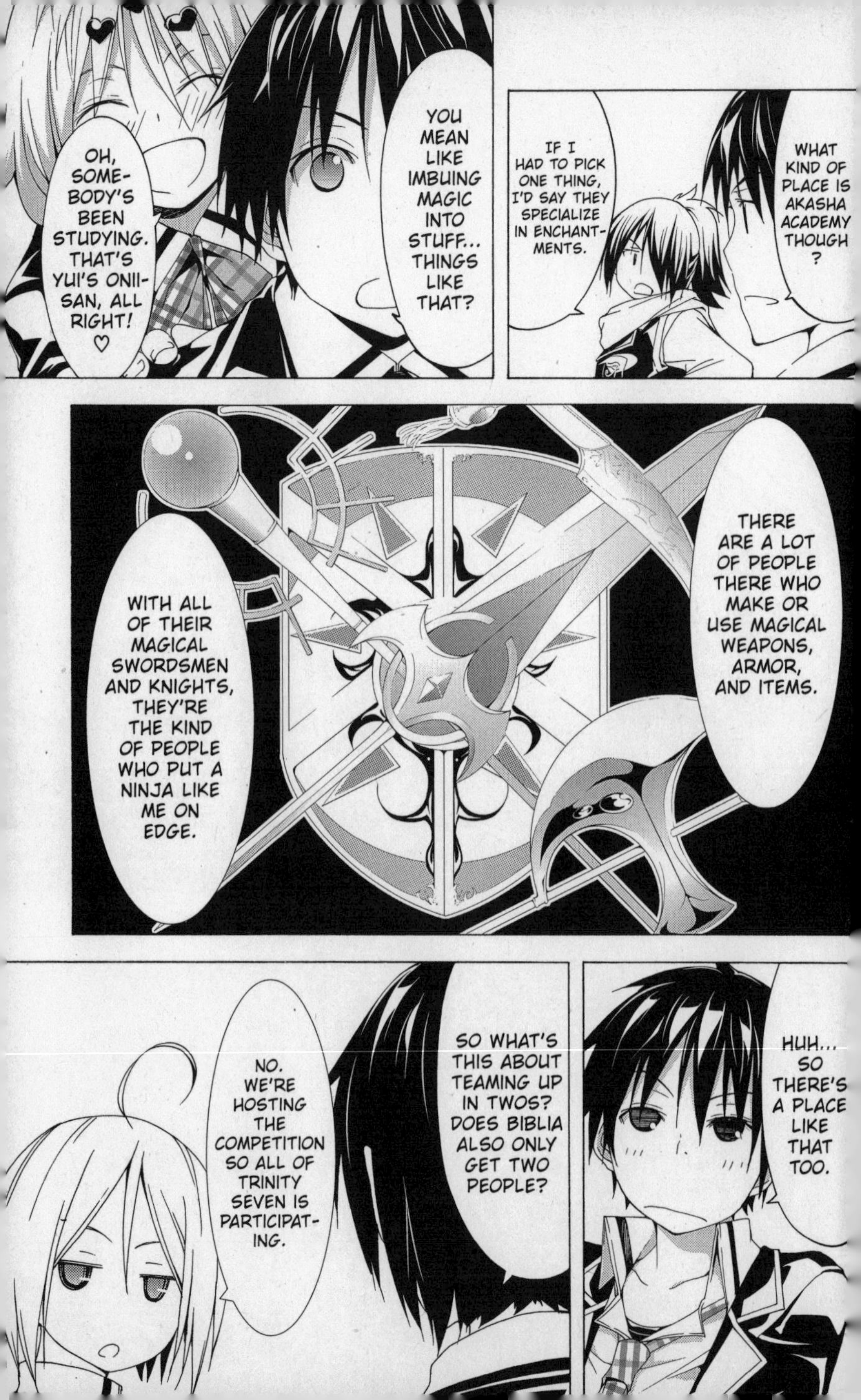
WHAT KIND OF PLACE IS AKASHA ACADEMY THOUGH?
IF I HAD TO PICK ONE THING, I'D SAY THEY SPECIALIZE IN ENCHANTMENTS.
YOU MEAN LIKE IMBUING MAGIC INTO STUFF... THINGS LIKE THAT?
OH, SOMEBODY'S BEEN STUDYING. THAT'S YUI'S ONII-SAN, ALL RIGHT! ♡
THERE ARE A LOT OF PEOPLE THERE WHO MAKE OR USE MAGICAL WEAPONS, ARMOR, AND ITEMS.
WITH ALL OF THEIR MAGICAL SWORDSMEN AND KNIGHTS, THEY'RE THE KIND OF PEOPLE WHO PUT A NINJA LIKE ME ON EDGE.
HUH... SO THERE'S A PLACE LIKE THAT TOO.
SO WHAT'S THIS ABOUT TEAMING UP IN TWOS? DOES BIBLIA ALSO ONLY GET TWO PEOPLE?
NO. WE'RE HOSTING THE COMPETITION SO ALL OF TRINITY SEVEN IS PARTICIPATING.

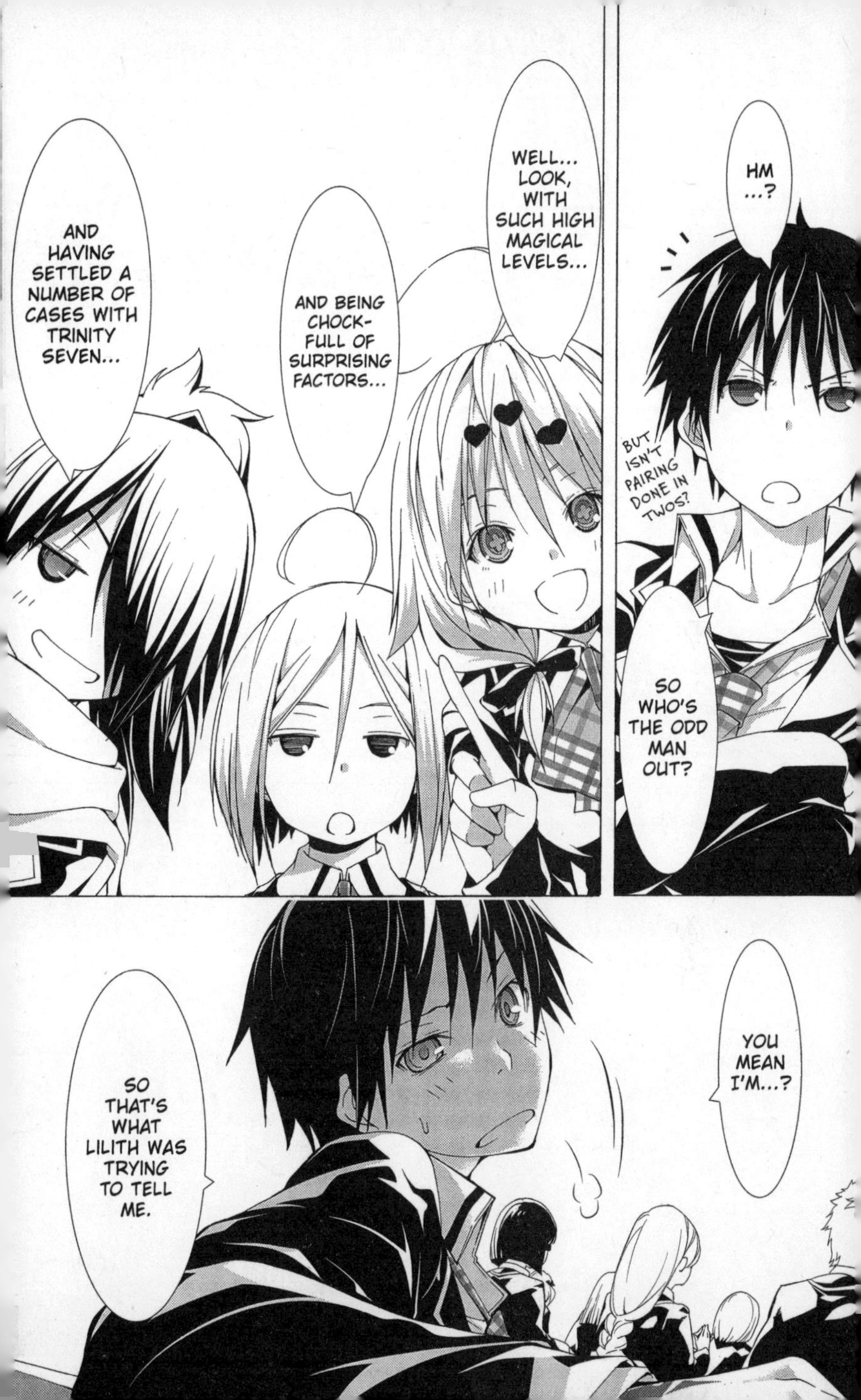
HM ...?
BUT ISN'T PAIRING DONE IN TWOS?
SO WHO'S THE ODD MAN OUT?
WELL... LOOK, WITH SUCH HIGH MAGICAL LEVELS...
AND BEING CHOCK-FULL OF SURPRISING FACTORS...
AND HAVING SETTLED A NUMBER OF CASES WITH TRINITY SEVEN...
YOU MEAN I'M...?
SO THAT'S WHAT LILITH WAS TRYING TO TELL ME.

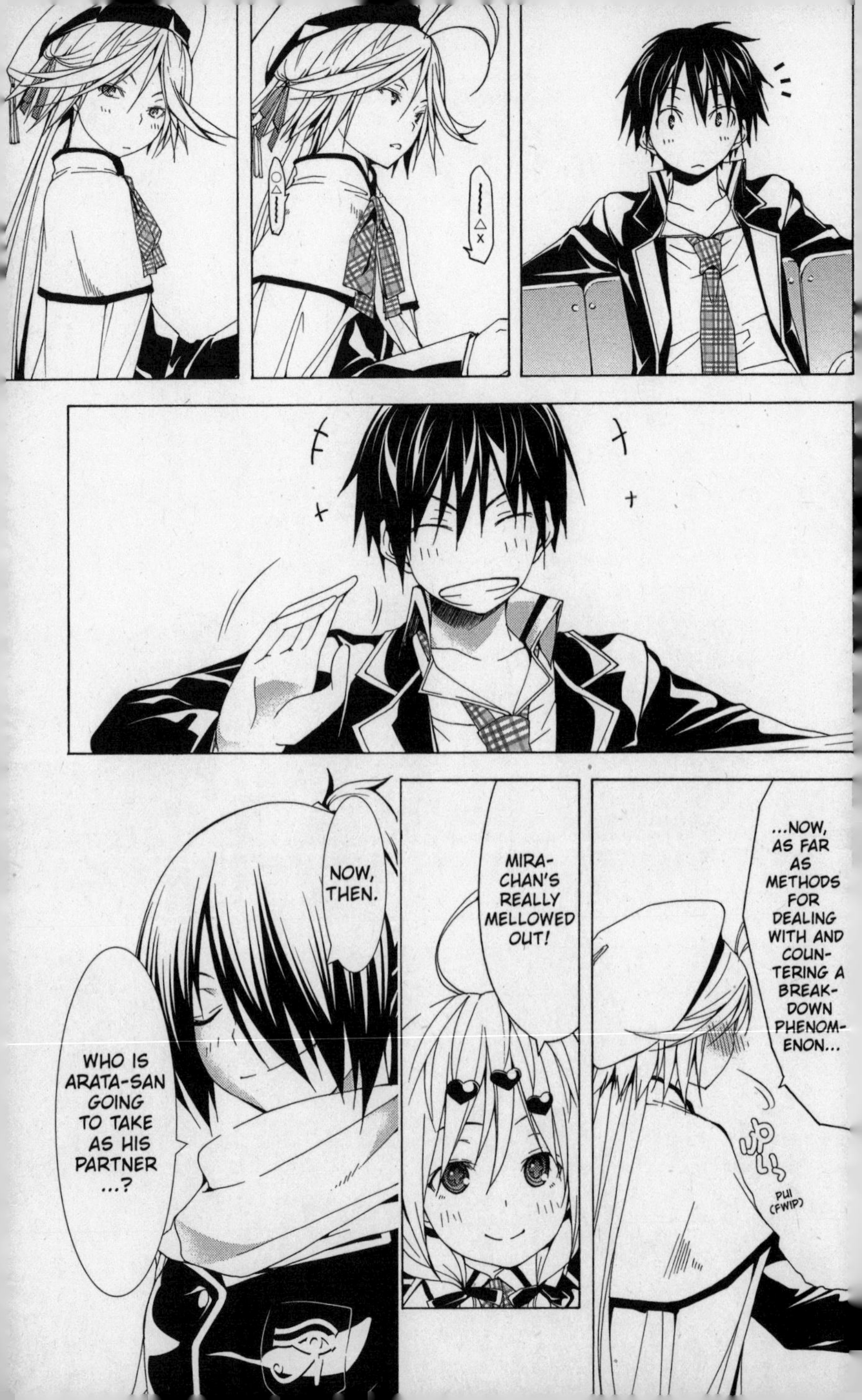
...NOW, AS FAR AS METHODS FOR DEALING WITH AND COUNTERING A BREAKDOWN PHENOMENON...
PUI (FWIP)
MIRA-CHAN'S REALLY MELLOWED OUT!
NOW, THEN.
WHO IS ARATA-SAN GOING TO TAKE AS HIS PARTNER ...?

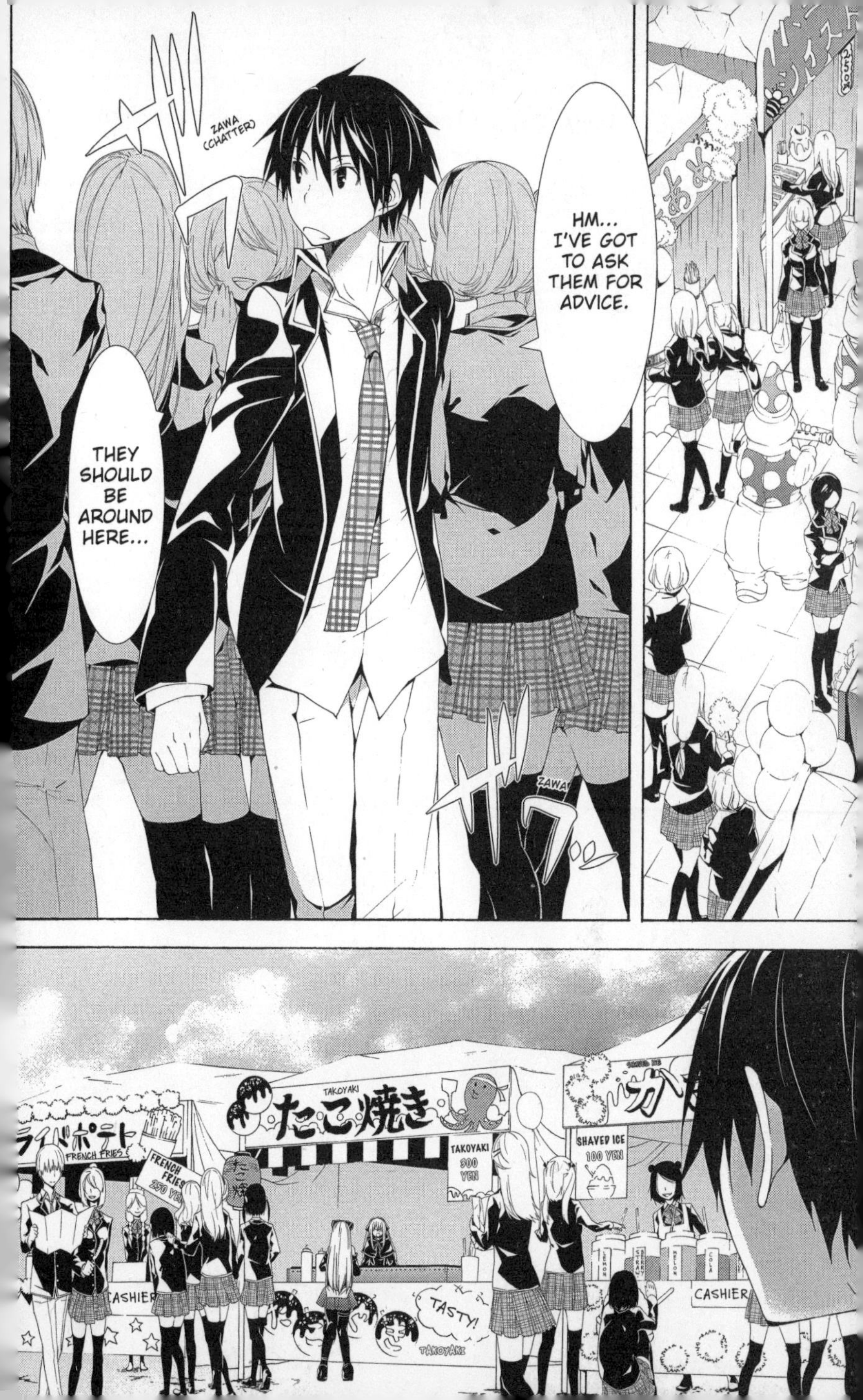
ZAWA (CHATTER)
HM... I'VE GOT TO ASK THEM FOR ADVICE.
THEY SHOULD BE AROUND HERE...
ZAWA
SHAVED ICE
SHAVED ICE 100 YEN
LEMON
STRAWBERRY
MELON
COLA
CASHIER
TAKOYAKI
たこ焼き
TAKOYAKI 300 YEN
TASTY!
TAKOYAKI
FRENCH FRIES
FRENCH FRIES 250 YEN

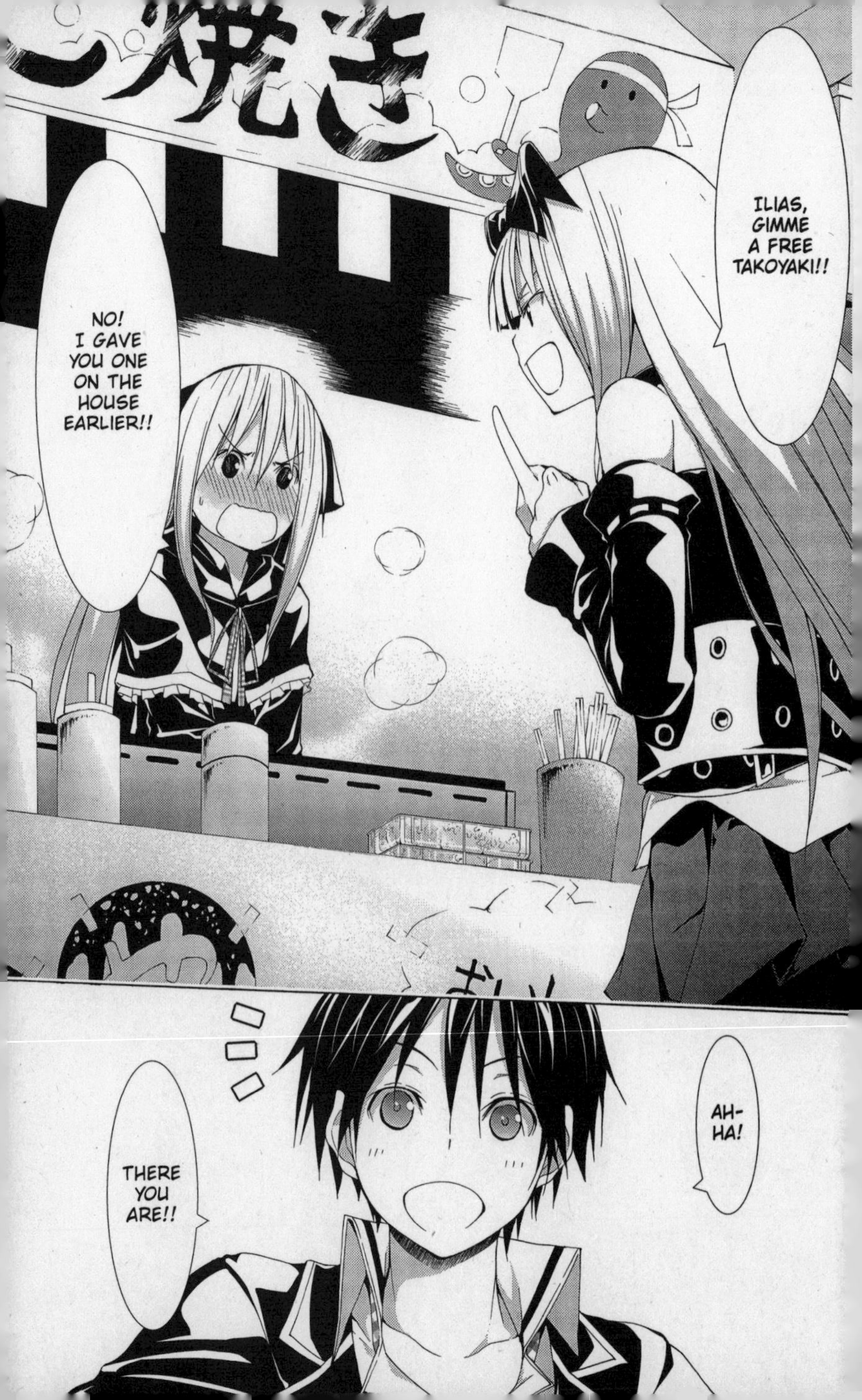

焼き
ILIAS, GIMME A FREE TAKOYAKI!!
NO! I GAVE YOU ONE ON THE HOUSE EARLIER!!
AH-HA!
THERE YOU ARE!!

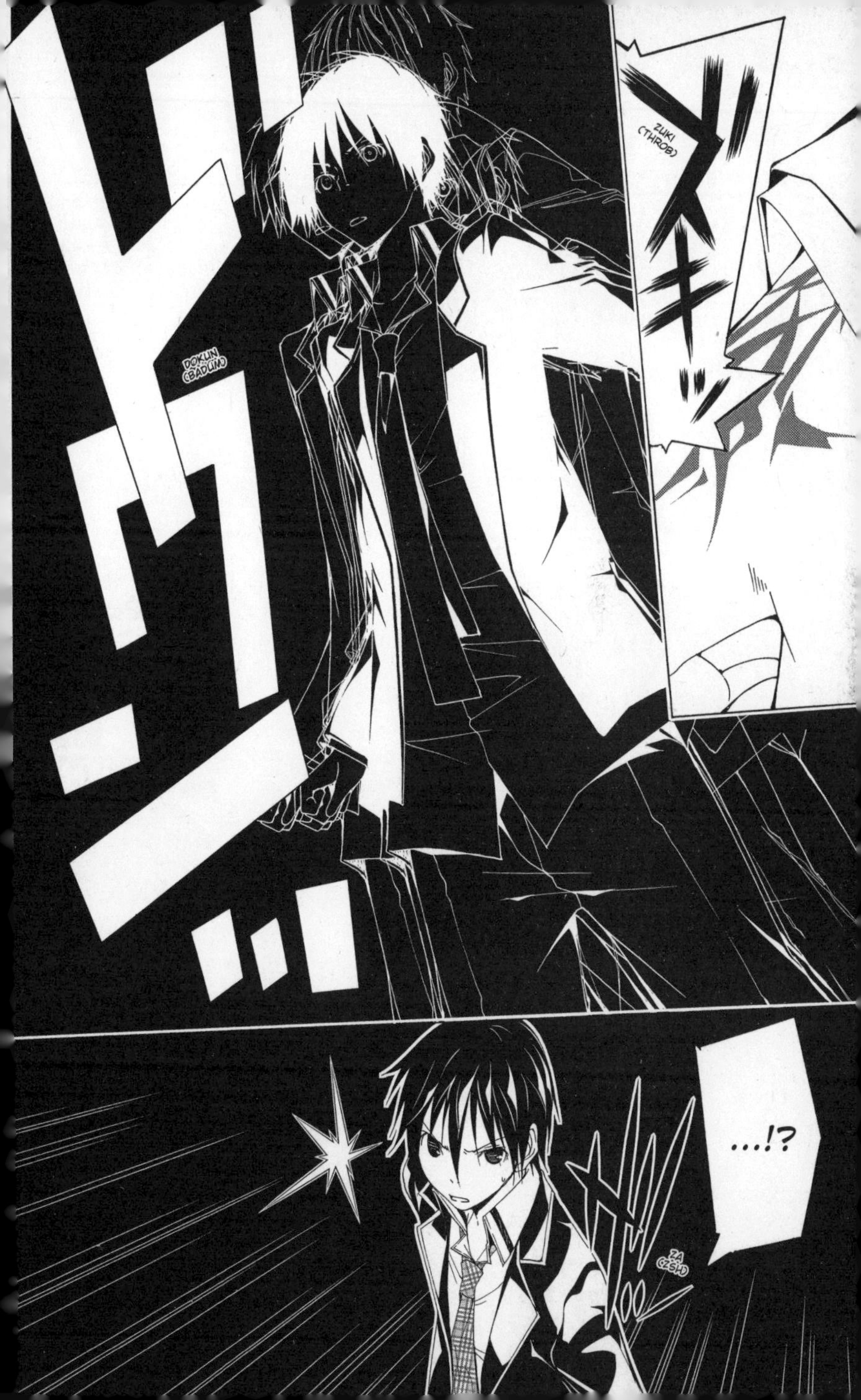
ZUKI (THROB)
DOKUN (BADUM)
...!?
ZA (ZSHD)

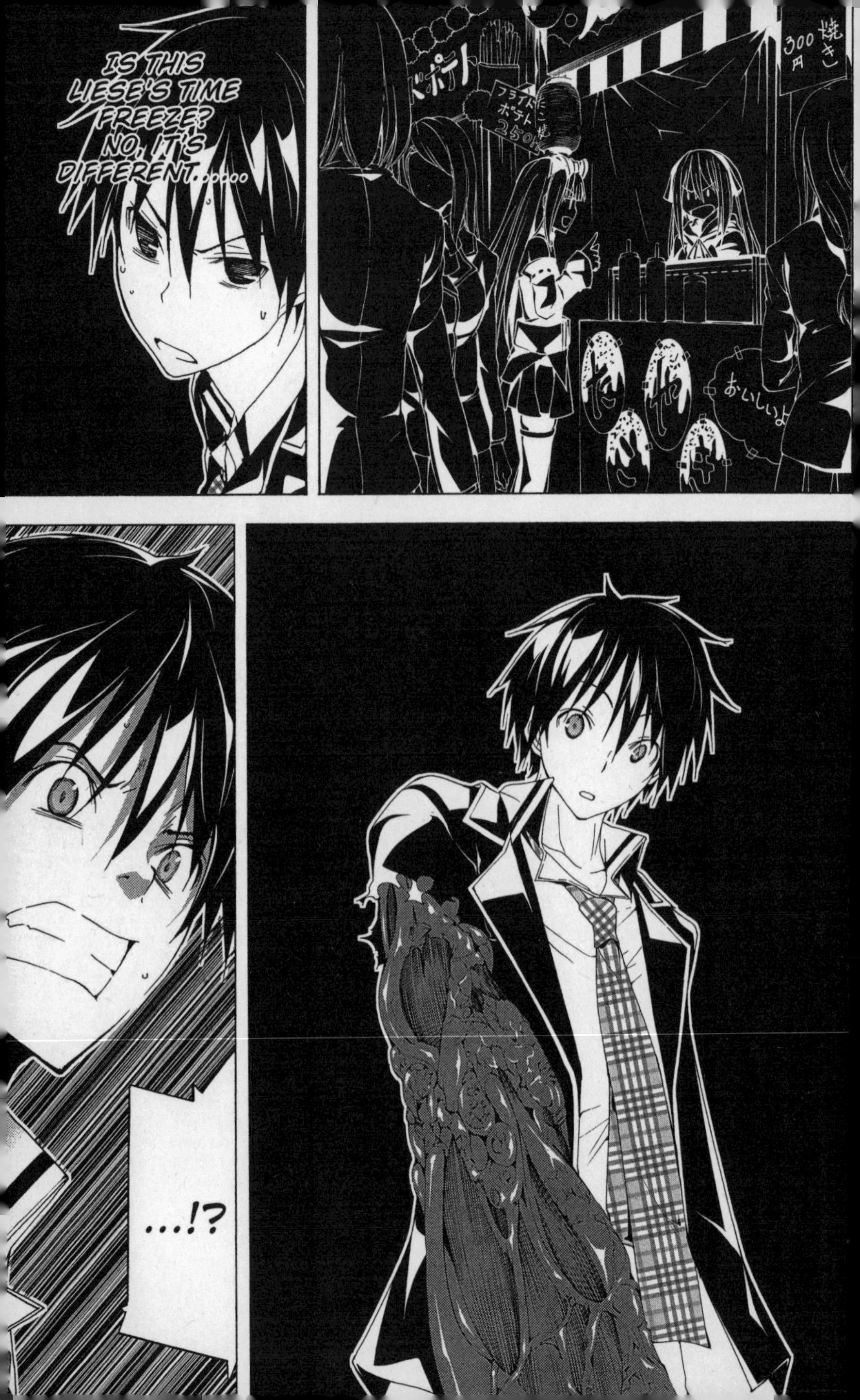
焼き 300円
ポテト
フライドポテト 250円
おいしいよ
IS THIS LIESE'S TIME FREEZE? NO, IT'S DIFFERENT......
...!?

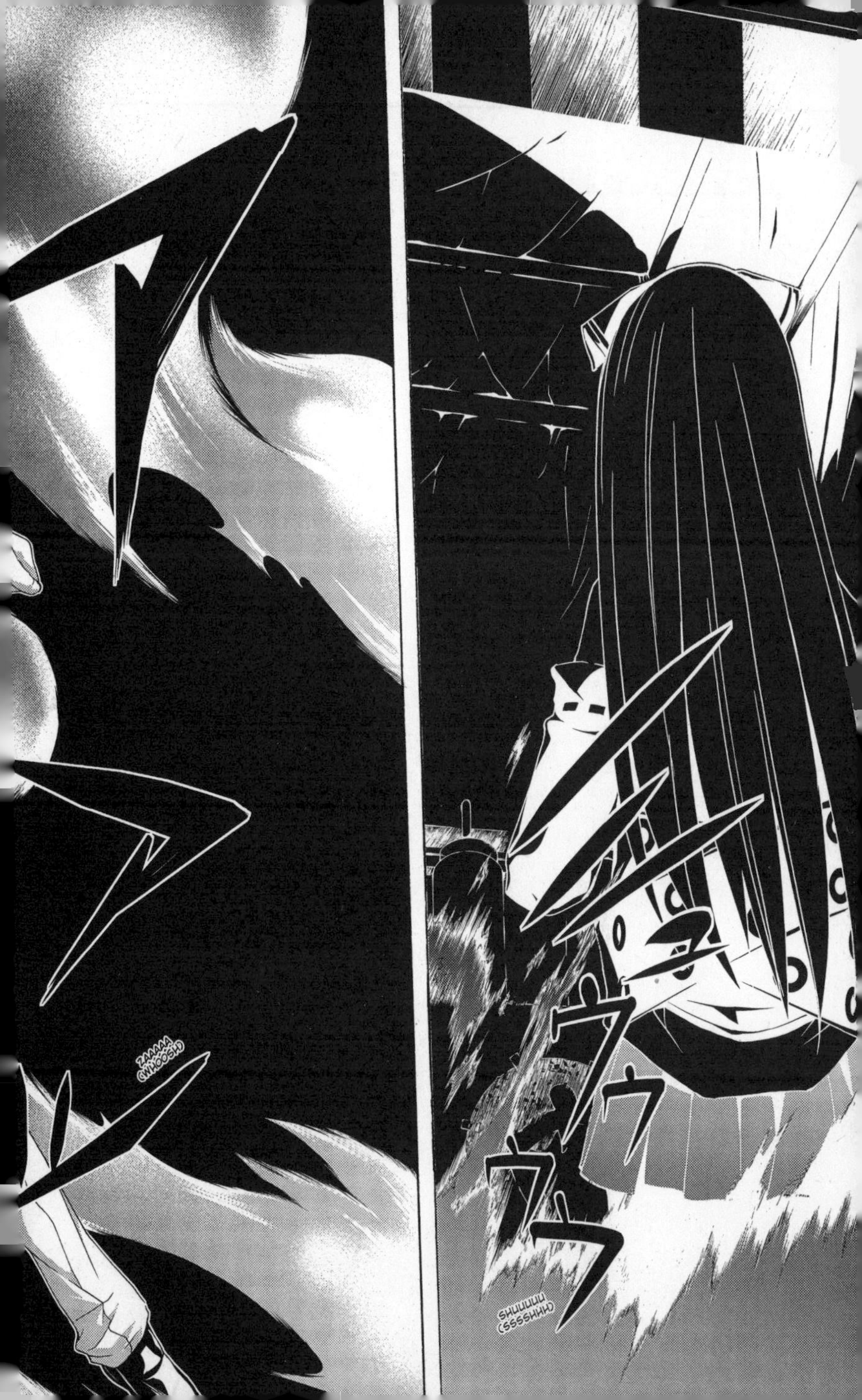
SHUUUUU
(SSSSHHH)
ZAAAAA
(WHOOSH)

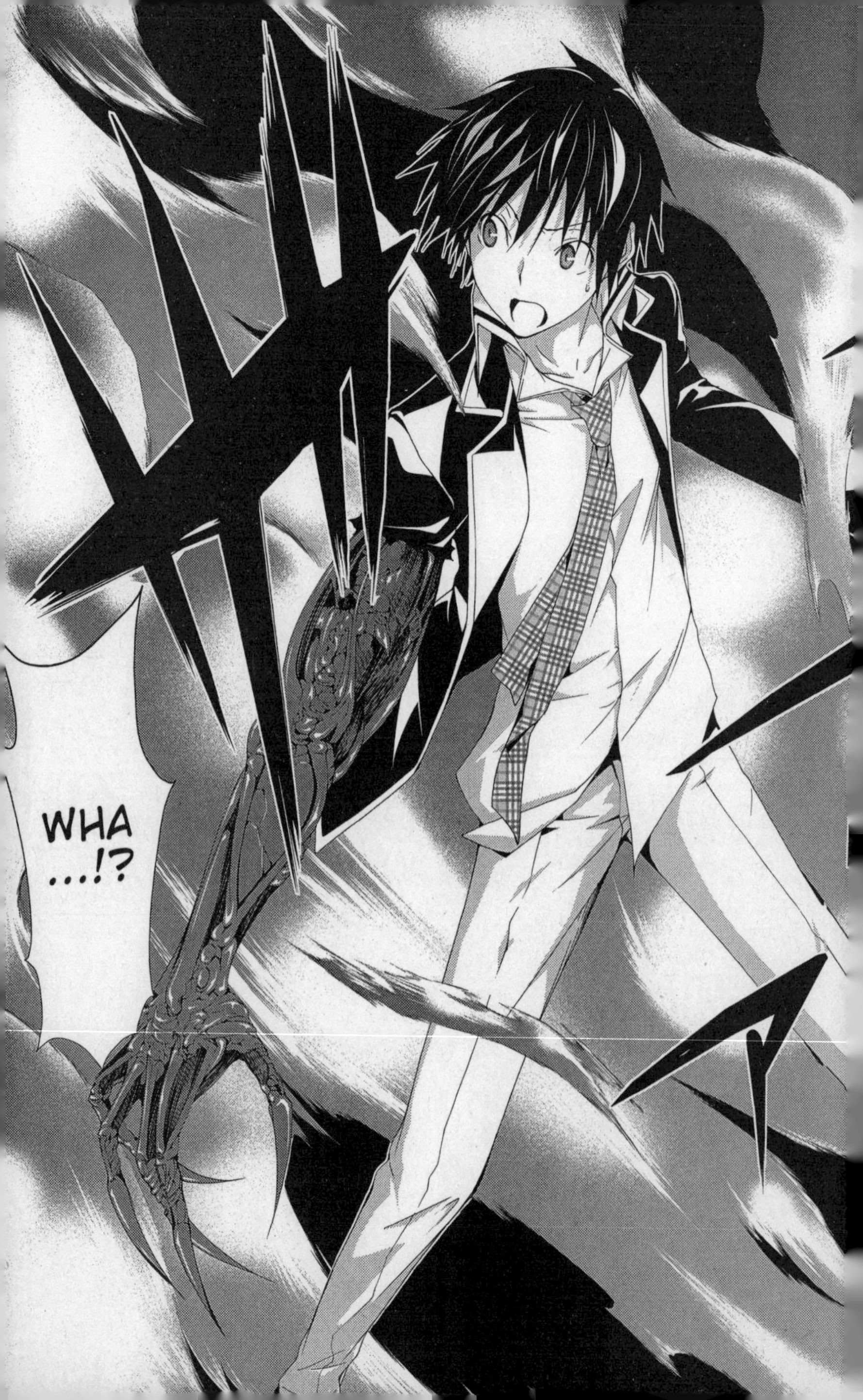
WHA ...!?

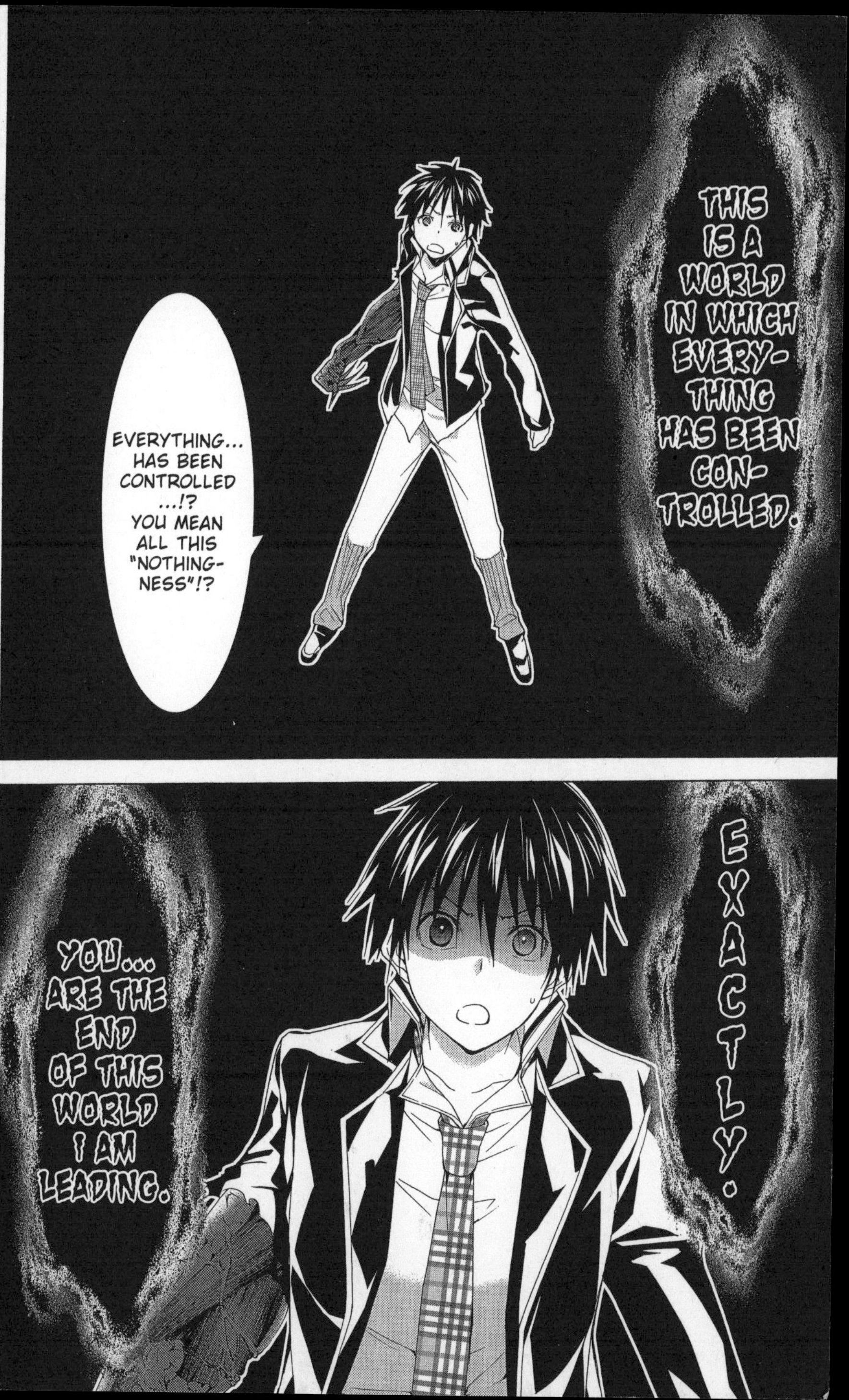
THIS IS A WORLD IN WHICH EVERY-THING HAS BEEN CON-TROLLED.
EVERYTHING... HAS BEEN CONTROLLED ...!? YOU MEAN ALL THIS "NOTHING-NESS"!?
EXACTLY.
YOU... ARE THE END OF THIS WORLD I AM LEADING.

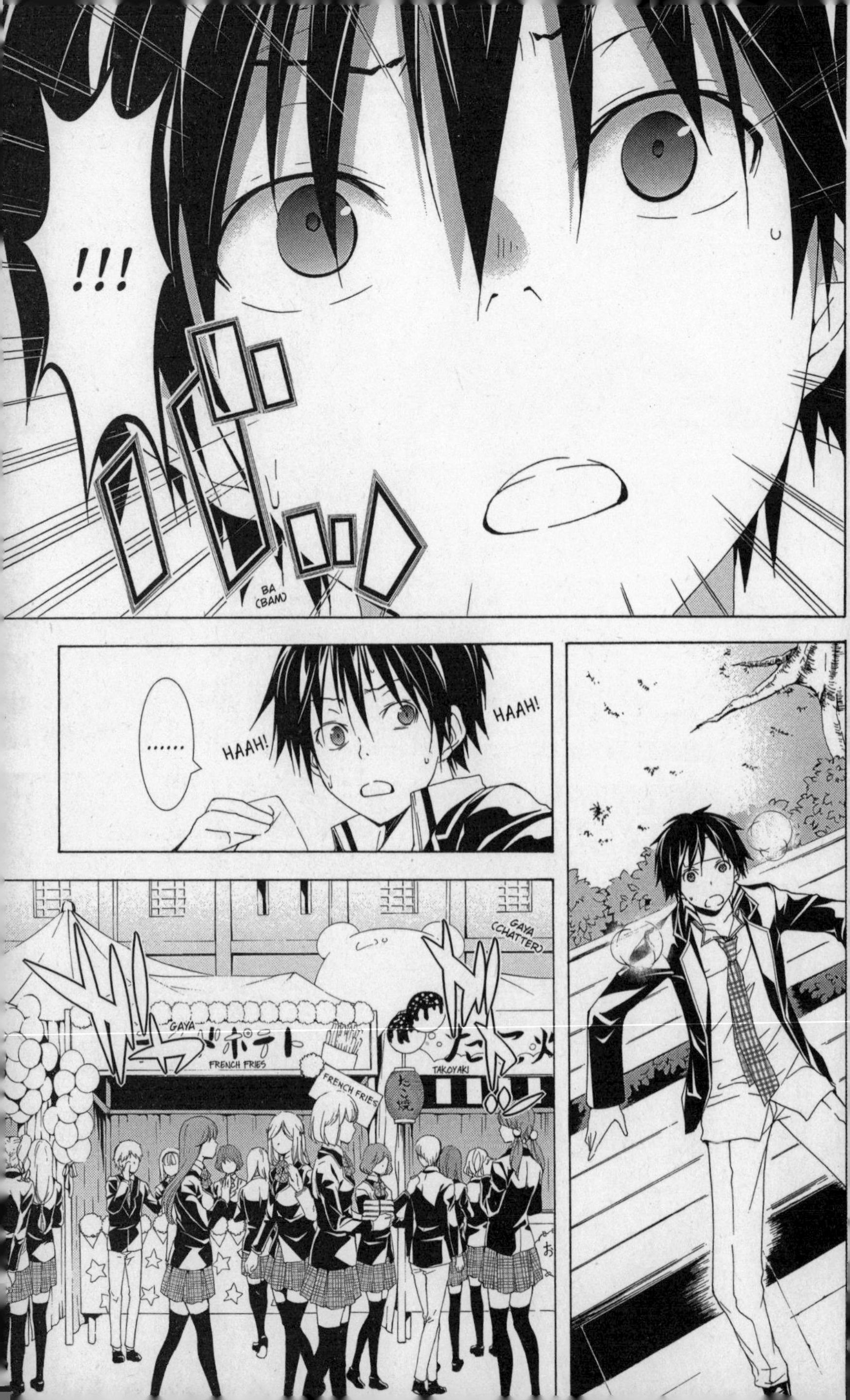
!!!
BA
(BAM)
HAAH!
HAAH!
......
GAYA
(CHATTER)
TAKOYAKI
FRENCH FRIES
GAYA
FRENCH FRIES

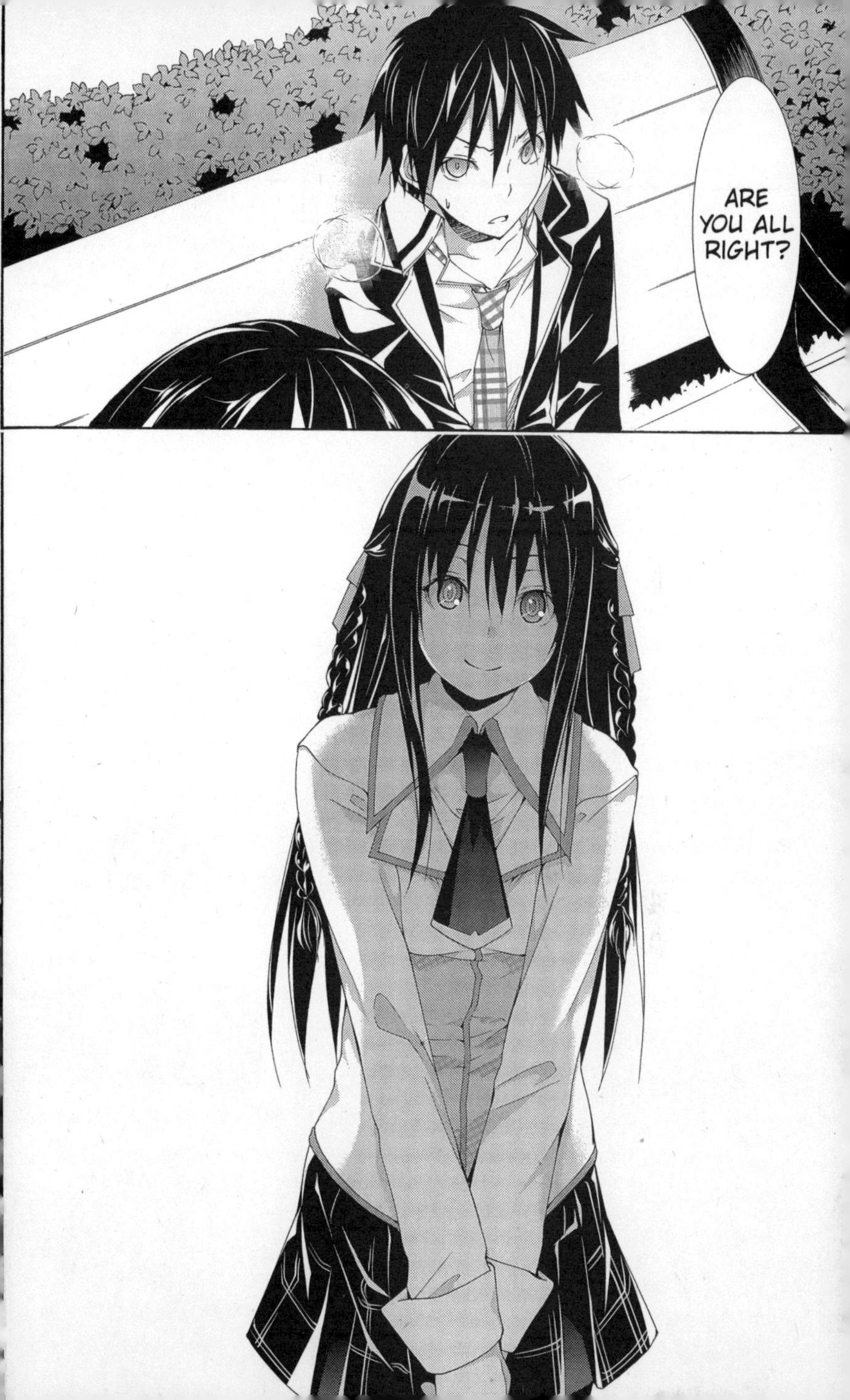
ARE YOU ALL RIGHT?

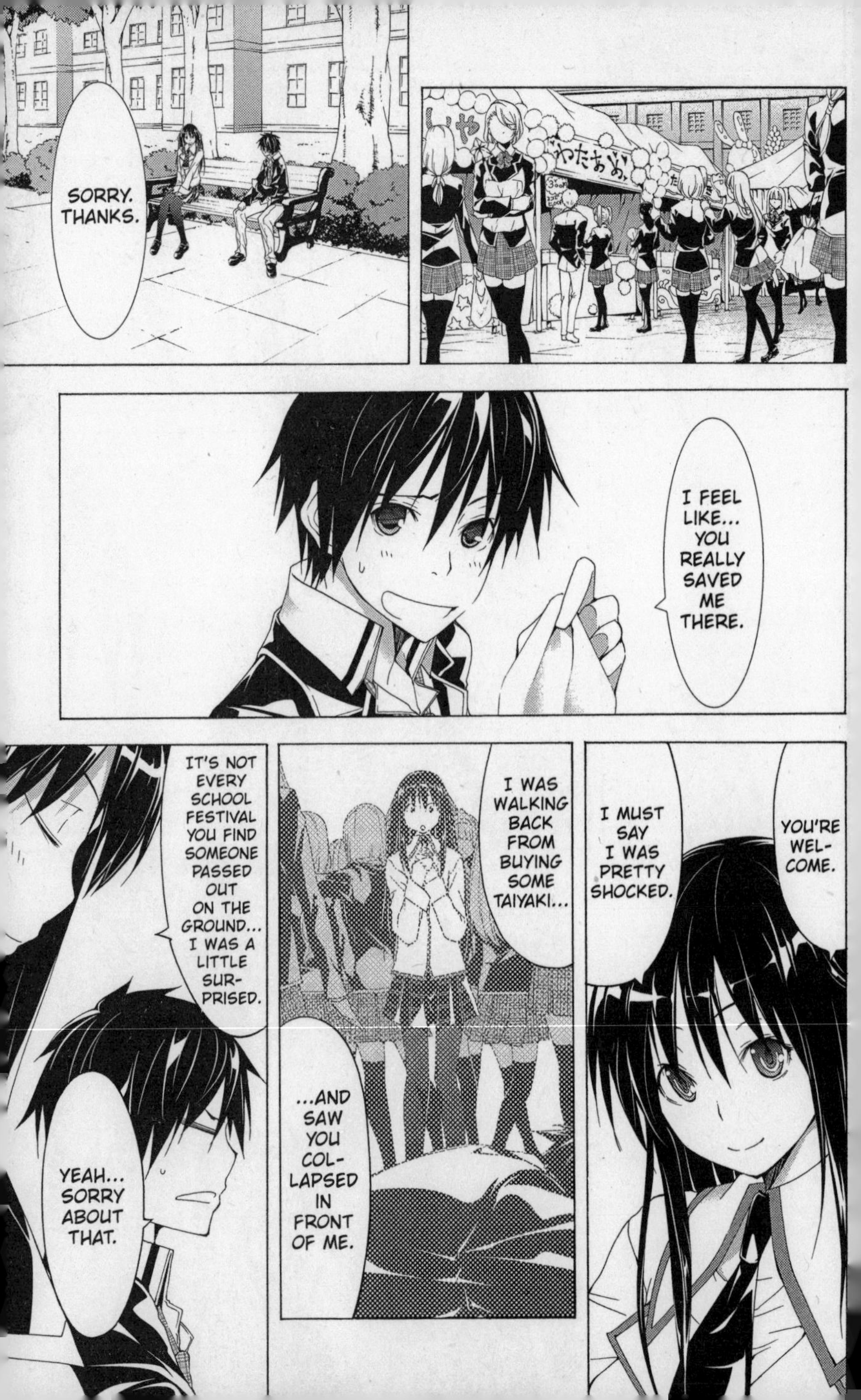
SORRY. THANKS.
I FEEL LIKE... YOU REALLY SAVED ME THERE.
YOU'RE WEL-COME.
I MUST SAY I WAS PRETTY SHOCKED.
I WAS WALKING BACK FROM BUYING SOME TAIYAKI...
...AND SAW YOU COL-LAPSED IN FRONT OF ME.
IT'S NOT EVERY SCHOOL FESTIVAL YOU FIND SOMEONE PASSED OUT ON THE GROUND... I WAS A LITTLE SUR-PRISED.
YEAH... SORRY ABOUT THAT.

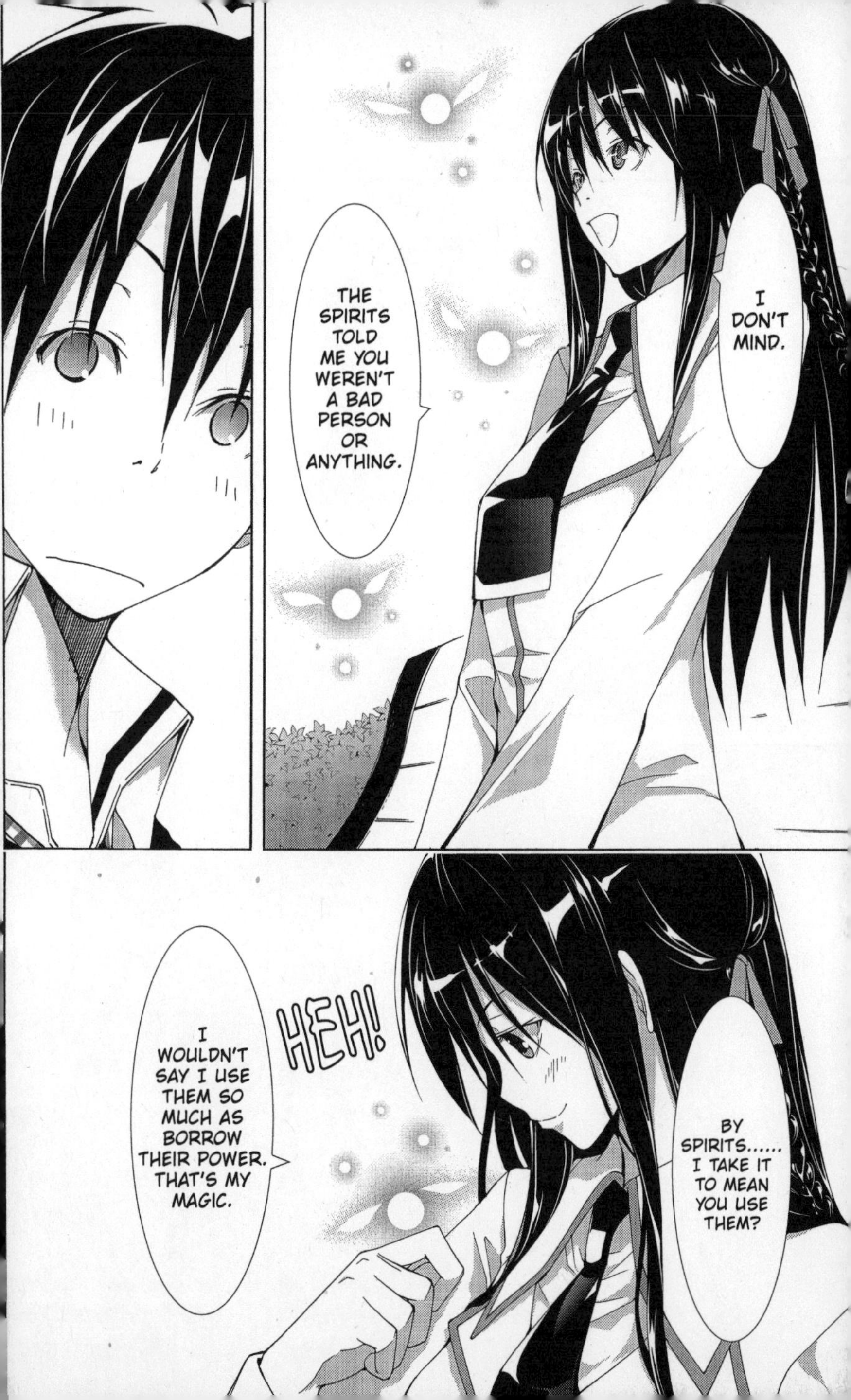
I DON'T MIND.
THE SPIRITS TOLD ME YOU WEREN'T A BAD PERSON OR ANYTHING.
BY SPIRITS...... I TAKE IT TO MEAN YOU USE THEM?
HEH!
I WOULDN'T SAY I USE THEM SO MUCH AS BORROW THEIR POWER. THAT'S MY MAGIC.

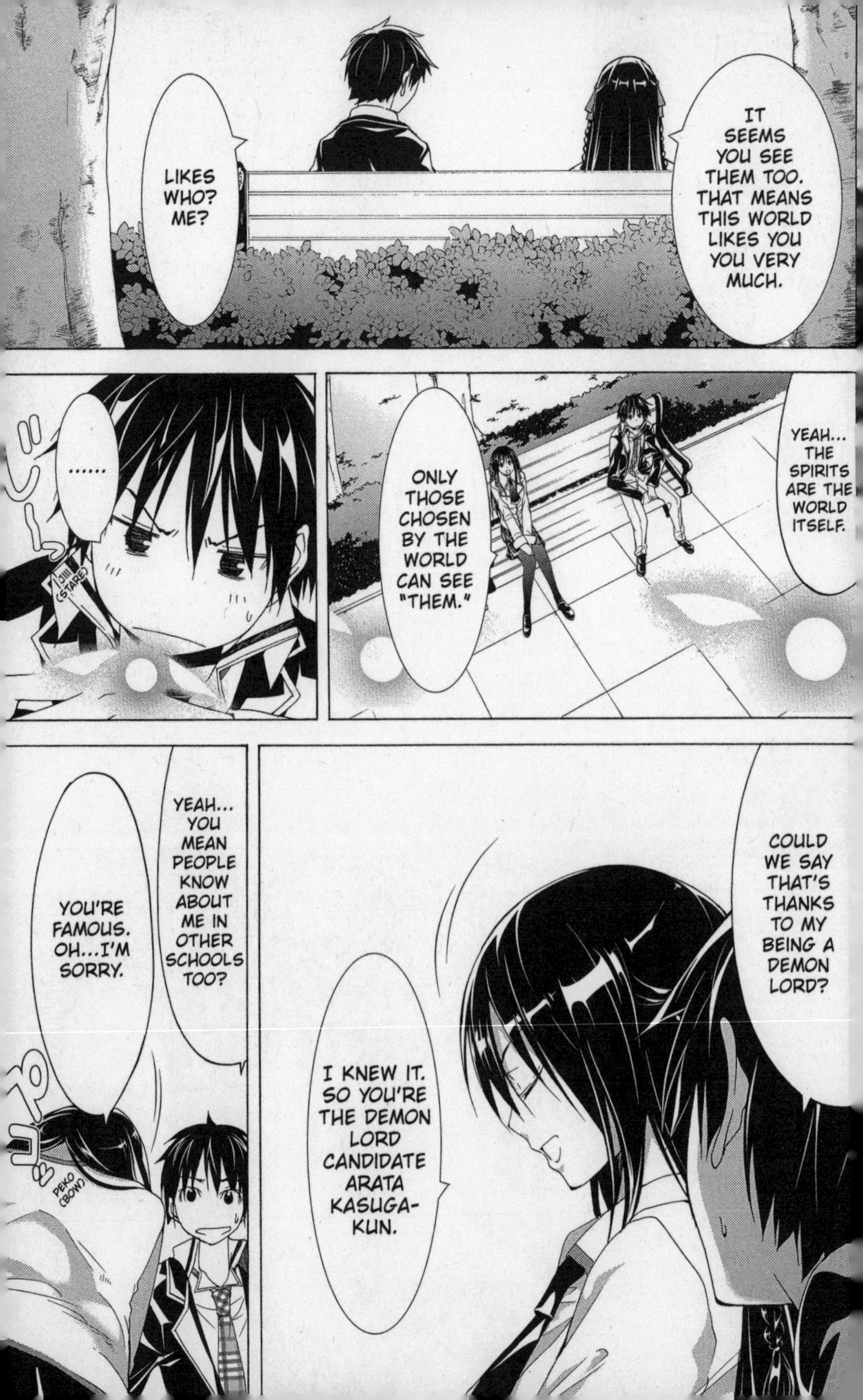
IT SEEMS YOU SEE THEM TOO. THAT MEANS THIS WORLD LIKES YOU YOU VERY MUCH.
LIKES WHO? ME?
YEAH... THE SPIRITS ARE THE WORLD ITSELF.
ONLY THOSE CHOSEN BY THE WORLD CAN SEE "THEM."
......
JIII (STARE)
COULD WE SAY THAT'S THANKS TO MY BEING A DEMON LORD?
I KNEW IT. SO YOU'RE THE DEMON LORD CANDIDATE ARATA KASUGA-KUN.
YEAH... YOU MEAN PEOPLE KNOW ABOUT ME IN OTHER SCHOOLS TOO?
YOU'RE FAMOUS. OH...I'M SORRY.
PEKO (BOW)

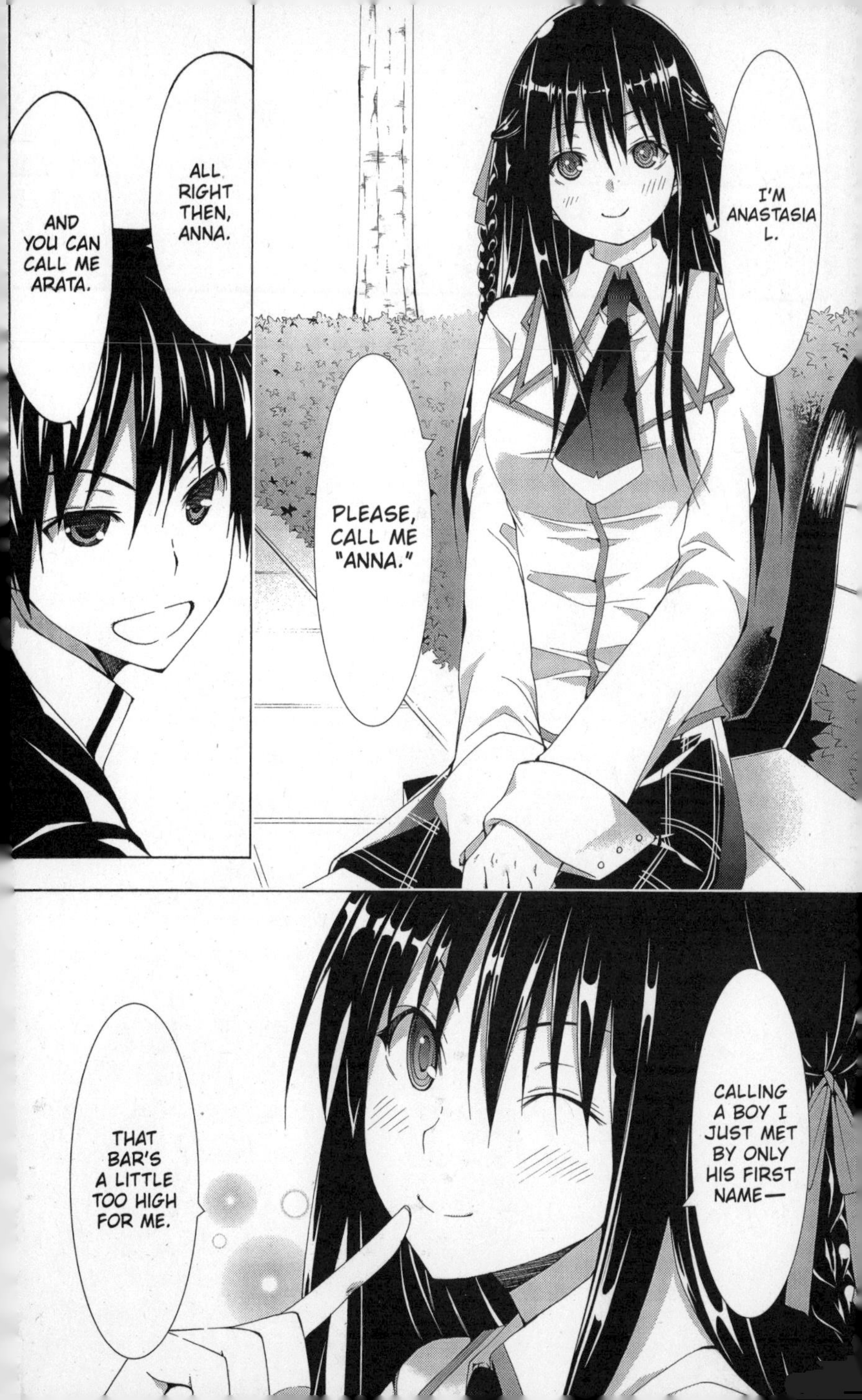
I'M ANASTASIA L.
PLEASE, CALL ME "ANNA."
ALL RIGHT THEN, ANNA.
AND YOU CAN CALL ME ARATA.
CALLING A BOY I JUST MET BY ONLY HIS FIRST NAME—
THAT BAR'S A LITTLE TOO HIGH FOR ME.

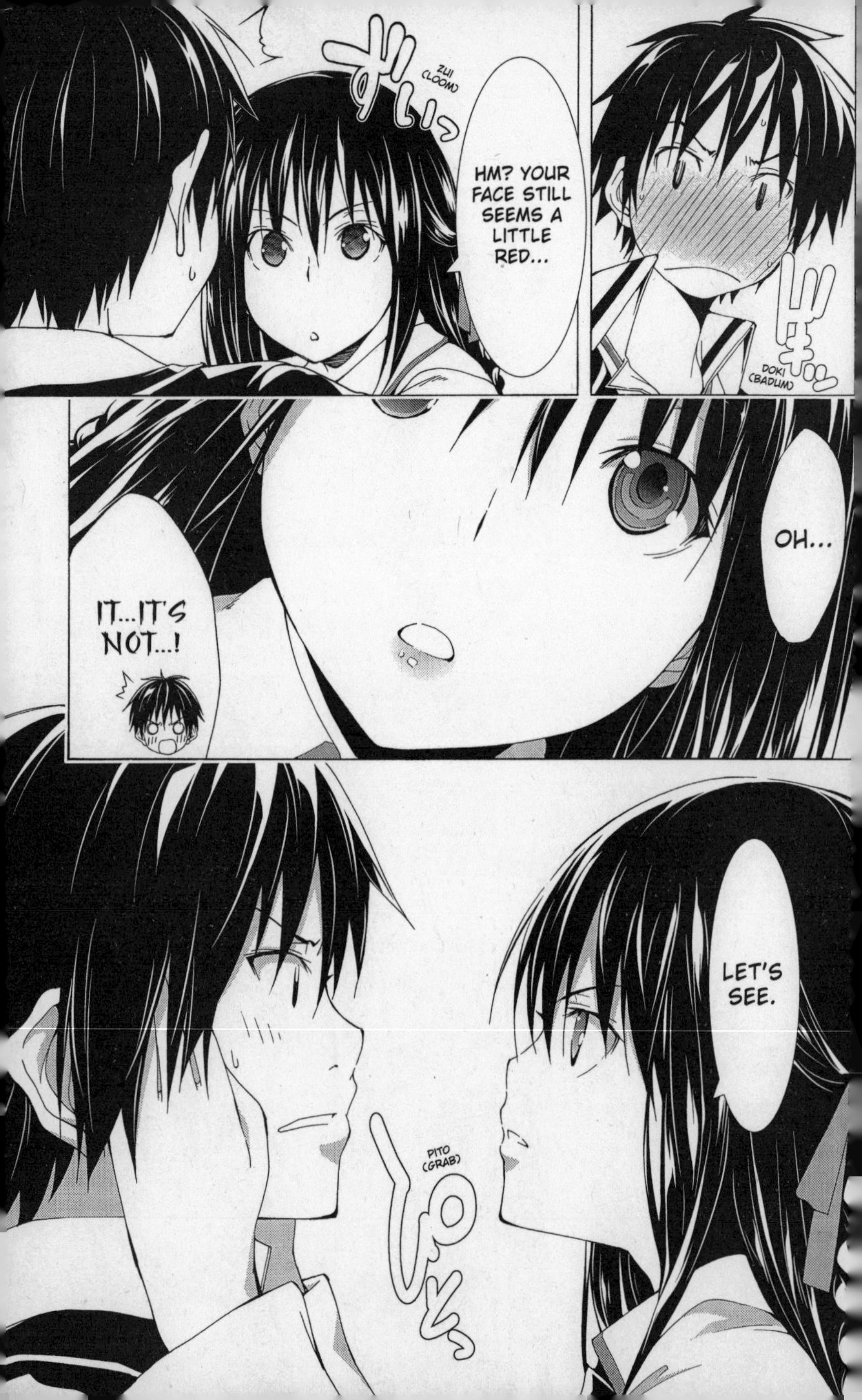
DOKI (BADUM)
ZUI (LOOM)
HM? YOUR FACE STILL SEEMS A LITTLE RED...
OH...
IT...IT'S NOT...!
LET'S SEE.
PITO (GRAB)

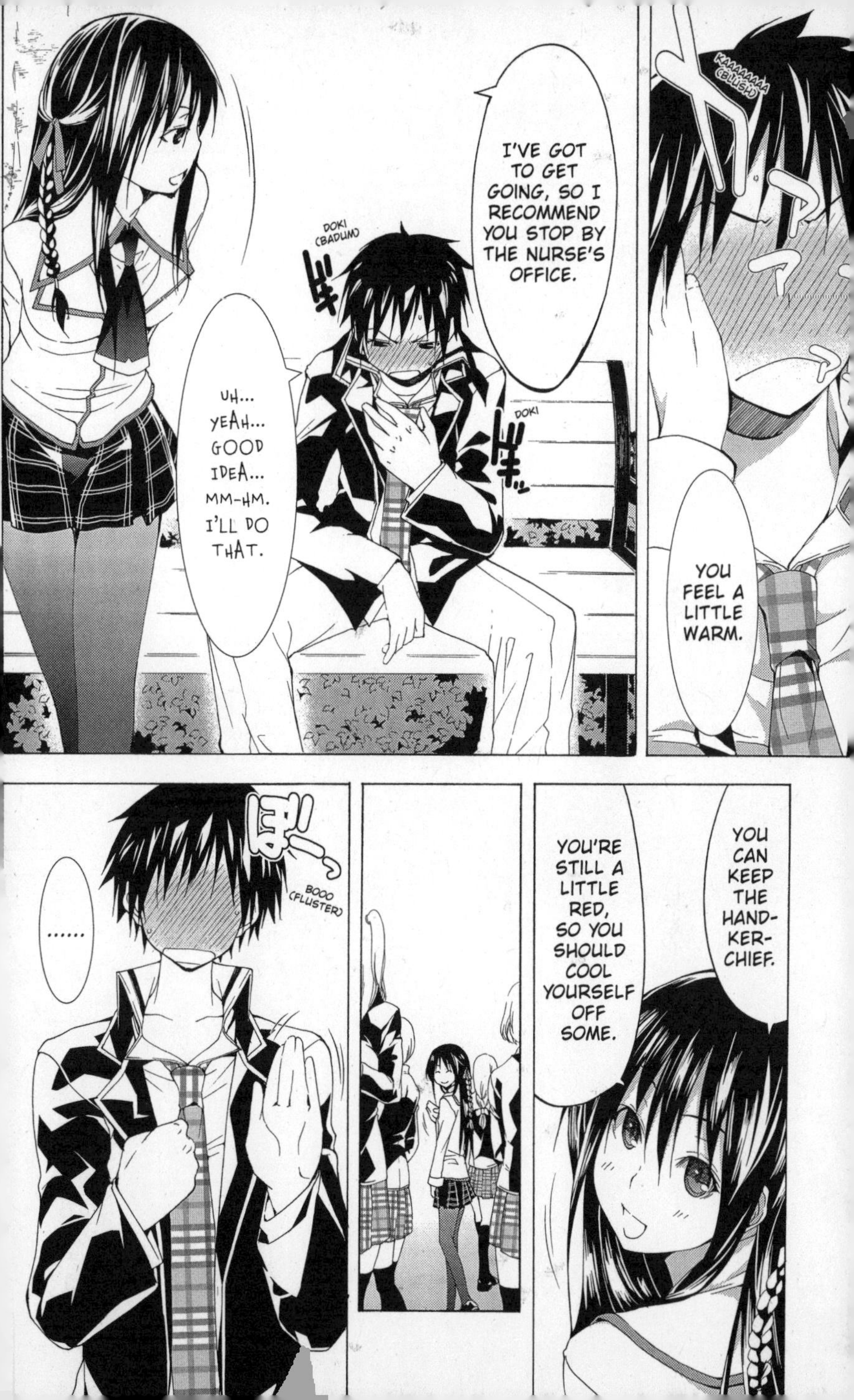
KAAAAAAA (BLUSH)
YOU FEEL A LITTLE WARM.
I'VE GOT TO GET GOING, SO I RECOMMEND YOU STOP BY THE NURSE'S OFFICE.
DOKI (BADUMP)
DOKI
UH... YEAH... GOOD IDEA... MM-HM. I'LL DO THAT.
YOU CAN KEEP THE HAND-KER-CHIEF.
YOU'RE STILL A LITTLE RED, SO YOU SHOULD COOL YOURSELF OFF SOME.
BOOO (FLUSTER)
......

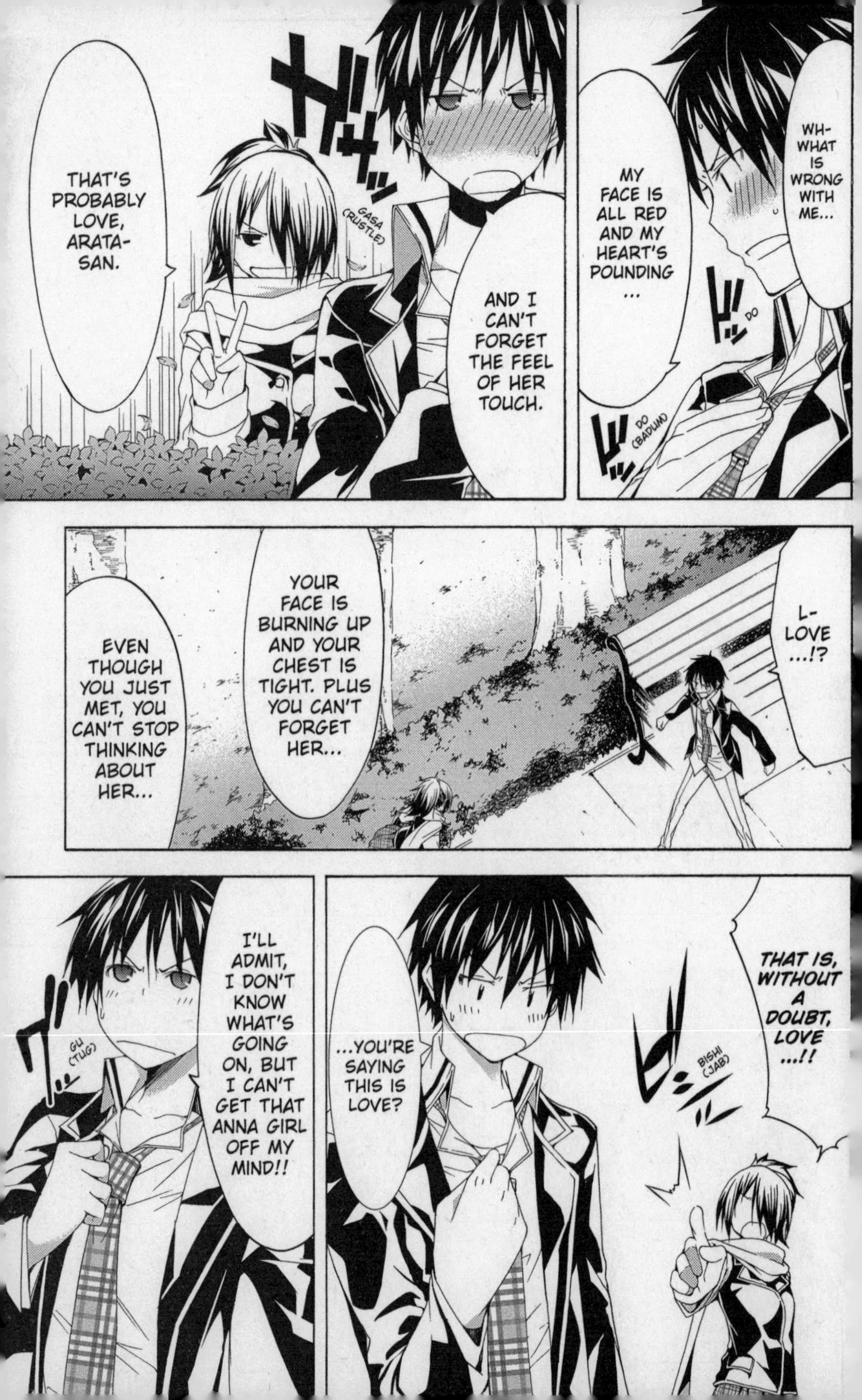
WH- WHAT IS WRONG WITH ME...
MY FACE IS ALL RED AND MY HEART'S POUNDING ...
DO
DO (BADUM)
AND I CAN'T FORGET THE FEEL OF HER TOUCH.
GASA (RUSTLE)
THAT'S PROBABLY LOVE, ARATA-SAN.
L- LOVE ...!?
YOUR FACE IS BURNING UP AND YOUR CHEST IS TIGHT. PLUS YOU CAN'T FORGET HER...
EVEN THOUGH YOU JUST MET, YOU CAN'T STOP THINKING ABOUT HER...
THAT IS, WITHOUT A DOUBT, LOVE ...!!
BISHI (JAB)
...YOU'RE SAYING THIS IS LOVE?
I'LL ADMIT, I DON'T KNOW WHAT'S GOING ON, BUT I CAN'T GET THAT ANNA GIRL OFF MY MIND!!
GU (TUG)

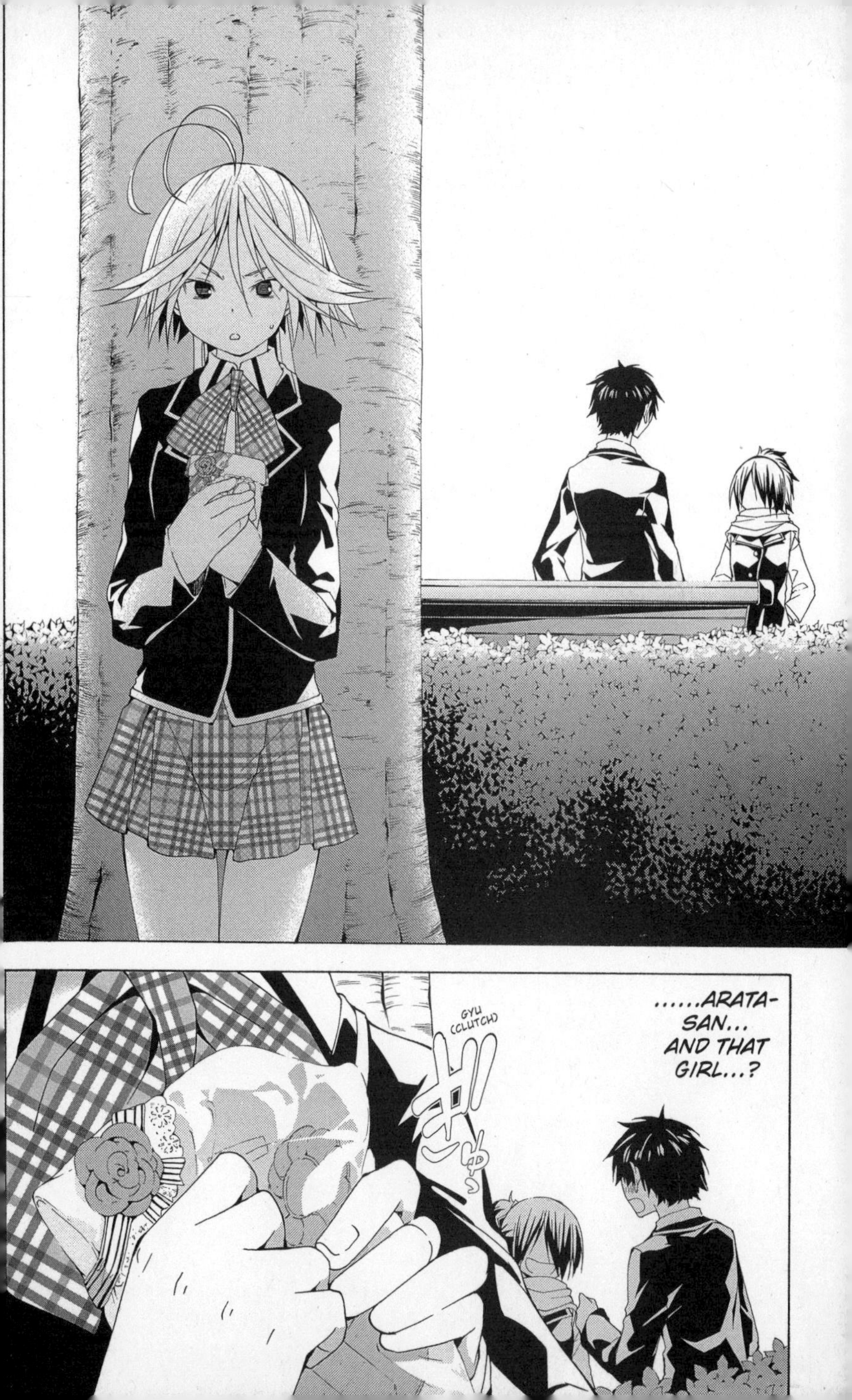
......ARATA-SAN... AND THAT GIRL...?
GYU (CLUTCH)